How To Keep Yo
Collector Car Alive

How To Keep Your
Collector Car Alive

Josh B. Malks

motorbooks

For my grandchildren, Sarah, Jonathan, Noah, Sadie, Cameron, and Teddy,
in hopes they will someday follow in Zaydee's tire tracks.

First published in 2008 by Motorbooks, an imprint of MBI Publishing Company, 400 First Avenue North, Suite 300, Minneapolis, MN 55401 USA

Motorbooks titles are also available at discounts in bulk quantity for industrial or sales-promotional use. For details write to Special Sales Manager at MBI Publishing Company, 400 First Avenue North, Suite 300, Minneapolis, MN 55401 USA.

To find out more about our books, join us online at www.motorbooks.com.

Library of Congress Cataloging-in-Publication Data

Malks, Josh B., 1935-
  How to keep your collector car alive / by Josh B. Malks.
    p. cm.
  Includes index.
  ISBN 978-0-7603-3290-0 (sb : alk. paper)
  1. Antique and classic cars—Maintenance and repair. I. Title.
  TL152.M2335 2008
  629.28'72--dc22

                                          2008005752

On the front cover: A car collector enjoying his 1960 Chevrolet Corvette. *Chris Endres/Hotridesphoto.com*

Sometimes the best way to pinpoint engine leaks is to treat the leaking fluid with fluorescent dye, run the engine, and then shine ultraviolet light on the area. *Tracer Products*

On the title pages: David Daggett of Santa Cruz, California, performs routine maintenance on his 1956 DeSoto Fireflite Sportsman. In the garage is David's 1941 Buick Special SSE sedanette. *Don Sherman*

On the back cover: Regular lubrication of the oiling points on the generator, distributor, and starter is vital to keeping your collector car alive.

About the Author:
Josh B. Malks has been a car guy since he was a lad, hanging out in local garages instead of playing punchball on the streets of the Bronx. While he has specialized in the exotic Cord, he has owned, driven, and maintained collectible examples of Oldsmobile, Plymouth, Kaiser, and others. He currently resides in Capitola-by-the Sea, California.

His books include *Auburn and Cord, Glenn Pray: The Man Who Brought Legends To Life, Cord: The Timeless Classic,* and *The Illustrated Duesenberg Buyer's Guide.* He is a past president of the Auburn-Cord-Duesenberg Club and the editor of its monthly magazine. He is also a member of Classic Car Club of America, Antique Automobile Club of America, Silver Ghost Association, and American Mensa.

ISBN-13: 978-0-7603-3290-0

Editor: Jeffrey Zuehlke
Designer: Mandy Iverson

Printed in Singapore

CONTENTS

ACKNOWLEDGMENTS

This book was written with the help of some extraordinary professionals and talented hobbyists. Some are currently active in their fields, others retired. All graciously offered their knowledge to help other enthusiasts preserve their precious vehicles. In addition to their other accomplishments, most of them love and maintain old cars, boats, and planes. I thank them profusely for their contributions.

First and foremost, I thank **Bill Kennedy**, a scholarly engineer and prolific writer. He serves as vice president, technical, of the Silver Ghost Association. Owners of these wonderful Rolls-Royces drive them extensively, way beyond what you and I might consider typical for cars that are between 82 and 102 years old. His many articles in the *SGA Tourer* have been an inspiration. He took the time to proofread and fact-check the text of this book, and offered many valuable suggestions. Any errors in interpreting his comments are mine. **Bob Adler** of Adler's Antique Autos is a specialist in the restoration and preservation of old cars in general and vintage Chevrolets in particular. His column, "Corrosion Lab," is featured in *Vintage Truck* magazine. **Ray Bohacz** writes the monthly column, "Mechanical Marvels," for *Hemmings Classic Car* magazine. He shared his experiences with the Evans coolant. **Bill Cannon** is founder and former Technical Editor of *Skinned Knuckles* magazine. I've tried to learn from Bill's meticulous documentation of the opinions he expresses. **Jeff Dreibus** is "The Old Carb Doc." He shared his wealth of experience in carburetion, fuel delivery systems, and the effect of new fuels on older car parts. **Douglas Godfrey** began his career in tribology at the NASA laboratory in Cleveland. He later joined Chevron Research, retiring in 1983. He has written 55 papers on tribology and has been honored by the Society of Tribologists and Lubricating Engineers. **Matt Joseph** is best known for his articles in *Skinned Knuckles* and *Cars and Parts* magazines. I thank him for his willingness to share his breadth of knowledge of matters automotive. **Robert C. Joseph**, Ph.D., is the author of the definitive history of the Ethyl Corporation. **Neil Maken** is editor of *Skinned Knuckles* magazine, whose subtitle speaks volumes: *Written by Restorers, for Restorers.* His comments and corrections helped make this a better book. **Gordon Millar** is a consulting engineer. Before he retired he was a vice president of the Ethyl Corporation. His love is antique boats, and he writes extensively for boating magazines. The late **Thomas S. Pendergast** was a mechanical engineer. His career included work with aircraft electrical systems and with aeronautical and industrial gas turbines. He drove and restored classic and collector cars and flew an antique plane. **Snick Quicker** is a retired engineer, whose background includes the design of automotive test equipment. He's a hobbyist and car collector. His special knowledge of the high-compression cars of the 1950s and 1960s was invaluable. **Fred Rau** is the former editor of *Motorcycle Consumer News,* a nonadvertising magazine that tests and rates motorcycle industry products. An electrical engineer, he operated a power plant for a major utility for 20 years. **Alexi Stiop** is director of research and development for D-A Lubricant Company. He and chemist **Al Rouch**, retired director of fuels and lubricants for United States Auto Racing, helped me understand the components of oil additive packages. **Joseph Tunick Strauss**, Ph.D., is a materials engineer specializing in metallurgy. His firm, HJE Company, builds machines that make metal powders. **David Zeckhausen** is president of Zeckhausen Racing. He provided a very professional perspective on the subjects of brake fluid and brake bleeding. The counsel of engineers **William Anderson** and **Robert Olree** on the subject of modern oils was most appreciated. In addition to those credited in the text, my thanks also to **Phil Angell of Solar PALS, Blackstone Laboratories, Corrosion Doctors, Tom Duffy of The Solar Biz, The Eastwood Company, Ethanol Promotion and Information Council, Griot's Garage, Herguth Laboratories, Hunter Engineering Company, KD Tools, Magnaflux, Optima Batteries, Rust Bullet, Smog-Check of Santa Cruz, Pall Corporation, John and Betty Schoepke, Winchester Auto Parts**, and **Wix Filters** for the use of photographs and drawings and other courtesies extended to me. And special thanks to **Gina and Shawn Bahten** of Quality Automotive in Santa Cruz, California, for their endless patience.

INTRODUCTION

The purpose of this book is to help you maintain your collector car as a driving vehicle. In 1995 I wrote *How to Maintain and Enjoy Your Collector Car* with a similar purpose. It was well-received, but went out of print a few years ago.

Worse than out of print, it went out of date. New materials and techniques have been developed, and some older ones have been rendered obsolete. In addition, the original book addressed itself primarily to cars through 1950 vintages. The updated book you are now reading brings us through the muscle car era.

When many of us bought our first car, it was often a vehicle between 10 and 15 years of age. Chances are that first set of wheels had seen better days, which was why we could afford it. We lavished months of effort on fixing it up. (Who knew then that this was called restoration?) We often attempted to improve on the original, mechanically and visually. We went on dates in it, hung around it, worked underneath it, told lies about it, loved it . . . and drove it. After all, that's what it was for. And it ran and ran.

Decades later, that same car has become collectible. The time and the money that a new owner puts into returning it to original appearance and condition are usually multiples of the car's original purchase price. In the 1950s and 1960s, collectible cars were often the grand classics of an earlier era. Today's popular collectibles are more likely to be cars originally intended for stylish or fast everyday transportation. And many of them are just like the car that the high school football captain got the prettiest girl with!

And what happens after these cars are restored? Lewis Carroll would have loved it. In a development worthy of *Alice in Wonderland*, Americans spend many millions of dollars each year buying and restoring machinery whose intended purpose was transportation, then consign that machinery to suspended animation under a car cover. Ironically, this is done in the interests of preserving these artifacts of another era. In practice, it's destroying them.

Idle mechanical devices deteriorate. Seals dry up, brake fluid congeals, rust begins to form. Cars that are started and idled only occasionally suffer the additional damage of acid corrosion.

Given reasonable care, the best thing you can do to preserve your collectible car is to drive it. The wear it will receive is far less damaging than the results of vegetating. At least once a week, my mid-1930s classic car goes out for exercise. Sometimes on my way home, I stop to visit a car-loving friend, or pause to fill the gas tank. Admiring passersby often ask: "Aren't you afraid to drive it?" Nope. As a matter of fact, I'd be afraid *not* to.

Even more important than the effect on the car is the effect on the driver. If your newly restored collectible wears out, it can be restored again. But you, the driver, can't. Every year in which you miss the fun of driving your prize is a year less in which you'll be able to do it.

Driving your collector car is good for the spirit, too. Drivers and passengers in other cars smile, wave, and applaud. Children stare at your rolling history lesson, and actually engage their parents in conversation.

In 1995 I wrote about the cloud gathering over that happy scene, in the form of environmental concerns. Sympathetic legislators have recognized that the low mileage that our collector cars are driven makes them minimal contributors to greenhouse gases. They also know that our cars, though old, are better maintained than the clunkers that they are trying to get off the roads. And it's true that our collector cars are still viewed positively by most of the population.

To remain so, they must be driven responsibly, with concern for the environment. Collectors themselves must participate in what has become a national debate on the place of the automobile in our society. To help our cause, we must become familiar with the facts and not rely on the platitudes of yesteryear. No matter where you stand on the issue of global warming, be aware that others have strong feelings on the subject. Make no mistake. The concept of the collector car as a benign artifact is under attack and must be wisely defended if it is to survive.

I should note that this book does not contain specific how-tos on subjects common to all cars, like engine tune-ups or paint touch-up. Neither will you find instructions for repairs or restoration. There are already many good sources, in print and online, where you can find such information. What you *will* find here, I trust, are answers to many of your questions, as well as a firm foundation for any deeper research you may care to do.

In some of the discussions in this book, I mention proprietary products and some sources. I have no financial interest in any of these products or sources and report only on my own experience with them or that of others whose opinions I trust.

Some of the concerns I raise regarding the protection of your car from the assaults of corrosion, abrasion, and other ills may seem extreme. Remember, though, that you may plan to keep your collector car for a much longer time than your everyday machine. Also, modern metallurgy and technology are incorporated in the new cars that we drive daily. These protect them from some of the ills that can beset our older treasures. To similarly protect our older cars, we need to work a bit harder. I've tried to provide the background that led to each of my recommendations. So pick and choose among my proposals, but at least consider them.

A decision you'll have to make before following some of the suggestions in this book has to do with how you, dear reader, use your collector car. While I hope that all readers are drivers, the ratio of driving-to-show-going will vary dramatically from car to car. For owners who do both, most of the suggestions in this book do not address modifying the appearance of the car. Many of the suggested visible modifications can be of a bolt-on nature, so they may be quickly replaced by original components when you exhibit (or sell) your car. Some improvements are permanent, but with ingenuity you can often render them near-invisible.

Let me tell you a little story. On a side street in London once, I watched a magnificent old Daimler limousine pull up in front of a small hand laundry. The uniformed chauffeur was alone in the car. He got out, went in, and emerged carrying a paper-wrapped package of shirts. Then he slid back behind the wheel and the gorgeous vehicle purred off. A classic worth a fortune had gone on a prosaic errand. Did that demean the Daimler? I don't think so; I think it elevated the laundry!

Driving your pride and joy is good for you and good for the car. Let's do it.

Josh B. Malks
October 2007

The author with Moonshadow, *his prized 1936 Cord 810 Westchester sedan.*

CHAPTER 1
WEAR AND LUBRICANTS

A restorer friend once showed me a project he was working on. It was a fine classic of the 1930s that had been purchased at a respected auction. This particular make had a reputation for excellent driving characteristics. The new owner found it otherwise, and sought help. My friend found some mechanical problems, which he repaired. What was most startling, however, was that except for the engine, transmission and rear end, there was not a drop of lubricant anywhere on the car! Door strikers and dovetails were chromed and grease-free. Hood and trunk props were literally squeaky clean. Steering linkage and tie rod ends, when dismantled, were actually rusty! This car gave new meaning to the word "clean." It was also well on its way to self-destruction by wear.

The study of the causes and effects of friction, lubrication, and wear is called tribology. An automobile is a big tribological device. Friction, lubrication and wear abound. Many parts of a car couldn't work without friction. Friction holds a nut on a bolt. Friction is required for a clutch to work, and for brakes to stop the car. Moving parts of the car, on the other hand, must be lubricated to reduce friction and prevent wear. Because lubrication is sometimes imperfect, some wear can still take place.

There's no need for you to become a lubrication engineer or a tribologist to keep your collector car running for many decades. This chapter will look at the causes of wear, and how lubrication helps prevent it. It'll be a simplified exposition of a complex subject. But an understanding of the causes of wear and how lubrication works will put you in a better position to make decisions on products to use, procedures to follow, and driving techniques to practice.

KINDS OF WEAR

To the unaided eye, polished metal surfaces look mirror-smooth. Crankshaft and connecting rod bearings, and the journals that turn in them, are examples. Under high magnification, though, these smooth-appearing metal surfaces actually show impressive projections called asperities. Wear occurs when these asperities come into contact with each other. Oil reduces friction between parts by preventing metal-on-metal contact—most of the time. Different operating conditions call upon different physical and chemical characteristics of the oil. The oil you use and the way you drive affect the lubricant's ability to protect your engine and drive, train from damage.

While there are at least 10 different kinds of wear that can occur in the moving parts of our cars, some of them are immune to any corrective action we can practically take. Happily, three of the worst car-destroyers can be controlled, if not completely eliminated, by proper maintenance and operating practices. Those top-three car-destroyers are abrasion, adhesion, and acid corrosion.

ABRASION

Abrasion is the gouging of metal surfaces by hard particles that are too large to pass freely through the clearance between a bearing and its journal. When your engine is running, a journal doesn't ride centered in the bearing. Most of the clearance is on the top; only a fraction is at the bottom. (Actually, the position of the clearances change as the load changes direction, but top and bottom are easy to visualize.) An oil film separates the surfaces. Film thicknesses are measured in thousandths of a millimeter, commonly called microns. (A micron is about .00004 inch.) So oil film thickness may range between .5 and 20 microns.

All circulating used engine oil carries solid particles. Some dirt enters the engine through the carburetor, and some through crankcase breathers. Dirt in the fuel eventually makes its way into the oil. So do abrasives from an often-overlooked source—dirt and metal chips left behind during engine overhauls. Other particles are the results of the wear of engine components.

Particles of grit circulating in the oil eventually will attempt to pass through the bearings. They'll cut their way through the soft babbitt surface of the bearing, or embed themselves in it. The Cummins Engine Company did extensive testing of the relationship of the size of grit particles to engine damage by abrasion. While the tests

HOW CONTAMINANTS GET IN THE OIL

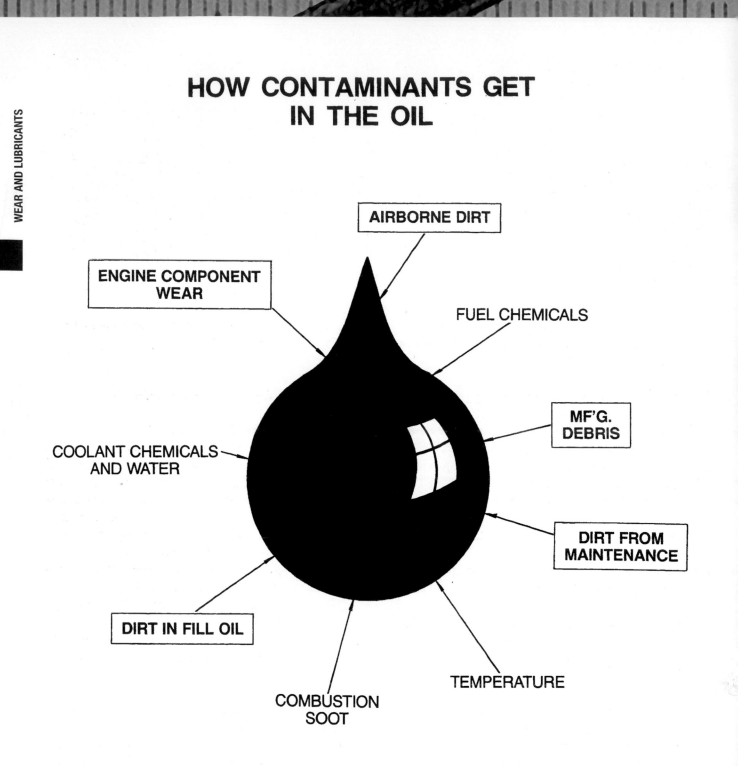

Well-designed filters control [SOLID] contaminants, reducing both wear and lube oil breakdown.

Pall Corporation

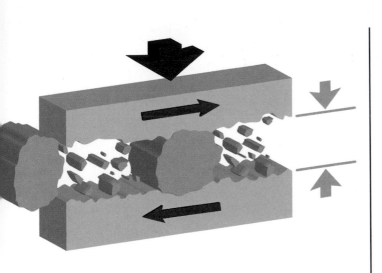

Wear by abrasion. Particles that are too big can't damage the surfaces. Neither can particles that are too small. Pall Corporation

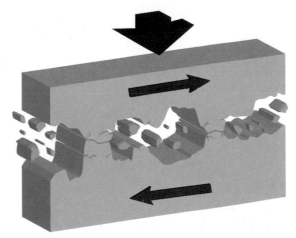

Wear by adhesion. When asperities touch, they weld together then tear off particles from each surface. Pall Corporation

were conducted on diesel engines, the principles hold true for our gasoline engines as well. What Cummins found was that the most wear was caused by the smallest particles. That's because particles that were much larger than the bearing's dynamic clearance couldn't enter the bearing at all.

Exactly the same results were found to apply to the cylinder walls. Most of the grit in this case enters with carburetor air. Findings were similar for cam lobes, cam followers, and the bushings used on the camshaft.

The meaning is inescapable. Cleanliness—clean oil, clean air, clean fuel—is a vital factor in achieving long life for all parts of your car and its engine. Achieving that cleanliness is a function of filtration, the topic of a later chapter.

ADHESION

Adhesion describes what can happen when actual metal-to-metal contact occurs in your engine. As we've seen, even the smoothest, most finely machined metal surfaces are rough when viewed microscopically. Because of this, when two metal surfaces are pushed together, the high spots begin to touch. The more the surfaces are squeezed together or loaded, more of the high spots touch. If the surfaces are sliding against each other, microscopic welds occur. As the welds are torn apart, metal is transferred from one surface to the other in a disorderly manner. The surface becomes increasingly rough, and even more likely to weld together. We see the result as scuffing.

Adhesion is prevented by keeping the surfaces from touching by using the proper oils and greases.

ACID CORROSION

Acid corrosion occurs on damp surfaces exposed to exhaust gases. While that seems to describe only the inside of your exhaust system, it applies equally to the cylinders of your engine. For every gallon of gasoline burned, about a gallon of water forms in your exhaust. Exhaust gases also contain sulfur, among other things; the combination of these produces sulfonic acid. Any acid that is permitted to condense on cylinder walls begins a corrosive attack on that wall.

You can minimize acid corrosion by choosing a motor oil with additives that neutralize acid. You can stop acid condensation, and the damage it causes, by proper starting, driving and stopping techniques. We'll discuss these in Chapter 19.

HOW ENGINE LUBRICATION WORKS

To lubricate our collector cars properly, and to avoid the problems described above, it's helpful to understand how lubricants protect moving parts. The engine, the most complex mechanism in your collector car, benefits from three regimes of lubrication.

HDL

When your engine is running at a constant speed, under moderate load and at moderate temperature, crankshaft and rod journals in their bearings act somewhat like pumps to produce a wedge-shaped film of oil on which

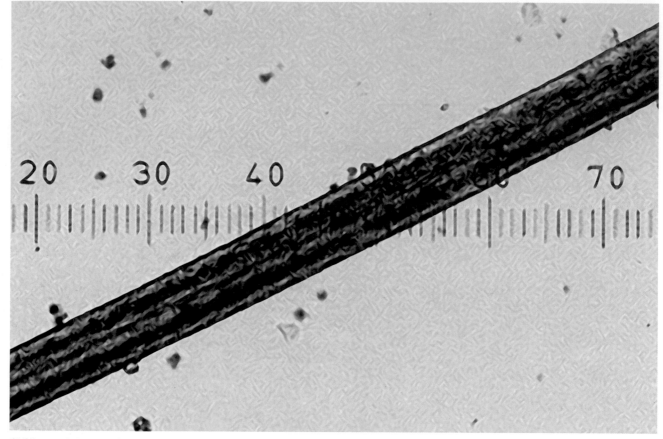

This human hair, magnified 500 times, actually measures about 70 microns in diameter. The small particles are about 10 microns in size. Particles like these can damage engine bearing surfaces. Pall Corporation

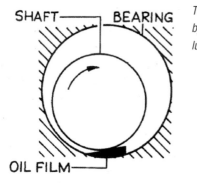

The wedge of oil created by hydrodynamic lubrication.

the journal actually rides without touching the shaft. This is HydroDynamic Lubrication or HDL. HDL is the best kind of lubrication; it results in low friction and extremely low wear. Note that the desirable wedge of oil characteristic of HDL is generated by hydraulic pressure developed by the rotation of the shaft. It is not solely a result of engine oil pressure, which by itself is insufficient to completely separate the moving metal

parts. Many of us have experienced HDL at work in the frightening phenomenon of hydroplaning. In this case rainwater is the lubricant, and the smooth tires and highway represent the surfaces of bearings and shaft.

In the best circumstances, other internal parts of your engine operate with HDL too. These include camshaft bushings, piston rings against the cylinder wall (except at top and bottom dead center), the valve lifter, the part of the cam lobe that's circular, and the valve stems in their guides.

BL

In earlier years, motor oil was essentially a refined petroleum with undesirable components such as wax removed. These base stocks met automotive lubrication needs if oil was changed often enough. Engine life in the 1930s through the 1950s rarely reached 100,000 miles, and then only with valve and ring jobs along the way. Striving to do better, chemists and engineers added small amounts of oil-soluble chemicals to base stocks. These additives have played a major role in the increased longevity of modern engines. They can play a similar role in the long life of your collector car.

One important additive function comes into play when a part of your engine isn't operating in the HDL regime. Some parts of the engine never experience conditions for HDL. These include the piston ring-cylinder wall contact at top and bottom dead center. As the piston slows, then stops, the oil wedge is lost. (Slow is a relative term in engine work; that piston may be slowing, stopping, and restarting 40 times a second!) If you've ever dismantled or rebuilt an engine, you've noticed that cylinder wear is greatest at the top and bottom of the piston travel. This is why.

When you accelerate suddenly, the relative speed of the crankshaft journals and bearings increases rapidly. But the load on those bearings increases even more rapidly. The oil film is ruptured momentarily. Actual metal-to-metal contact may occur.

Into the breach to prevent catastrophic failure springs boundary lubrication, or BL. It's called that because the boundaries or surfaces of the metals are involved. BL occurs between surfaces sliding at relatively slow speeds under high temperatures and high loads. The burden for providing BL falls mostly to additives dissolved in the oil by the refiner. These antiwear agents react chemically with the metal surfaces, just when temperatures rise due to initial metal-to-metal contact. They form thin inorganic films with a high melting point. Think back to sliding along in your stocking feet on a bare wood floor. Now recollect the sensation on a waxed floor, and you can visualize the action of the films formed by the antiwear additives.

EHL

When hard metals contact each other at concentrated spots under great pressure, an extremely thin film of oil prevents actual contact. Pressures like these actually cause the metal parts to deform where they touch. You've seen strobe pictures of a golf ball flattening when the club hits. The elasticity of the material permits it to regain its original shape as soon as the pressure relaxes. Hard steel is also elastic, and ball and roller bearings deform in exactly this way. So do gear teeth. In an engine, so do the cam lobes and the lifters on which they push. The flat area is extremely small, and the oil film extremely thin. Under these enormous pressures the oil actually turns to a very viscous material almost like nylon. It liquefies again when the pressure is removed. This kind of lubrication is elastohydrodynamic lubrication, or EHL.

The lubricating regimes described above do occur in your engine and other parts of your car. Mixed HDL, BL, and EHL conditions also occur. Some components operate in more than one regime, and some go quickly from one to another.

You may find this discussion of tribology either interesting or boring. The important knowledge for us as car owners is that the survival of our machinery depends on our providing lubricants that are capable of maintaining the lubrication patterns described above, and in treating the machinery in a manner that interferes as little as possible with the conditions of good lubrication.

Remember too that the oil washing the bearings does more than keep metal surfaces from touching. It carries away any wear particles so they may be trapped by the oil filter and removed from circulation. Even more vital, it plays an important role in carrying away heat from the bearings and journals. The hot oil returns to the oil pan, where it gives off some heat through the walls of the pan. Highly stressed engines may use aluminum oil pans, often with fins, to improve heat transfer. Racing engines use small oil radiators, called oil coolers, to remove even more heat from the oil before it recirculates.

OIL PRESSURE

The most important thing about oil pressure is to have some. Normal oil pressure varies from engine to engine, and with engine speed. Pressure is higher when oil is cold and viscous, and drops as it warms up. Look for oil pressure that doesn't change dramatically from one drive to the next. As long as pressure remains within the range indicated as normal on the car's gauge, or the oil pressure light stays off, there's little need for concern. (But remember that some oil-pressure sending units won't turn the warning light on until pressure has dropped to four pounds per square inch.)

A sudden drop in gauge pressure that stays down, or a gauge that falls to zero at driving speeds, or a light that comes on suddenly, is reason to *immediately* pull off the road and stop. If a check reveals that oil level is correct, call the tow truck. If you continue to drive you'll still need the tow truck, a few miles and a seized engine later.

CHAPTER 2
NEW OILS, NEW PROBLEMS?

The quart of oil that you put in your collector car's engine is far more than just refined petroleum. It's a complex chemical combination designed to provide the three types of lubrication discussed in Chapter 1, as required by different conditions, and in different combinations. Before considering the additives in the can, it's useful to understand the most important consideration in choosing a motor oil—its viscosity.

Viscosity is the property that primarily governs the thickness of the oil film in HDL. It's the measure of an oil's resistance to flow. Thicker oils have a higher viscosity, thinner oils lower. Viscosity is measured in units of centipoise, centistokes, or Saybolt Universal Seconds. None of these laboratory measurements is used to identify the motor oil that you buy for your car. The Society of Automotive Engineers (SAE) has set up a numbering system that's more familiar. It's commonly referred to as weight; engineers prefer the term grade. For automotive purposes, SAE grades range from 5 to 50. The grades are arbitrary numbers that indicate the viscosity range at a temperature of 100 degrees Centigrade (212 degrees Fahrenheit). A "W" added to the number indicates that the measurement of viscosity was taken at a temperature of 0 degrees C (32 degrees F). Because of the importance of viscosity, the SAE classification system refers to viscosity alone, and makes no reference to any other physical or performance characteristics.

Using oil that's more viscous than required creates several problems. In cold temperatures it may not pump as quickly to all parts of the engine. An oil that is too viscous may create cooling problems because it doesn't carry heat away from bearings as quickly. Higher fluid friction will also increase gasoline consumption. Oil that's thinner than required will (surprise!) have its own set of problems. Of most concern is its lower film strength, and inability to separate moving parts as well as it should. Related problems are increased oil consumption, potential leakage and increased engine noise.

Oils are sold in single grades, like SAE 30, or multigrades, like SAE 10W-30. Many collector cars were designed during an era when oil came only in single grades. Most oil refiners still supply high-detergent single-grade oils, usually SAE 30 and 40. *There is nothing old-fashioned or inferior about these oils.* The additive package is usually the same as in the multigrade oils, testified to by the same API service classification on the bottle or can. More about this later.

Multiviscosity oils are supposed to have the characteristics of each grade at different temperatures. A 5W-30 oil is supposed to behave like a 5-grade oil at 32 degrees F, and like a 30-grade oil at 212 degrees F. That does not mean that it gets more viscous as it gets warmer. All oils become less viscous as they get hot. This 5W-30 oil gets thinner more slowly than one would expect of a 5-grade oil, so when 212 degrees F is reached it's no thinner than 30-grade oil would be at that temperature.

Multiviscosity oils are created by starting with a very low viscosity base stock. Then viscous polymers are added. These have little effect at low temperatures. At high temperatures, they keep the low viscosity base stock from getting even thinner. Refiners call these additives Viscosity Index Improvers, or VI Improvers for short. They're a mixed blessing. At heart, wide range conventional (not synthetic) multiviscosity oils are 5W or 10W base stocks. Keeping their viscosity up at high temperatures demands the use of a lot of polymers. Fewer polymers are better for all engines, because it's the oil that does the lubricating; polymers don't.

SYNTHETIC OILS

Viscosity index is the area in which so-called synthetic oils shine. Synthetic lubricants, like conventional oils, are made from petroleum. It's the treatment that's different. There are different types of synthetics, so any definition must be broad. Generally, synthetic lubricants are the result of reactive chemical processes that create substances of higher molecular weight than the original reacting substances, with planned and predictable physical properties. That's the key difference between synthetics and familiar conventional oils.

A petroleum motor oil starts out as a base stock with a grab bag of ingredients and properties. Some of the harmful molecules are separated out by distillation, extraction and filtration. What's left are the most useful molecules from the original crude oil stock, but the molecules themselves are largely unchanged. Chemicals are then added to bring the final blend as close as possible to the requirements of an engine lubricant. A synthetic motor oil is produced by chemical reactions, and its molecules are tailored to meet the specific needs of engine lubrication. So synthetic oils require far smaller quantities of additives to meet those needs.

Synthetic oil technology goes back to the 1920s. Synthetics saw some use in World War II (1939–1945) but came to the public's attention when they became the only lubricants that could handle the heat and pressure of the new jet airliner engines, and the extreme cold of the Alaska pipeline. Today synthetics for automotive use are produced by nearly all major oil companies, as well as by specialty oil suppliers like Red Line and Amsoil.

The several classes of synthetics that are applicable to automobile use each have multisyllabic names. If you're interested in the chemistry, texts are available at your library or online to elaborate on this subject. For our purposes, using a synthetic oil produced by a well-known supplier is safe advice.

The major advantage of synthetics is their inherently greater viscosity stability over a wide range of temperatures. Essentially, they are thinner all the time. Thinner oils give higher gasoline mileage, which in turn permits auto manufacturers who recommend their use to calculate a lower average mileage for the modern cars they sell, to meet government standards. On the other hand, several years ago the head of crankcase oil research for an oil refiner that has invested much in synthetic oil technology said that he did not think there was any application for synthetic oil in antique cars. Still, research and development go on and things may be changing for the better. And there is anecdotal evidence that collector car owners have used synthetics with positive results.

Early synthetics displayed some problems of compatibility with neoprene and other seal compounds used in older engines and transmissions. Synthetic producers largely solved these problems, but caution is still advised. If you decide to try synthetics, keep an eye out for leaks for the first few thousand miles of driving. Sometimes a seal that held oil because it was nicely coated with years of engine gook starts to leak when cleaned up by the tendency of synthetics to dissolve sludge and lacquer deposits. A new seal may be needed to fix the leak.

Marketplace decisions are bound to become even more complicated with time. Most major refiners now offer blends of synthetic and conventional motor oil. As might be expected, the ads claim the best of both types at half the price of synthetic.

DOUGHNUTS AND STARBURSTS

The crude base oil stock, no matter how carefully refined, is not capable of meeting the lubrication needs of engines running today, whether modern or vintage. In addition to VI Improvers, refiners add chemical compounds to the base oil to deal with specific problems created by the operation of internal combustion engines. These are generally referred to as additives, and they're in every container of oil that you can buy today.

Antiwear agents provide boundary lubrication. *Dispersants* help control deposits. A pinch of *silicone* controls foam. *Corrosion inhibitors* reduce rust and neutralize acids.

The typical car driver is in no position to evaluate the additive packages or real-world capabilities of a quart of engine oil. So in 1958 the American Petroleum Institute (API) created service classifications for motor oils. Oils were graded in tests conducted by the American Society for Testing and Materials (ASTM). Three gasoline engine categories were established: ML, MM, and MS, for Light, Medium, and Severe service. This grading method didn't prove entirely satisfactory, and a joint effort by API, ASTM, and SAE resulted in a new system that better communicates between the oil producers and the engine manufacturers. This system is defined as SAE J183 Engine Oil Performance and Engine Service Classification. In 1988 API established the symbol that appears on containers of motor oil to help motorists match the needs of their engines to the quality of the oil. It's popularly referred to as the "doughnut."

The API "doughnut" on the back of a container of oil.

The ILSAC "starburst" on the front.

The first letter of the API service category indicates the kind of engine this oil was intended for. It stands for the type of ignition system. "S" (Spark) is for gasoline engines, "C" (Compression) for diesels. Many oils are suitable for both, and bear both service category labels. The next character—a letter for gasoline engines and a letter-number combination for diesels—designates oil quality. Each new category does not replace the previous one. Instead, it indicates that the motor oil has passed tests designed to meet the increasingly stringent needs of newer engines.

The International Lubricants Standardization and Approval Committee (ILSAC) includes representatives of the engine manufacturers, oil suppliers and additive makers. In 1995 ILSAC created standardized tests that motor oils must pass to receive the ILSAC "starburst" classification. As standards change, ILSAC applies new and higher numbers to its ratings; current in 2007 was GF-4. The starburst, the gear-shaped symbol containing the words, "For Gasoline Engines," appears on the front of containers of motor oils that meet the standards. It is referred to as an evergreen symbol. This means that even though the technical requirements needed to display it will change, the symbol itself will not. The intent was to have a consumer-friendly symbol, hoping that once consumers learned that oils marked with the starburst are good oils, they will not need to know much more. Consumers would not have to decipher the API codes to determine the performance standard of that oil.

Since our collector car owners are more sophisticated, the starburst symbol means little. And since the starburst symbol specifically identifies oils that give better gas mileage, those oils will tend to be of lighter weights. So keep your eye on the doughnut.

EXIT ZINC

It was once assumed that the higher the letter on the doughnut, the higher the quality of the oil. This may have been the case until 2007, when questions began to be raised about the effects of the latest formulations on collector car engines.

The most widely used antiwear additives in motor oil, as they have been since the 1950s, are compounds of zinc and phosphorous. Popularly they are just called zinc. Zinc dialkyldithiophosphate is often abbreviated ZDDP; zinc dithiophosphate, ZDP. The films that ZDDP (or ZDP) form on the metal surfaces are sacrificial. That is, they wear away as they protect. When fresh metal appears again, the additive causes new films to form. Zinc is used up as it performs its function. This is one of the reasons why owners should replace their motor oil regularly.

The most modern motor oils have seriously tampered with additive chemistry, and concerns, some of them shrill, have been raised about the possible detriment to our older engines. Specifically, zinc and phosphorous have been gradually reduced during the past several years, more rapidly since 2007. That's because they are suspected of reducing the effectiveness of (and eventually destroying) the now-universal catalytic converters on modern cars, as the oil reaches combustion chambers by way of imperfectly sealing rings or worn valve guides. Catalytic converters are required on over-the-road diesel engines as of 2008, so the zinc and phosphorous in oils intended for such use is being drastically reduced as well.

The last API classifications before the most precipitous reduction in zinc were Service SL for gasoline engines and CH-4 for diesels. Service SM and later contain diminished amounts of the ZDDP additive—usually .08 to .10 percent by volume. Another way of saying this is 800 to 1,000 parts per million (ppm). Some reports from the field seem to indicate that the latest oils can create serious problems in older engines, particularly engines that use flat tappets. (The Internet, with its unprecedented abilities in mass communication, has made it possible to frighten more people more quickly than ever before. And it should be noted that some of the alarms have been sounded by the makers of aftermarket oil additives, who themselves have axes to grind.)

Somehow the scary stories have a familiar ring. They sound much like the "death knell of old engines" that followed the removal of tetraethyl lead from American gasolines in the 1970s. Despite the total removal of lead from gasoline, despite the relatively small number of older engines that have had hardened valve seats installed, and despite the rarity of owners who pour lead substitutes into their gas tanks, collector cars soldier on. Will this be the case with ZDDP-less motor oils as well?

The answer is not yet clear. There is little doubt that engineers consider zinc, along with improved metallurgy and manufacturing precision, to be a highly significant factor in the virtual doubling of engine life between 1950 and 1970. It is also important to understand that the widely reported instances of camshaft and lifter scuffing when using the new oils were related to the startup of new or newly rebuilt engines. The engineers call this break-in scuffing. Engines that have been running for some time and are well broken-in appear to be at far less risk.

And yet, accusations that uncaring oil companies are prepared to sacrifice our old cars on the twin altars of environmentalism and government-mandated mileage standards persist. Bob Olree, himself a collector car enthusiast, is the chair of the ILSAC/OIL Committee. In a 2004 SAE paper coauthored with Michael L. McMillan of General Motors Research and Development, Olree states that the test engines for the Service (SM, for example) and starburst (GF-4, currently) designations are a Nissan 2.4-liter single overhead camshaft engine, and a General

PREOILING

The subject of preoilers comes up regularly in hobby publications. Preoilers are devices that pump oil under pressure into the engine's oil galleries *before* the engine is started. The purpose is to prevent dry starts. Figures have been bandied about in print suggesting that every start takes years off the life of an engine. Some of the prose has been so graphic that the reader could almost hear the engine's bearings and cylinder walls shriek in protest. So the idea of separating the journal from the bearing with prestart oil pressure certainly seems like a good one.

Preoilers are an attractive concept. But the purpose of spending money on such a device would be to add life to your engine by eliminating dry starts. All the tribologists with whom I have spoken say that dry-start damage is mostly a creation of the advertiser's imagination.

The basic theory is that the crankshaft journals, cylinder walls and cam lobes are "dry" when your engine is not running. In fact, most of the oil film that was on them when you stopped the engine is still there when you start it again. It's held by capillary action at the points of HDL, BL, and EHL contacts. What about storage over the winter? While the combination of a cold start and a long sitting time is not a happy one, doing this once a year will not destroy your engine. Interestingly, synthetics have a poor affinity for metal and will cling to engine parts less well than mineral oil. This is one of several of the reasons that synthetics are not necessarily a good match for collector cars.

But what about pressure? Don't the journals and bearings touch until the engine oil pump can supply full pressure? Nope. It's the oil *film* that separates journal and bearing. The wedge of oil is created by the turning action of the journal, independent of any outside oil pressure. (Remember the example of hydroplaning?)

Another point worth considering is the risk of damage to your engine if the preoiler's check valve should fail. (For this reason at least one industrial engine manufacturer voids the warranty if a preoiler is installed.)

I love gadgets, but I think you should pass on this one.

Motors 3.8-liter overhead valve engine. This latter engine has flat tappets. One of the tests, the Sequence IIIG test, is meant to simulate an overhead-valve engine with flat tappets in a truck pulling a load of cattle across a desert on a hot day. Service SM oils pass this test. Sounds good.

The authors of this paper also point out that SM oils contain about the same amount of ZDDP --- up to .08 percent --- as the motor oils of the mid-1950s, and substantially more than the .03 percent included in the oils used in pre-World War II cars. High-load passenger car engines, like the powerful cars of the 1960s and 1970s, created a need for even more ZDDP, up to .010 or .012 percent. It is this peak amount that has now been reduced to about .08 percent again. So, these engineers maintain, it is unlikely that the use of API-SM oils will result in catastrophic failure of our old engines. (They do caution that additives like GM's EOS are recommended for starting up flat tappet engines. And muscle car drivers appear to have cause to be wary.)

These engineers are experienced lubrication professionals, and their words should not be dismissed lightly. But technology moves on, at an accelerating rate. Current tests may not always tell us how well modern oils will serve our old cars *over the long term*. The authors of the paper agree that further reductions in zinc and phosporous are coming, and may provide proper protection only for newer cars. They even wonder aloud how much interest there will be in the future in protecting old and obscure engines.

So will current and future oils affect the ultimate longevity of our collector cars? At this writing, there may be some cause for concern.

Oil companies are under pressure to assist engine manufacturers in wringing the most miles per gallon out of their fleet averages, and appear to be, for now, willing to trade mileage for longevity. That is exactly the opposite of the interests of collector car owners. At the same time, the oil companies are aware of the effect of the removal of ZDDP from motor oils on older cars. Zinc-based additives are not the only way to achieve antiwear chemistry and most of the major companies are working on and incorporating substitute antiwear additives. But new engines do not require the level of antiwear protection that our older metallurgy and designs do. So it is possible that the antiwear package in future oils may never again reach the levels that we require.

The current discussion has brought to the forefront another key issue: parts quality as a factor in engine wear. Coating camshafts with phosphate, for example, is known to markedly reduce startup camshaft scuffing. Be aware of who makes your parts, and where they are made. Seek references before you permit a rebuilder to install critical new parts like camshafts and lifters.

WHAT OIL TO USE

Motor oils on the shelves of your auto supply store are all Service SM or higher now. And oils intended for racing, while higher in ZDDP than API-graded motor oils, are often designed with an additive package that is intended to deal with the stringent short-term needs of highly stressed racers, not necessarily with the longevity we seek.

If you prefer a synthetic, Amsoil's well-known AMO (10W-40) and ARO (20W-50) motor oils contain, at this writing, over 1200 ppm of ZDDP. They are not API-rated. For a non-synthetic, consider Classic Car Motor Oil. The Indiana Region of the Classic Car Club of America worked with the Department of Research and Development of D-A Lubricant Company of Indianapolis, a respected formulator of lubricants for the racing and trucking industries, to develop a formula specifically for older cars. Their new 15W-40 oil includes a balanced package of additives, including 1,600 ppm of zinc as ZDDP. In addition, the oil contains detergent/dispersants, as well as important preservatives to keep the oil on engine components even when the car is stored and not driven regularly.

WHAT ABOUT DETERGENTS?

Detergents are added to crankcase oil to allow the oil to suspend dirt and control acids and other undesirable products of combustion. Detergents also prevent engine-damaging deposits from being formed. Some of the most significant wear possible in an engine can be caused by sticking or stuck components—piston rings, for example.

Some hobbyists choose to use oil grades and compositions that were recommended by the original manufacturer. This is not a problem for cars manufactured in the 1950s or later, as motor oil contained detergents by then. Even for earlier cars, detergent oil would seem to be beneficial. You may have read that modern oils with detergents should not be used in old engines. You've heard that they will loosen dirt and particles, which will then clog passages and result in burned bearings. It's theoretically possible for this to occur in an engine with very small oil passages. But do you personally know of a case where an expert mechanic could confirm that this actually happened? What's misleading is the term detergents. It conveys the idea that they are cleaning agents. For accuracy, detergents in oil are better described as detergent/dispersants. They do keep interior surfaces clean, but their primary job is to hold dirt particles in

CCCA Indiana Region's new motor oil for collector cars.

temperatures, the viscosity rating will be appropriate to your engine's needs. You can feel comfortable resisting the siren song of synthetics and other exotic lubricants.

If you live where winter temperatures are cold, and if you plan to drive your car on very cool spring and fall days, take advantage of the lower viscosity of multigrade oil when it's cold. If it's 10 degrees in your garage in the early morning, 10W-30 oil flows better than straight 30 does. Oil can do its job best with the fewest additives necessary, VI improvers included, so choose the narrowest viscosity span for the temperatures you're likely to encounter.

I use a multigrade oil in the engine of my older collector car. I do this because I can drive the car year-round where I live. The multigrades are thinner at engine start-up on cold days and so permit oil under pressure to fill all the galleries more quickly, and because with a hot engine at highway speeds, they stay thicker than the SAE 30 specified by the manufacturer 70 years ago.

CHECKING OIL

Make it a habit to check your engine oil every time you take your car out of the garage. Do it before you start the engine. Leaks can occur even when the car is standing still, and there may be less oil in the crankcase than when you last drove the car. (If your car has an automatic transmission, check the dipstick on that unit too.)

CHANGING OIL

We established earlier that oil becomes laden with suspended dirt and combustion products through normal engine operation, and that these unwanted particles contribute to engine wear. So your collector car's oil must be changed at reasonable intervals, and the engine really should have an oil filter. (More about filters in Chapter 5.) If the car is equipped with an oil filter, a reasonable interval means changing the oil no less than once a year regardless of mileage and no less often than every 3,000 miles. If your car does not have a filter, I would not exceed 1,000 miles between oil changes.

And what could be simpler than an oil change? Put a pan under the engine, remove the drain plug, wait for the oil to drain, replace the plug, refill with oil. Actually, it's often not quite that simple. Removing and replacing the drain plug can be an uncomfortable exercise involving contortions and bad language. And drain plugs can sometimes be a source of leaks later.

The really simple way is to replace your plug with a Fumoto drain valve. This is a small solid-brass ball valve

suspension so they may be carried to the oil filter and trapped there, or removed when the oil is drained.

Still, if the thought of oil passage blockage in your 1930s car keeps you awake at night, it's worth your peace of mind to seek out a nondetergent oil.

The best viscosity for your engine is a grade that will maintain proper HDL, yet not result in excessive consumption. If multiviscosity oil was recommended for your engine by the automaker, follow that recommendation. Single-grade oils were originally specified for collector cars built in the years before multiviscosity oils were available. If your collector car dates to this era, you have choices to make.

If you live where winter temperatures are very mild, the single-grade oil recommended by your car's owners manual will serve you well. The oil will flow sufficiently when starting to lubricate engine parts quickly. At high engine

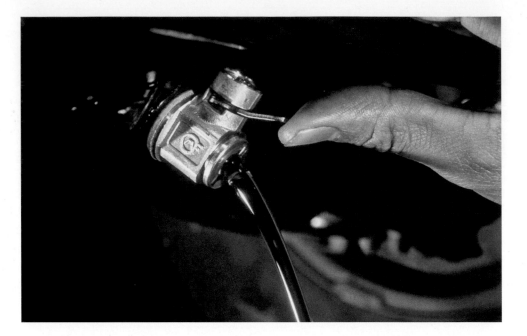

A Fumoto valve makes oil changing easy.

operated by a lever. A quarter-turn opens the valve; a quarter-turn back seals it. For security, you have to lift the lever against slight spring pressure to open it.

I can change the oil on my 1936 Cord without getting under the car. I slide my oil drain pan under the car by its long handle, look down to be sure that the pan is under the valve, then reach down and flick the Fumoto valve open. When the pan is fully drained—I leave it overnight—I reach down and push the lever closed. Pull out the oil drain pan, and I'm ready to refill the crankcase.

CHAPTER 3
GREASE JOBS AND OTHER LUBRICATION

The grease job is a thing of the past, as far as modern cars go. If you take your new iron to a quickie lube place, you'll note when they're finished that they've marked "N/A" next to most of the potential lubrication points on their checklist. (That's after you've paid your $35 to $50!) Modern cars use sealed grease points, which are intended to last the life of the car, such as that is.

Some classics of the 1930s were equipped with Bijur lubrication systems that delivered oil to every greaseable point. Fords and Mercurys in the 1950s offered a similar system as an option. But on most of our precious collectables, nearly every point in the steering linkage had a grease fitting. So did kingpins and some ball joints. So did suspension arms. On some cars the pedal linkage had grease fittings too. In addition, several points on the engine and drivetrain required grease or light oil periodically.

Lubricate your car yourself. It's a great way to feel close to your toy, and to know that what you're doing has a direct, positive effect on its longevity. You'll also get a regular opportunity to inspect undercarriage items for safety or potential failure.

You want to get the car up in the air a bit to do this job comfortably and safely. Before you do that, I strongly recommend that you first read Chapter 13.

Grease can be defined as a semisolid lubricating compound. Its purposes include reducing friction and wear, providing protection from corrosion, and sealing the greased component from water and contaminants. A good grease resists leakage and dripping and is compatible with the seals meant to contain it.

Greases are essentially oils gelled with compounds called soap. A variety of gelling agents are used commercially to make grease. The grease is often named for the gelling agent. If a sodium soap is used, the grease is called sodium-based. The same for calcium soaps and lithium soaps. Some greases are gelled with synthetic chemicals, or specially treated fine clay called bentone. Generally, the more soap used with the oil, the harder the grease. Nearly all of today's name brand chassis greases are lithium-based.

Greases are classified by the National Lubricating Grease Institute (NLGI). NLGI numbers describe the hardness of a grease, and in that sense relate to the amount of soap in it. The numbers run from 000 to 6, with the lower numbers denoting softer greases. Chassis grease, for comparison, is usually No. 2.

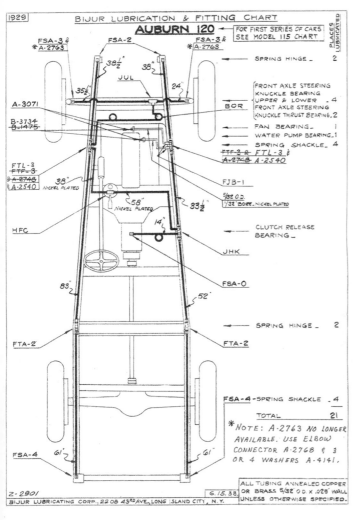

A Bijur central lubricator chart from the 1930s.

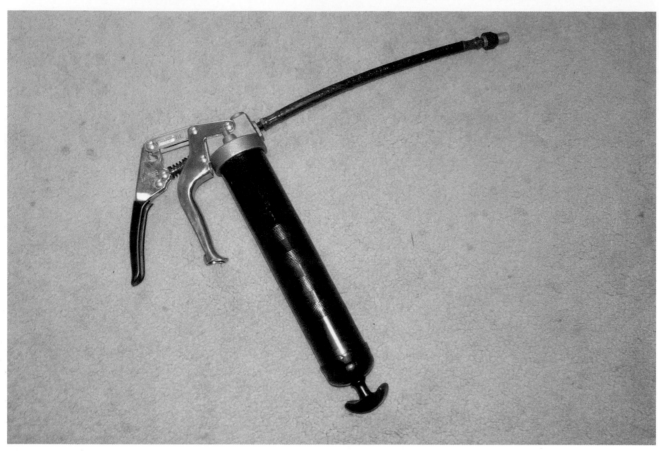

A modern grease gun by Alemite, with flexible extension for tight places. Clever linkage permits you to choose between high pressure and high volume.

This coupler can hang onto the grease fitting by itself.

A grease fitting cap from Niagara, with a ring that secures it to the fitting. You can use these to keep your brake bleeder screws clean too.

Using a grease rather than oil avoids the need for oil reservoirs, pumps, and tubing. The bulk of the gelled compound that we call grease is just the soap carrier. The oil weeping out of the grease does the lubricating job. The soap simply holds the oil.

Greases are not as good as oil for lubricating for several reasons. Since grease does not circulate, it does not carry away heat. There's no pressure moving the lubricant in grease to where it's needed, as there is with motor oil. So if the grease was not introduced into all the spots where it might be needed, the possibility of oil starvation exists. Further, wear fragments and contaminants in grease remain in the immediate vicinity of the lubricated parts, and can damage them. Lastly, it's difficult to completely flush these contaminants out of a greased bearing without complete disassembly.

Most of the points on collector cars that require lubrication with grease are in the steering and suspension systems. Generally these are equipped with Zerk-type fittings, and are lubricated with a grease gun.

Your main tool will be a grease gun made for a 14-ounce grease cartridge. That's the standard size sold in auto supply stores everywhere. (Avoid the miniguns. They have to be refilled often, and the selection of available lubricant cartridges for them is very limited.) I recommend getting a gun with a flexible neck that will enable you to reach some half-concealed fittings. The coupler at the end of the nozzle is supposed to be pushed over the end of the grease fitting and held there while you pump grease. Throw it away and buy a coupler that locks onto the grease fitting by turning a collar. There'll be times when you'll need one hand to hold the gun, and one hand to pump the lever. That's when you'll appreciate that the nozzle hangs on to the grease fitting by itself.

Keep a bunch of shop towels with you as you grease. You'll want to wipe off each fitting before you lock the coupler onto it. That's because dirt will have been sticking to the grease film on the fitting. If you don't clean it off, you'll push it right into the polished surfaces of the ball joint with your first pump of the grease gun handle. Wipe the fitting afterward to minimize the dirt that it will collect. Better yet, snap a nylon cap onto each grease fitting. Some caps have a ring tab that stays on the fitting and keeps the cap from falling to the ground and rolling around in the dirt while you grease the fitting.

As you pump grease into the fitting you'll see dirty grease coming out. Some instructions suggest that you stop pumping when you see grease emerging. I like to pump until I see clean grease follow the dirty grease that comes first. Then I know that clean grease has reached the working parts of the joint I'm greasing. It's messier, and may cost another nickel's worth of grease, but I prefer it. Wiping off the surplus grease will use up those shop towels.

Be careful, though. Many later collector cars have air- and water-tight grease seals over some joints. Ball joints are an example. So if the seal stays intact, the grease should technically stay in there forever. And in fact, if you put too much grease in there, you may even rupture the seal.

AUTOMATIC AND MANUAL TRANSMISSIONS

Modern automatic transmission fluids nicely meet the needs of the automatic transmissions that may be found in collector cars. Automatic transmission fluid (ATF) doesn't take the beating from combustion processes that engine oil does, but it is subject to a great deal of heat from the workings of automatic transmission clutches. Still, your collector car's automatic transmission should be able to run for several years before a fluid change is needed.

Your nose is a good tool for checking the condition of your ATF. If the fluid starts to smell like burnt toast, it needs changing now, in hopes of preventing major damage. Drop some ATF from the dipstick onto a clean paper towel. Examine the spot after a minute has gone by. If the fluid has spread out and is pink like the new stuff, or red or light brown, it is probably requires no action. If the spot hasn't spread out and is dark brown, the ATF has oxidized and should be changed. There are several different types of ATF, so check your owner's manual for the correct one for your car.

Unless you're a skilled mechanic, I don't recommend changing the fluid yourself. Just dropping the pan and draining the fluid can still leave most of the ATF in the torque converter or fluid coupling. Find a service station that will work with you, and let their equipment do a proper fluid change.

Manual transmissions benefit from the extreme pressure (EP) additives found in lubricants rated GL-4 and GL-5 by API. EP additives typically work by attaching themselves to the metal surfaces of the gear teeth. When microscopic asperities on the teeth come into contact with each other, creating high local temperatures, the additives provide boundary lubrication to prevent the metal surfaces from welding at the contact points. EP additives contain compounds of sulphur and phosphorous. Both of these can corrode what the techies call yellow metals. These include the bronze synchronizer cones used in your older car. (Some older cars have bronze bushings in the gears too.)

The level of EP additives in GP-4 gear oils is sufficient to protect the gear surfaces of manual transmissions. ASTM's D-130 Copper Strip Corrosion Test measures the corrosiveness of a gear lube to copper, which is a component of bronze. Grades range from 1a to 4b. GL-4 lubricants must pass this test with a grade of no less than 1b, which is the second-from-the-best rating. Pennzoil Gearplus SAE 80W-90 is one petroleum oil that meets the GL-4 spec; Amsoil Manual Transmission & Transaxle Gear Lube SAE 75W-90 and Red Line MTL and MT-90 are synthetics that do so too.

Generally speaking, GL-5 lubricants should not be used in manual transmissions. They have a higher level of EP additives, and are not required to get a high score on the D-130 test. If your ride is a muscle car or Corvette, though, consider a GP-5 gear oil that claims the API's MT-1 designation in addition to GP-5. (The designation usually is shown on the bottle as GP-5/MT-1.) The MT-1 spec originally was created for heavy-duty, unsynchronized truck and bus transmissions, and requires a grade of no lower than 2a in the D-130 test. This is considered the lowest acceptable grade for transmissions like ours. Lubriplate's APG series of gear lubricants is one that bears the GL-5/MT-1 designation. Their engineers assure me that the corrosion-causing reactivity of the EP additives in these lubes only comes into play at elevated transmission temperatures, as when shifting repeatedly under heavy load. And even then, say they, it is sufficiently controlled to merit the MT-1 rating. That's not the way most of our collector cars are driven, although only you can be the judge of this for your own car.

Like motor oils, transmission lubricants come in single- and multiviscosity forms. Your choice should be based on the manufacturer's recommendations, and what you learned about viscosity in Chapter 2.

Different brands of gear lube, even though they appear to have identical ratings and viscosity, may cause better or poorer shifting. Be sure to consult the website and print publication of your marque club for the brands that other owners have tried, and whose shifting characteristics they prefer.

DIFFERENTIALS

Most differentials in our collector cars, including post-1949 Ford products, use hypoid gearing. This results in quieter gears, but subjects them to severe sliding action that can wipe the lubricant off the gears. They can make good use of a GL-5 lubricant, in the grade specified by the car maker.

Limited slip differentials (LSDs) require fluid especially designed for them. While Chevrolet's trademark Positraction has become virtually generic, several different internal designs have been used in LSDs since Packard pioneered their use in automobiles in 1956. Consult your car's manuals or your car club's publications for the correct lubricant specification.

Penrite makes a steering box lubricant that's especially good for older cars.

MANUAL STEERING BOXES

This simple-appearing mechanism has several contradictory needs. Pressures are great between the gears and cams and rollers, so an antiscuff or extreme-pressure lubricant would seem desirable. But most older steering boxes used felt seals, and many incorporated bronze bushings. Neither works well with the common EP additives. Oil, even a viscous oil, tends to leak out of older steering boxes. Chassis grease won't leak, but the gear teeth cut channels through it and don't get lubricated.

One answer is a lubricant made especially for steering boxes. These products are viscous enough not to leak, but soft enough not to channel, even in cold weather. They are laden with EP additives of a type compatible with steering box components. One such product is Penrite Steering Gear Lubricant, imported from Australia. I've used it for years, with good results.

The Penrite lube is pretty thick when it's cold. While it is possible to warm the plastic bottle in a pan of water to make it runny, I've found that to be unnecessarily complicated. So I just "spoon" it out of the bottle with a Popsicle stick and stuff it into the steering box. It usually takes several shots, separated by a short time, for the lubricant to drift down into the gears.

POWER STEERING

Many later collector cars are equipped with power steering. A steering box similar to the manual variety was still in place, supplemented by a belt-driven hydraulic pump, hoses and a pressure cylinder.

The two most common power steering complaints are noise and leaks. A slipping drive-belt on the power steering pump can produce a loud squeal, especially when turning sharply. You can adjust this belt, just like a fan belt. Other noises, and leaks at hose couplings or at the pump should be dealt with by a repair shop.

The only regular owner maintenance for a power steering system is to check the level of the fluid periodically. Running the system low can ruin the pump. If low, check for possible leaks, before adding fresh fluid to the pump reservoir. Use a fluid recommended by your car's manufacturer; not all power steering fluids are compatible with all systems.

WHEEL BEARINGS

The bearings on which the nondriven wheels turn are lubricated by grease. There's usually a pair of them, the inboard ones slightly larger in diameter than the outboard ones. Most are of the tapered roller design, although ball bearings are used in some cars.

Periodically the old grease should be cleaned out of these bearings, and replaced by fresh grease. In a collector car, replacement every two or three years is sufficient. Use a grease specifically labeled for use in wheel bearings. The process is referred to as repacking.

Wheel bearings are enclosed in the wheel hub, so you'll need to remove the brake drums and hubs to get at them. Instructions for removing and replacing the drums will be found in your car's service manual. Here are some additional tips:

Degrease bearings carefully in fresh solvent, and keep them surgically clean. We've all seen the service station mechanic throw bearings into a hubcap as he removes them. That's a no-no. Remember that whatever you put into a greased bearing stays there. A bit of abrasive can do a remarkable job of destroying a freshly greased bearing.

Lay parts out on a clean paper towel. The time to inspect a bearing for wear or abrasion is while it is clean. Look for rough spots, pits, or anything other than a nice shiny smooth surface. Any discoloration or roughness is an indication of trouble. Bearings cannot be repaired.

A bearing packer that is used with a grease gun. Lisle Corporation

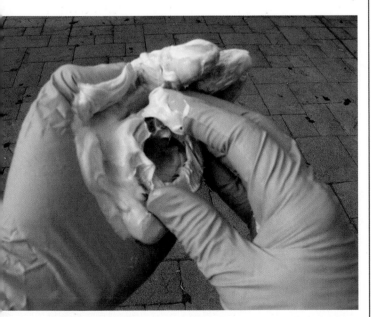

You can pack bearings by hand, too, but be sure all the old grease is pushed out.

A bearing packer that is operated by hand. It works well, but takes a good deal of effort. Lisle Corporation

Don't forget the oiling points on the generator, distributor, and starter.

They must be replaced. In the case of tapered roller bearings, the outer race (the cup) or the inner race (the cone) can be replaced separately, but if one is damaged the other may be as well.

There are two types of home garage bearing packers. One uses a grease gun to pump grease in. The other requires pushing the grease through with manual pressure. It works well, but can require a lot of muscle.

You can repack bearings with your fingers too, which wastes less grease. Use your palm and fingers to work grease through until it comes out all around the other side of the bearing. Just be sure that all the bearing crevices are full.

Tapered roller bearings must have a bit of end play. When you reinstall the drum assembly, use large channel pliers (the so-called water pump pliers) to tighten the nut firmly. This will seat all the parts. Then loosen the nut and tighten it back up snugly by hand. In the unlikely event that a slot in the nut lines up with the cotter pin hole in the spindle, put the pin in and you're done. If it doesn't line up, back off to the next slot. If that position feels too loose, tighten by one slot.

If you are really fussy, you can set the bearing clearance more accurately. You'll need a package of arbor shims, which you can purchase in a tool supply shop. Get them with an ID the same as the diameter of the spindle at the nut end. Before reinstalling the nut and its washer, add a single arbor shim underneath. Pick a thickness at random. Tighten the nut by hand again. Keep trying different washers until one of the nut slots lines up with the hole. It's tedious, but it'll give you just the right end play and contribute to the longevity of the bearings. (The importance of this adjustment was well-known to car owners in the 1950s. A two-piece nut marketed as The Educated Nut made it simple to get this adjustment right. I guess not enough owners of what are today's collector cars thought it was worth the three bucks.)

OTHER LUBRICATION

There are many other points on your car that need to be lubricated as well. If two surfaces rub together, they will eventually wear each other out. Only the film of grease between them keeps the surfaces from sticking together, squeaking, wearing rapidly or failing altogether.

In our collector cars' heydays, makers of lubricants put out charts that showed all lubrication points, helpfully noting which of their products should be used on each. (You can find these charts at swap meets or online now and then.)

As with motor oil additives, there are always new products claiming to solve all of the world's lubrication problems. Me, I prefer the tried and true. White lithium grease is available in tubs and spray cans. It can be used on door, hood, and trunk hinges. Cheap, narrow paintbrushes can get grease into irregular spaces. Stick lubricant works well on door strikers, trunk latches, hood latches, and trunk props. Silicone

sprays repel moisture. They are kind to rubber, so you can use them on squeaky weatherstrips. Some use them in door locks. I'm old-fashioned and prefer to squirt graphite in there.

There may be oil cups on the generator and starter bushings, and on the distributor. A wick under the distributor rotor may need some oil. So may the clutch throwout bearing. Don't be lavish with oil on these parts. The excess runs into the mechanism, and neither generator commutators nor clutch plates (with one exception) will benefit from a dose of oil. Check the lube chart to be sure you're not missing any spots.

The aforementioned exception was Hudson's "wet" clutch, which the company used for over 40 years. A bath of oil, or Hudsonite, as it later became known, provided smooth engagement between the clutch plate and a disc containing hundreds of small round cork inserts. Owners need to maintain the fluid level.

Keeping grease and oil on everything that needs it, in the right amounts, is one of the most important paths to longevity for your collector car. Doing it on a sunny weekend morning can almost make you feel that George Burns and Gracie Allen should be coming out of the car radio.

CHAPTER 4
ADDITIVES AND OTHER KINDS OF SNAKE OIL

Your local auto parts store probably stocks between five and 20 brands of motor oil additives. Few list their ingredients. All offer "Increased Engine Life and Better Gas Mileage in a Bottle." Most include effusive testimonials, some from respected racing professionals. Who can you believe?

Some years ago Fred Rau, then editor of *Motorcycle Consumer News*, did an intensive investigation of four basic groups into which motor additives can be placed. Here is a condensation of the results of his research, with some updates on the zinc issue.

TESTIMONIALS VS. SCIENTIFIC ANALYSIS

Most producers of oil additives rely on personal testimonials to advertise and promote their products. A typical print advertisement may include letters from satisfied customers stating something like, "I have used Product X in my engine for two years and 50,000 miles and it runs smoother and gets better gas mileage than ever before. I love this product and would recommend it to anyone."

Researchers refer to such evidence as anecdotal. While it has its place in the examination of any product or process, it is used responsibly only as an adjunct to scientific testing. Instead, we find it most commonly used to promote such things as miracle weight loss diets. Compiling personal testimonials for a product is one of the easiest things an advertising company can do—and one of the safest, too. As long as they are only expressing someone else's personal opinion, they don't legally have to prove a thing.

PRODUCTS WITH PTFE ADDITIVES

These used to be among the most popular oil additives on the consumer market. However, their popularity has declined as car owners have become more informed. But they are still on store shelves, so you should know about them.

These are products whose primary or substantial ingredient is PTFE powder suspended in petroleum or synthetic motor oil. PTFE is the common abbreviation for polytetrafloeraethylene. (DuPont Chemical Corporation sells it under its trademarked name Teflon.) Some heavily advertised brands fall into this category. While they must sell well, since they are still on the shelves, oil additives containing PTFE have also garnered their share of critics among experts in the field of lubrication.

The most damning statements originally came from DuPont, inventor of PTFE and holder of the patents and trademarks for Teflon. The company stated: "Teflon is not useful as an ingredient in oil additives or oils used for internal combustion engines."

DuPont threatened legal action against anyone who used the name Teflon on any oil product destined for use in an internal combustion engine, and refused to sell its PTFE powders to anyone who intended to use them for such purpose. Some additive makers simply went to Europe to buy their PTFE powders. Others filed suit. The courts ordered DuPont to resume selling their PTFE to the additive producers. The additive makers claim this is proof that their products work. In fact, it is proof only that the American legal system works. The decision against DuPont involved restraint of trade; you can't refuse to sell a product to someone just because there is a possibility they might use it for a purpose other than for which it was intended. The court's decision made no mention of PTFE's effectiveness as a motor oil additive.

The additive-makers claim that PFTE, in the form of suspended solid particles, coats the moving parts in an engine. Hard to believe. In manufacturing PFTE-coated cookware, the base material must be rendered scrupulously clean and free of oil during manufacturing in order to get the PFTE to stick to it. Those are hardly the conditions inside your engine.

Indeed, PFTE solids seem more inclined to coat nonmoving parts, such as oil passages and filters. And if your engine's oil filter is doing its job, it will collect as much of the PTFE as possible as quickly as possible. This can result in a rapidly clogged filter element. To assure

Lots of products to "improve" and "repair" your engine may be found on the shelves of your favorite auto supply store.

oil pressure, the filter's bypass valve will open and your engine will lose the benefits of oil filtration until the filter is next changed.

The PTFE sellers state that their particulates are of submicron size, and thus capable of passing through an ordinary oil filter unrestricted. This may be true when the additive is first poured into your car's crankcase. But PTFE expands when exposed to heat. So even if those particles are small enough to pass through your filter when you purchase them, they very well may not be so small when your engine reaches normal operating temperature.

In 1997, three subsidiaries of Quaker State Corporation (the makers of Slick 50) settled Federal Trade Commission (FTC) charges that ads for Quaker State's Slick 50 Engine Treatment included false and unsubstantiated claims. The ads claimed that:

> Every time you cold start your car without Slick 50 protection, metal grinds against metal in your engine . . . . With each turn of the ignition you do unseen damage, because at cold start-up most of the oil is down in the pan. But Slick 50's unique chemistry bonds to engine parts. It reduces wear up to 50% for 50,000 miles.

In fact, the FTC said, "most automobile engines are adequately protected from wear at start-up when they use motor oil as recommended in the owner's manual. Moreover, it is uncommon for engines to experience premature failure caused by wear, whether they have been treated with Slick 50 or not."

Testimonials in favor of oil additives often come from professional racers or racing teams. In the world of professional racing, the split-second advantage that might be gained from using such a product could be the difference between victory and defeat. Virtually all of the detrimental effects attached to these products are related to extended, long-term usage. For a short-life, high-revving, ultra-high performance racing engine designed to last no longer than one race or one racing season, the long-term effects of oil additives need not even be considered. Readers of this book, on the other hand, are primarily concerned with engine longevity. For this purpose, no laboratory tests have indicated any reduction in long-term wear in engines using PFTE as a motor oil additive. Instead, such tests have raised concerns regarding increased wear, clogging of oil filters, and potential starvation of bearings as a result of clogging of oil passages by accumulations of the particulate in the additive.

Regardless, manufacturers and publicists persevere, while continuing to produce new products and shouting claims about technological breakthroughs. Future tests will determine the accuracy of these claims. At this writing, however, there is no credible evidence that adding PTFE to your motor oil in any form will result in increased longevity for your precious collector car engine.

PRODUCTS WITH DETERGENTS AND SOLVENTS

Many of the older, better-known oil treatments do not make claims nearly so lavish as the new upstarts. Old standbys like Bardahl, Casite (now a line of Honey brands), and Rislone instead offer the benefits of quieter lifters, reduced oil burning, and a cleaner engine.

Most of these products are made up of solvents and detergents designed to dissolve sludge and carbon deposits inside your engine so they can be flushed or burned out. Usually, their active ingredients will be found in a base of standard mineral oil. One popular brand adds Stoddard Solvent (mineral spirits). Another, coal tar distillates. Other brands use kerosene, naphthalene, xylene, naptha, acetone and isopropanol.

In general, these products are designed to do just the opposite of what the PTFE additives claim to do. Instead of leaving behind a coating or a plating on your engine surfaces, they are designed to strip away such things. All of these products will strip sludge and deposits out and clean up your engine, particularly if it is an older, abused one. The problem is, unless you have some way of determining just how much is needed to remove your deposits without going any further, such solvents also can strip away the boundary lubrication layer provided by your oil.

Overuse of solvents is an easy trap to fall into, and one that can promote harmful metal-to-metal contact within your engine.

PRODUCTS WITH THE ADDITIVES ALREADY FOUND IN MOTOR OIL

Though some additives may not contain anything that could harm your engine (and some may contain things that could be beneficial), most experts still recommend that you avoid their use. The reason for this is that your oil, as purchased from a major oil refiner, already contains a very extensive additive package. This combination of additive components is blended to achieve a specific formula that will meet the requirements of your engine. Usually several of these additives are synergistic. That is, they react mutually, in groups of two or more, to create an effect that none of them could attain individually. Changing or adding to this formula can upset the balance and negate the protective effect the formula was meant to achieve, even if you are only adding more of something that was already included in the initial package.

Think of your oil as a cake recipe. If the original recipe calls for two eggs, will adding four more eggs make the cake better? Not likely. Instead it will probably upset the carefully calculated balance of ingredients and ruin the entire cake. Adding more of a specific additive that is already contained in your oil is likely to produce analogous results.

ZINC: LOOK BEFORE YOU LEAP

We live in an era of swiftly changing technology. This is both a blessing and a curse; those of us whose motoring tastes are stuck in an earlier century need to be keenly aware of what's happening around us.

Zinc dialkyldithiophosphate, or ZDDP, has been included in the standard additive package of every major brand of engine oil sold over the past several decades. As described in Chapter 2, ZDDP has become a focus of serious discussion in the first decade of the twenty-first century as motor oil formulators begin to reduce the zinc compounds in their products.

As we also read in Chapter 2, other additives are replacing zinc, albeit slowly. But they will be designed primarily to protect new engines. So you may be inclined to add a shot of a product that claims to include zinc to your favorite existing brand of oil. This may not be the simple solution it sounds like. With everyone leaping on

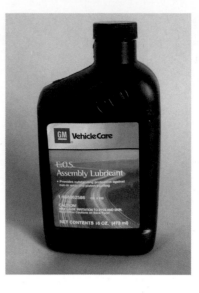

GM's EOS is intended to protect engines during startup. It's needed more than ever today.

the zinc bandwagon, products being sold as replacements may contain neither the correct quantity nor the correct formulation. Indeed, it has been shown that excessive zinc content can lead to deposit formation on engine valves, spark plug fouling and even bearing corrosion. In this case, more is not necessarily better.

One additive that has a loyal cadre of followers is GM's EOS, for Engine Oil Supplement. It was unavailable for a while, but is now back on the market as GM part number 88862586. GM intends it to be used as a crankcase oil additive to protect cams and tappets when the engine is started for the first time, but some collector car owners use it at every oil change.

At this writing, supplemental antiwear additive technology continues to be a developing science. At least one antique car club has commissioned chemists to develop a non-zinc antiwear additive for its members' cars. For the rest of us, the best sources of information on helpful and safe products, in my opinion, are hot rod and street rod magazines. Their editors and contributors are fine technicians and engineers, and often do the comparative testing that the collector car owner cannot do.

Additives with zinc compounds are easy to identify. The zinc phosphate they contain is a known eye irritant, capable of doing serious harm if it comes in contact with eyes. Therefore, products that contain zinc phosphate carry a federally mandated warning label indicating that they contain a hazardous substance. If you want to use one of these products, wear protective goggles and exercise extreme caution.

CHAPTER 5
FILTERS

If a single enemy to the longevity of internal combustion engines were to be named, it would be *dirt*. Thankfully, filtration technology has improved dramatically over the decades, and is one reason that engines last so much longer today than they did in the eras of our collector cars. So what can we learn from modern usage, and how can we adapt some of these new techniques to make our beloved cars last longer?

Filter manufacturers have spent decades testing how contaminated air, oil, fuel and coolants affect engine wear. Ditto for piston ring and ,valve manufacturers. Much of the data presented here is excerpted from their technical bulletins and test reports.

AIR FILTERS

Imagine you could have only one filter on your precious engine: Which filter should it be? Oil? No cigar. The component that your engine uses more of than anything else is *air*. And, unfortunately, air is the dirtiest component of the liquids and gases that enter your engine.

A typical six- or eight-cylinder engine inhales about one million gallons of dirty air for every one hundred gallons

A centrifugal air cleaner of the 1920s.

Oil-bath air cleaner on a 1957 Ford police car.

of gasoline it burns! The particles in that air include sand, clay, carbon, vegetable matter, insects, soot, and tire dust. Hard particles gouge and scrape at metal surfaces. They tear away oil films and cause frictional heat and wear.

In the 1950s, a piston ring manufacturer released an analysis that indicated 40 percent of piston ring failures were the result of excessive abrasive wear. An air-cleaner manufacturer determined that the wear rate for cylinder bores not protected by an effective air cleaner was 40 to 50 times greater than when an efficient air filter was in use.

The first carburetor air cleaners were introduced about 1925. They were designed to extract, by centrifugal force, the larger particles being carried by the air stream. In that era, 20,000 miles was a normal interval between ring jobs. The next step was the copper mesh filter. In this design the air passed through a copper mesh, like a potscrubber. The mesh was wetted in oil. Every 1,000 miles or so, the mesh was supposed to be cleaned in

Air cleaner with an oil-wetted mesh element.

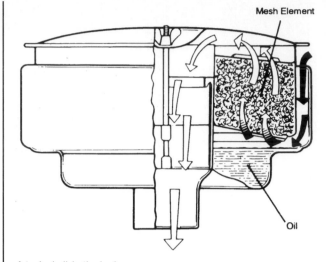

A typical oil-bath air cleaner.

Two styles of replaceable paper air filters.

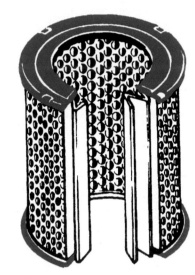

kerosene and redipped in oil. While this design would seem to deny entry only to insects and to the largest particles of dirt, it actually did trap some of the harmful particles. The effective element was the oil, which used the mesh as a lattice from which to hang. As the oil dried out and became clogged with dirt particles, the efficiency of the filter plummeted. Copper mesh filters remained in use until the 1950s.

By this time, oil bath filters were available for most cars—although they were standard equipment only on higher-priced lines. Introduced on expensive cars in the early 1930s, the oil bath filter still used a mesh filter as its primary element. The filter design forced the air to make a 180-degree turn across the surface of a pool of oil. As the dirt-laden air made the turn, some of the heavier particles of dirt stuck to the surface of the oil, eventually settling to the bottom. The air, carrying droplets of oil with it, then passed through a mesh element where more dirt was caught. This device was supposed to be cleaned and the oil replaced every 2,000 miles. Oil bath air cleaners are about five times as effective as copper mesh filters (which, we should note, can only be considered

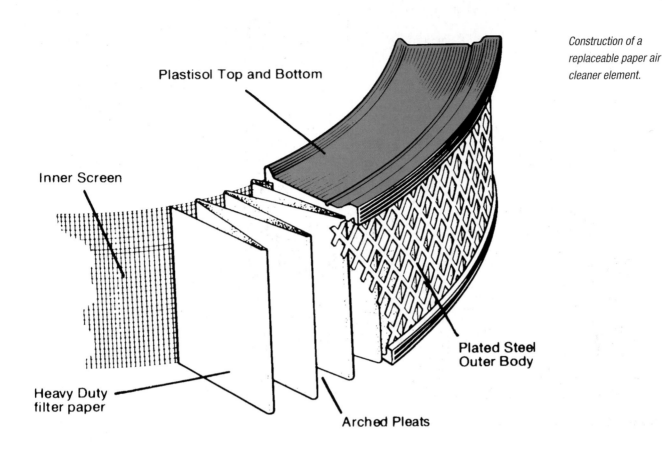

Plastisol Top and Bottom

Inner Screen

Heavy Duty
filter paper

Arched Pleats

Plated Steel
Outer Body

Construction of a replaceable paper air cleaner element.

as better than nothing). But even the best oil bath air cleaners are only effective if the mesh and the oil bath are scrupulously maintained.

Replaceable paper air cleaner elements were introduced on American cars in the 1950s. Since then, they've been joined by reusable polyurethane filters. When properly used, either can provide 98 to 99.9 percent clean air to your engine's induction system. If you care for your car, these are the *only* types of air filter that you should use.

The key to air filter design is to provide adequate filtration while not restricting the engine's enormous appetite for air. Manufacturers generally refer to their paper air filter elements as *light duty* or *heavy duty*. Light-duty filters are designed for cars. Since space is restricted, so is the size of the element. Paper filter media that block the smallest particles would clog up quickly. So the porosity of the filter element is a compromise, balancing free breathing and filter media efficiency. Heavy-duty paper filters are used in trucks and large equipment, where space is of less concern.

Larger elements can be used, with tighter porosity to trap smaller particles.

The Society of Automotive Engineers (SAE) has established standards for air cleaner testing. These standards are quantified with a test procedure, SAE J726. That standard has been adopted by the International Standards Organization (ISO) and is now ISO standard 5011. In the industry, this is referred to as a coarse dust test. For testing, dust is graded to sizes between 5.5 and 176 microns, with half of the dust being 50 microns. You remember that a micron is 1 millionth of a meter, or about .00004 inch. (It's interesting that this is referred to as a "coarse" dust test.) As we learned in Chapter 1, most engine wear is believed to be caused by particles that are about 10 to 20 microns in diameter. Paper filters frequently are rated to capture 98 percent of this particle size when they are new. As they age, they become more restrictive and actually capture more; but they should not be overloaded, as they can in some cases release particles that had been previously captured.

PAPER AIR FILTER CALCULATIONS

The major concern with retrofitting a paper air filter element is having enough filter area. For those who like numbers, here are some useful formulae.

By pleating the filter paper material, it is possible to have a relatively large filter in a small space. The minimum acceptable area for a paper filter used in a four-stroke engine can be found with the formula below, provided by Bill Kennedy. The boost figure is there to make the formula applicable to supercharged engines. In normally aspirated engines this figure is zero.

$$A = \left(\frac{\left[\dfrac{14.7 + Boost}{14.7} \right] \times CID \times RPM}{20,839} \right)$$

Where:

A = the area of the filter required, in square inches;
Boost = the boost pressure in pounds per square inch;
CID = the cubic inch displacement of the engine;
RPM = the maximum speed of the engine in revolutions per minute; and 20,839 = a constant.

Note: The 14.7 is atmospheric pressure at sea level and 70 degrees. If you live at a very high altitude—such as 5,000 feet—use 12.23.

Paper air filter packaging does not usually state the area of the filter inside. To arrive at a pretty close estimate of the area of a candidate filter for your conversion, use this formula:

$$A = (P \times 2) \times \frac{(OD - ID)}{2} \times L$$

Where:

A = Filter area, in square inches
P = the number of pleat edges, measured around the OD of the filter
OD = the outside diameter of the filter
ID = the inside diameter of the filter
L = the length of the filter element

Several manufacturers, including K&N and Amsoil, make air filters that use one or more densities of oil-wetted polyurethane foam or gauze. These filters are not discarded like paper elements, but instead are cleaned and reoiled at intervals. Tests have shown these filters to be a bit more effective than paper air filters. Considering the low number of miles that most collector cars are driven, however, I don't think that the additional expense and added maintenance of oil-wetted filters make them worthwhile.

If your collector car provided a replaceable air filter element as stock or optional equipment, consider yourself lucky. If your car predates the era of the replaceable element, you'll need to fit one. This may require some ingenuity, but it's a rare car for which this can't be accomplished.

Fortunately for us collectors, manufacturers have never been able to standardize the lengths or diameters or shapes of air cleaner elements. There are literally dozens of shapes and hundreds of sizes. To retrofit your air cleaner, you'll need to do some calculations first.

Because of the variety of air cleaner designs, it isn't possible to present specific plans in this book. But here are some suggestions. If you can find a stock air cleaner that uses a modern element, resembles the original, and will fit your car properly, consider using that. Candidates are those made for a later year of your car, or a more expensive make and model by the same manufacturer. Failing that, consider converting your stock filter to use a modern element. Physically, a paper or polyurethane element will have to be larger than the copper mesh fitted to an older air cleaner enclosure. Thus you can't just replace one with the other. Such a conversion may require destructive modifications to an original air cleaner. This is a last resort, but balance this vandalism against the protection of an original engine.

To choose an element, check the interchange charts for the size of engine this element was originally fitted to. Look for the same displacement as your engine, or larger. If you'd like to work out the numbers for yourself, see the sidebar above.

Just because they aren't as messy or obvious as water or oil leaks, don't ignore air leaks. Filter elements have soft plastic sealing surfaces that must fit tightly against the air cleaner. Also watch for and correct leaks that could permit dust-laden air to enter around the carburetor throat or around any tubes into the air cleaner.

Once fitted, maintain your air cleaner element religiously. Replace paper elements once a year. While polyurethane elements can go longer before cleaning and reoiling are needed, it's best to do this on the same yearly schedule. For simplicity, do your element maintenance every spring before the touring season starts.

CRANKCASE VENTILATION AND BREATHER FILTERS

There are only four ways for dirt to get into your engine. We've discussed the major one above. Next in order is the breather for the crankcase ventilation system.

Ventilation of the crankcase is necessary to remove acid fumes (which encourage the creation of sludge), and to prevent pressure in the crankcase from pushing oil out through the seals. Well into the 1950s, most American car engines ventilated the crankcase by means of a road draft tube. The tube opened into the crankcase and pointed down toward the road. Its bottom end cut at a 45-degree angle. The resulting mild vacuum when the car was moving was supposed to draw air through the oil filler cap and out of the tube, carrying with it noxious crankcase vapor. The fumes were released into the air. Tests of the era showed the emissions from road draft tubes often equaled those from the tailpipe as a source of polluting hydrocarbons!

The Positive Crankcase Ventilation (PCV) valve was invented during World War II to allow tanks to ford streams without drawing water into their engines. By the mid-1960s PCV valves and their associated piping were standard equipment on cars sold in the United States. Tubing incorporating the PCV draws fumes from the crankcase into the intake manifold, where they are burned with the incoming fuel charge. Makeup air is drawn in through the carburetor air cleaner, already filtered.

If yours is a pre-PCV car, the breathers through which makeup air enters the crankcase are usually part of the oil filler cap, and are most often equipped with the simple mesh filter used on early carburetor air cleaners. To eliminate this source of entry for engine-destroying dirt, you'll again need to adapt modern filter technology.

Unlike the situation with the large carburetor air cleaner-silencer, you probably will not be able install a replaceable element in your crankcase breather cap without modifying its appearance. So consider using an ugly but effective filter for driving, and replace the original cap only for shows.

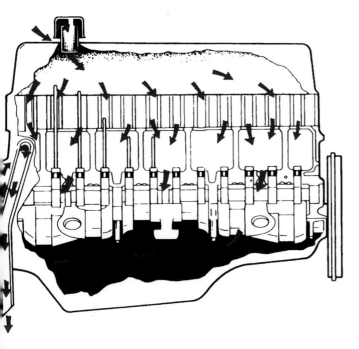

How the road draft tube system works. Air enters the crankcase from the breather at the top and is sucked out through the tube at the bottom.

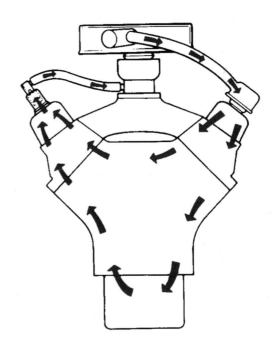

An early PCV system. Filter air was drawn from the air filter and vapors then pulled from the crankcase into the intake manifold during periods of high vacuum.

A lawnmower or motorcycle air filter "sock" can be adapted to filter air entering through the car's oil filler cap.

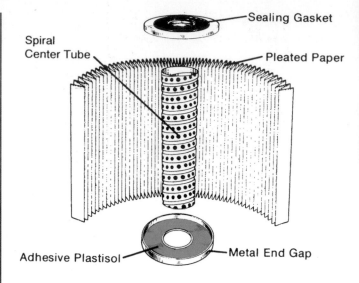

Construction of a full-flow oil filter element.

Replaceable air filter elements are made for the small gasoline engines used on lawnmowers. They're essentially a polyurethane foam sock, and may be just the right size to fit over the cap of your crankcase breather. They come in a variety of proportions too, to suit the location of your cap and the clearances available. Similar foam elements are available from motorcycle shops, some using the latest oil-wetted technology.

OIL FILTERS

As with air cleaners, the vital engine-saving potential of oil filtration was increasingly recognized with the passing decades. Few cars of the 1920s had any type of oil filter. By the 1930s and 1940s bypass filters were offered as standard or optional equipment on some cars, although most still had no filters at all. For these, aftermarket bypass filters were available. Integral full-flow oil filtration gradually became standard equipment in the 1950s.

Matt Joseph calls engine oil "a sewer for an engine's wastes," so an oil filter element has a tough job. Sludge, varnish, wear particles, soot, water, unburned fuel, carbon, and miscellaneous debris all circulate in the oil. The filter must attempt to remove these as they pass through. And it must remove the smallest particles it can, without plugging up too quickly. This is where the compromises begin.

The concept of bypass filtration is simple. Oil leaves the engine through a port that's fed from the main oil gallery. The oil passes through the filter before being returned to a point on the engine from which it drains into the crankcase. The bypass filter is not in the main line of oil circulation. It taps off and filters about 10 percent of the oil on each pass. The line to the filter is usually a 1/4-inch pipe or tube. Opening a hole of that

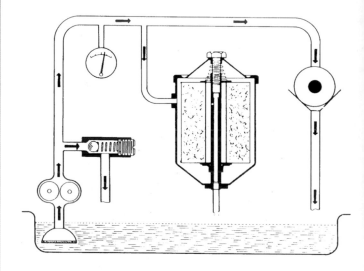

The principle of bypass oil filtration. Only some of the oil is filtered with each pass.

size in the engine's pressure lubrication system could cause a serious pressure drop. So a calibrated orifice in the line into the bypass filter restricts the volume of oil to an amount that will not cause a drop in oil pressure. Over a period of driving, all of the oil in circulation probably will pass through the filter.

Full-flow filters install directly into the main line of oil circulation. All engine oil passes through the filter, so all

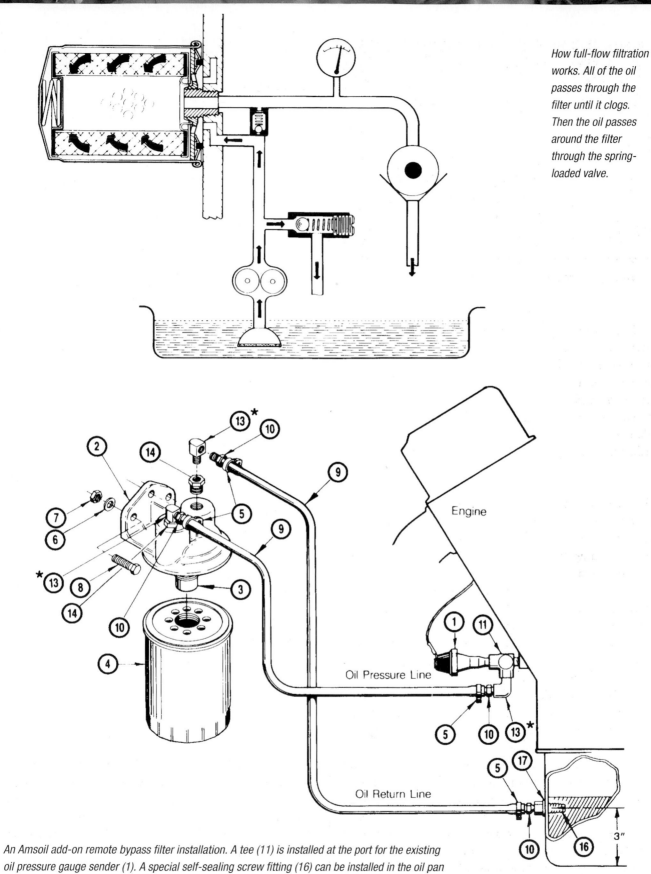

How full-flow filtration works. All of the oil passes through the filter until it clogs. Then the oil passes around the filter through the spring-loaded valve.

Engine

Oil Pressure Line

Oil Return Line

3"

An Amsoil add-on remote bypass filter installation. A tee (11) is installed at the port for the existing oil pressure gauge sender (1). A special self-sealing screw fitting (16) can be installed in the oil pan for the return line. Amsoil, Inc.

the oil is filtered all of the time. That would seem to be a more positive arrangement than the bypass filter system, but its effectiveness depends on proper maintenance. By the nature of their work, filters clog. The particles removed by the filter gradually block the filter's pores. Delay long enough between filter changes, and the filter element may plug completely. When this happens in a bypass filter, no more oil can flow through it. This doesn't cause damage. Oil pressure continues to be provided directly to the main oil gallery, and the engine simply runs on unfiltered oil until you get around to replacing the filter element. The full-flow filter element, by contrast, is in the main line of all circulation. If it clogged and blocked the flow of oil, the results would be catastrophic. So the base of each full-flow filter—the part to which you screw the "spin-on" element—is provided with a bypass valve. This spring-loaded device opens if the filter begins to clog, and permits oil under full pressure to flow around the filter element. (The valve may also open when the oil is cold and very viscous, and would have difficulty flowing through the filter.) In both bypass and full-flow systems, the result of a dirty filter element is the same—full volume of oil flowing through the engine, but with no filtration.

Since the entire volume of engine oil must pass through them, the pores of full-flow filter elements are far more open than those of bypass filters. If a full-flow filter element were as effective as a bypass element, the filter would clog in a very short time. Cummins Diesel's study indicated that most engine damage is done by particles of five to 20 microns in size. While many automobile full-flow filters will remove five-micron particles, some will permit particles as large as 20 microns to pass. By contrast, in tests by respected laboratories using the standard J806 SAE protocol for filter testing, bypass depth filters have removed 99.9 percent of particles 3 microns and larger. The thirsty fibers of bypass filters remove water from the oil as well. But remember that a bypass filter works on only some of the oil with each pass. Before it actually filters all of the oil, abrasive particles may have made many passes through engine bearings. Still, it's a far better solution than no filtration at all.

Before the 1950s, most cars that provided oil filtration at all used bypass type oil filters. (As late as 1955 neither the venerable Chevrolet "stovebolt" six nor the brand-new small-block V-8 offered an oil filter as standard equipment. A bypass filter was available as an option on both engines.) In many cases, filters were added later by the owner or dealer. These were always of the bypass type. Elements varied in composition and density. Filter

housings and the elements for them were supplied by manufacturers such as Fram, AC, Purolator and others.

Cars manufactured between the mid-1950s to the mid-1960s usually were equipped with full-flow filters of the canister type, with a replaceable element. But since replacement was a messy job, the canister types were superseded by spin-on elements, which are easy to obtain and install. Kits for converting the canister-type filter to a modern spin-on element are available for popular collector cars. They do affect authenticity; but for convenience and lack of mess they're worth it. If you need to look perfect for judging at shows, the original filter can be reinstalled in a relatively short time.

If your car originally used no filter at all, you can significantly improve your engine's longevity by installing a bypass filter. You can respect authenticity by using a filter housing dating to the era in which the car was built. The depth-type cartridge elements that these filters used are still available in the replacement market. Remove the old element and wash it—you should find the manufacturer's name and a part number. Most dealers can locate an exact replacement of the same brand or an interchangeable one from another. If you can't identify your element, contact the technical support service of a filter manufacturer like Wix, which can help specify an element based on its dimensions. I've found these folks to be very knowledgeable and equally friendly.

Avoid NOS bypass filter elements that can be purchased at flea markets. They may be many years old. Two of the major components of oil filters are glue and paper. Both dry out with time, rendering the element useless.

If your car is one for which no original filter was ever available, or if you want to improve on its stock filter, several manufacturers offer remote bypass filtration systems. These are intended as additions to the stock full-flow filters found on all modern vehicles, to provide the last full measure of filtration. But they will still be of great value as the sole filter on cars that originally had none. Amsoil offers a spin-on pleated paper filter element that's easy to change. While the design is similar to a full-flow filter, the pores are far smaller. Filtakleen and the venerable Frantz filter manufacture depth-type filters. The Hepo Company offers two levels of depth filters, tradenamed Oilguard and Hepo. The Filtakleen has a cast-aluminum housing. Several sizes are available, matched to the engine's oil capacity. The Franz unit is stainless steel, available polished as an option. Filtakleen's element looks like a roll of toilet paper in a gauze bag. It's made for them from a fiber grown in

Filtakleen USA

Bypass filter installations by Filtakleen (LEFT), Frantz (BELOW), and Amsoil (BOTTOM).

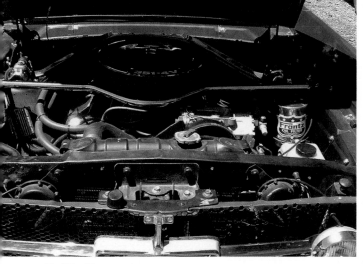

We Filter It!

Amsoil, Inc.

(ABOVE) *The Filtakleen depth element. It resembles a roll of toilet paper. But it's made of a special paper to industrial standards, densely wound.* Filtakleen USA

bar

Finland especially for the purpose. Frantz's filter element doesn't just look like a roll of toilet paper. It *is* a roll of toilet paper. (The Frantz filter has been on the market since the 1960s. It was substantially upgraded in 1999.) The Filtakleen unit is more expensive to buy, and its

elements are certainly more expensive than the Frantz's toilet paper. But the Filtakleen element is at least 50 percent more dense than a similar-size roll of toilet paper, and its consistent composition would seem to afford more reliable filtration than would the possible variations between brands and qualities of toilet paper.

Oilguard and Hepo filters are aimed primarily at the trucking industry, and their brawny machined cases and brackets reflect this. Their very efficient element looks like a roll of twine. It's wound more tightly toward the center. It filters from the outside toward the center tube, unlike the Filtakleen and Frantz, which filter from the top end of the paper roll to the bottom. Hepo claims less likelihood of channeling, in which the oil will cut passageways through or around the soft paper. And the Hepo and Oilguard's screw-on design makes servicing the element much easier than the rolled paper units.

To protect your car's authentic appearance as much as possible, you can install the remote filter in a hard-to-notice location. The Filtakleen, Frantz and Oilguard filters are all approximately the size of the bypass filters of the 1950s. The Hepo comes in a smaller, easier-to-hide size. All the manufacturers offer kits for installation on cars. Because the filter housing is under pressure, it may be mounted in any position. Just be sure that there are sufficient clearances and access for comfortable element replacement. Each of these filters requires a different style of access, so have your filter in hand while you are determining the best location for it.

Oil to a bypass filter is usually picked up from a tee at the oil pressure sender port, traveling from there to the filter through hoses made for this purpose. Returning the oil to the engine may require a bit more imagination. Amsoil provides a self-tapping, self-sealing fitting to return oil to your crankcase through a hole you drill or punch in the oil pan. It sells a punch tool too. Your engine may have a more

convenient return location where you won't have to make a new hole. Hepo offers an adapter to replace your car's oil drain plug, through which filtered oil can be returned to the crankcase. If you don't mind the appearance, Amsoil offers a swivel fitting that returns the oil through the oil filler cap. All these parts can be purchased separately, and used with any brand of bypass filter.

From 2003 to 2006, the U.S. Department of Energy conducted a three-year test of bypass oil filtration on a variety of gasoline-engine vehicles. The study used a

Amsoil's punch for making a hole in a sheet metal oil pan and the self-tapping fitting that screws into it.

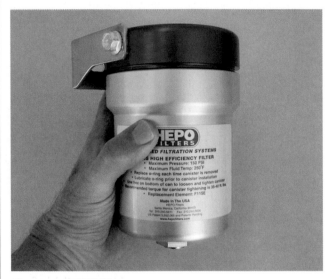

The compact HEPO filter.

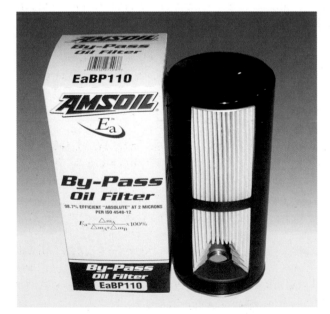

Amsoil's pleated paper bypass oil filter element. Amsoil, Inc.

The HEPO depth element screws into the machined top. So does the canister.

depth-type filter medium similar to the kind used in the Filtakleen. Analysis of the oil every 3,000 miles showed that oil changes could be reduced by 75 percent while still maintaining oil quality.

We are not seeking extended oil change intervals in our collector cars. But the cleaner oil provided by depth filtration seems like a good way to extend the life of an engine not originally equipped with a filter. While the various manufacturers may quibble over the precise level of filtration that their particular design offers, it seems clear that any filtration is a huge step beyond none at all. And yes, in some cases adding a bypass filter involves modifications to an authentic car. Only you can decide whether it's worth it.

Bob Adler, Chevrolet truck guru and owner of Adler's Antique Autos (www.adlersantiqueautos.com) offers a serious caution. Most installations of bypass filters require piping that can run four feet in length or even more. Typically, neoprene hoses designed to stand 250 pounds of pressure are used. Adler warns that these hoses are carrying full engine oil pressure. If the flexible line should break as a result of abrasion or other mishap, the engine's oil could be lost in a matter of minutes with catastrophic consequences. He feels that the potential danger outweighs the benefits of bypass filtration. I don't, but am plumbing my bypass filter with hard tubing, AN fittings, and stainless-covered hose just to be sure. These are the materials used on racing machines, available from Earl's Performance Plumbing. They cost a bit more than neoprene hoses, but in the quantities needed for a bypass filter installation this should not be an issue.

MAGNETIC DRAIN PLUGS

The lubricants in your transmission and differential enjoy a much easier life than motor oil does. But while they are subjected to far less dirt and abuse, transmissions and differentials do generate abrasive particles continuously as gear teeth slide against each other. These particles are steel, and what better way to capture them than with a magnet?

A practical way to put a large magnet right into the flow of lubricant is to attach it to the transmission or differential drain plug. Heavy equipment and aircraft have followed this practice for decades. Magnetic drain plugs used to be a popular aftermarket item for engine oil pans too, but I have not seen them in auto advertising for some years.

Before you install a magnetic drain plug in a transmission or differential, be sure that the magnet projecting into the housing will not interfere with any rotating parts.

Before removing your fuel filter, screw down these clamps onto the hoses on each side.

FUEL FILTERS

As with air and oil, the key word in the operation of a fuel system is cleanliness. A speck of dirt in the carburetor needle valve can cause engine flooding. Internally, carburetors have a multitude of small passages. Dirt in any of them can cause serious problems with engine operation.

Dirt gets into fuel systems in several ways. Gasoline caps that don't seal properly can admit airborne dirt. Rust can flake off inside of gas tank and fuel lines of old cars. Poorly executed attempts to seal the inside of the gas tank can be disastrous. If faulty techniques or improper materials are used, the result can be particles of sealant floating in the gas. And, once in a while, improperly filtered gas enters the tank from your local gas pump.

Many mechanical fuel pumps have a brass strainer in the bowl. So do many electric fuel pumps. Pleated paper disposable in-line filters are an excellent supplement. They are inexpensive and easy to install and replace. I recommend installing these filters on the input side of the fuel pump. When installing or replacing an in-line filter, use clamps to close down the rubber hoses before removing the filter.

Gasoline is a familiar fluid, but a very dangerous one. Be sure all parts of the car are cool before you begin opening gas lines. Be sure there's no one smoking and no open flames anywhere near where you're opening a gas line.

COOLANT FILTERS

A lot of junk circulates through the cooling system of your older car. Engine blocks in decades-old cars have been found to still have core sand from the manufacturing process in them! In our older cars, the installation of a coolant filter will help keep scale, rust and other particles from reaching and clogging the radiator.

One such device is the Gano filter. It comes in several sizes. The filter element is mounted in a clear plastic

Installed coolant filters from Tefba (ABOVE) and Gano (RIGHT).
MAKO Marketing

tube so you can watch your coolant flow. That's pretty and useful, but not authentic. With only a bit of head-scratching you should be able to invisibly install the two parts of the filter/strainer in an existing hose or tube. The Gano filter also includes a neat trap to keep captured particles from reentering the coolant stream.

The Gano filter's chief drawback is that you must partially dismantle some hoses and pipes to clean the filter. An Australian filter called the Tefba eliminates that need with a screw-off cap mounted on a vertical canister that holds the filter. Two screen meshes are provided. The company suggests that you start with the coarse filter. Once the major junk has been removed you can install the fine filter element. To service either type of filter, you may have to drain some coolant to below the filter level.

If you install a filter, be sure to clean it at least once a year (more often after you first install it). A filter plugged with crud restricts coolant flow.

Gano Filter Company

Bringing the filters on your collector car up to modern standards can be a chore. The outlay in time and money, while not enormous, may still be substantial. You won't see immediate changes in performance, comfort, or appearance. But no other improvements can have as profound an effect on your car's longevity.

CHAPTER 6
THE ENVIRONMENT AND US

Most people will agree that we have done damage to our natural environment. If you are not a believer, step outdoors on many days in Los Angeles or Pittsburgh or a host of other cities, and breathe deeply. Most of us can also agree that some steps need to be taken. First, we have to reduce the rate at which we are causing damage. Then, we need to find ways to undo some of what we have already done.

Collector car owners are a diverse population united by a common interest. That diversity has driven a variety of responses to our government's actions to restrain pollution and reduce our contribution to global warming. Some of us, convinced as we are of the righteousness of our cause, rely on Americans' love of liberty—and of the automobile—to protect our hobby. Others impute dark and devious motives to the bureaucrats, and vow civil disobedience. Still others throw up their hands and predict an end to car collecting as we know it. And a vital few to whom we are all beholden examine the issues and recommend actions that can influence the future of car collecting.

Reams of paper and miles of film have chronicled America's love affair with the automobile. Most collector cars are still exempt from the plague of regulations, inspections and licensing procedures that increasingly engulf modern cars. That's so because most citizens still view old cars on the highway as a friendly phenomenon. But there are strong forces who feel otherwise, and who write and lobby with a degree of vehemence a car-lover will find shocking. Many want our cars regulated and taxed off the highways, and they want it now.

Stanley I. Hart and Alvin L. Spivak are typical of those who prefer to rely on government coercion to implement their agenda. In *The Elephant in the Bedroom,* they call cars and trucks "the most wasteful element of our consumer society." Their remedy? Taxation of gasoline at "between five to nine dollars per gallon," with the revenue to be diverted, of course, to the construction of public transportation. The authors acknowledge that such extortionate taxation might decrease the usage of gasoline, so "the tax may have to be adjusted to even higher levels in the future."

While we bask in the smiles and admiration of fellow drivers on the road or at shows, we must not mislead ourselves about the fickleness of the public. With each repetition of even the most outrageous statement, more people believe it. When that statement has a germ of truth, and where ignoring it may carry risks to our health and that of our loved ones, a tipping point in public opinion is not far off. The Harts and Spivaks of the nation are not in the majority yet, but only our organized opposition will keep them from making the rules for our game.

To influence the future, and just to live with the changes of today, require a basic level of understanding of matters chemical and governmental that was unnecessary in the earlier years of our hobby. Still, one of the hallmarks of the successful car hobbyist has been the ability to integrate new knowledge and adapt it to

Emissions testing has become a big business. In most states collector cars are exempt from these periodic tests.

our needs. If we can learn to weld and to spray-paint, we can learn what we need to know about fuels and pollution and emissions testing.

Three major air pollutants are created by the burning of gasoline in cars. You ought to know these terms, because you'll find them referred to wherever pollution control is spoken. They are volatile organic compounds, carbon monoxide and nitrogen oxides. (The Environmental Protection Agency also tracks lead, particulate matter and sulfur oxides, but these are of less importance when discussing pollution caused by automobiles.)

Volatile organic compounds (VOCs) are sometimes referred to as hydrocarbons. They contribute to the formation of ozone, the primary component of smog. Ozone contributes to the damage of biological tissue, and to respiratory problems.

Carbon monoxide reduces the ability of the body to deliver oxygen to organs and tissues. It creates a special problem for those with heart conditions.

Nitrogen oxides (NOX) irritate the lungs, and are another ingredient of smog.

Concerns about the unarguable pollution of the air we breathe are responsible for governmental fiats that affect car collectors. Two that are of immediate concern are changes in the fuel our cars run on, and potential pressures to make it increasingly difficult to drive our favorite cars on the public way. Further in the future, but looming large, are intrusive and expensive testing procedures that may no longer exempt collector cars, as most of the current regulations do.

Why is all this being done? If you begin with the notion that pollution is a creation of big government, and that everything would be fine if we were only left to our own devices, then you can't help solve the problem. We do have a pollution problem to deal with. The issue is how to get those whom we elect to make our laws to respond to the hard facts that we can marshal for our cause.

When this book was written, the legislation that governed federal and state actions with regard to pollution control was the Clean Air Act Amendments of 1990. This legislation identifies 100 areas of the country where there is a problem with air cleanliness. It calls these airsheds. It establishes acceptable levels of pollution, and sets dates by which those levels must be attained. It mandates inspection programs for vehicles. These are called I/M programs, for Inspection and Maintenance. And, it gives the Environmental Protection Agency (EPA) the authority to work with

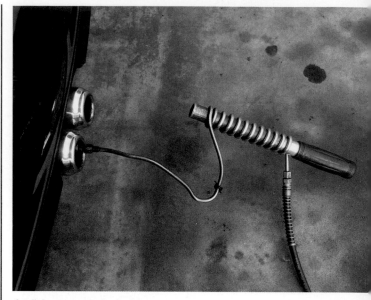

A tailpipe sensor collects data.

The computer gathers the data and checks them against permissible levels. In California, the information is sent directly to the DMV from this machine.

states on the development of solutions. Among these is the providing of incentives to those who contribute to air pollution to do things that will eliminate pollution. This last provision is the rationale for car-crushing programs. Instead of spending millions to clean up its own smokestacks, an oil refinery can crush cars and gain "pollution credits" to offset the damage that it does to the environment. So long as legislators and regulators believe old cars to be a major source of environmental damage, these programs will flourish.

EPA statistics are often broken down by "mobile" and "stationary" sources of pollution. Mobile sources include cars, trains, planes, lawnmowers, tractors, boats. If it moves, it's mobile. Stationary sources are everything else: homes, factories, refineries, steel mills.

Considering all the rhetoric, you may be surprised to discover that 1990 figures indicated that, on a national level, cars were NOT the major source of two of the above three pollutants. Stationary sources produced 48 percent of the VOCs, while cars produced less than 18 percent. Stationary sources produced 60 percent of the NO_X, cars only 11 percent. Only carbon monoxide is produced more by cars than by stationary sources: 31 percent to 20 percent. In all three categories, the pollutants produced by cars have gone down since 1970 by 5 to 9 percentage points, while those produced by stationary sources have gone up 3 to 8 points. This trend continues.

So why pick on old cars? It's hard to pinpoint all the exact motives, but generally there are three:
1. To the EPA, destroying old cars has a "green" feeling, and sells well to the Congress that appropriates funds to government agencies.
2. The more cars that are destroyed, the more that will have to be manufactured and sold to replace them. The term "harvesting" of cars has even been used.
3. Perhaps most important, note who attends the state and federal legislative committee meetings where regulatory decisions are made. Nearly everyone represents an industry that is regulated by these laws. It stands to reason that they'll be pushing for the best deal for themselves. Unorganized hobbyists and our cars become the chess pieces in the game.

So what do we do? First, we must clearly understand the issues. We must not act before we think, because that will simply destroy our credibility with the public and with legislators. In the world of politics, the good guys are not protected because they are good, or because they have reason and logic on their side. They are protected because they are organized. So organize we must. That will make it possible for us to make our case reasonably, accurately and persistently to those who make the laws. As voters and taxpayers, we *can* get our message across. But we must do it together.

Join the groups that lobby on our behalf. Among them are SEMA Action Network (SEMA-SAN) and Clean Air Performance Professionals (CAPP). Membership dues, for those groups that charge them, are a tiny fraction of your investment in your car.

Public opinion will be a vital factor in determining the future of our hobby. There are ways that we car lovers can show our best face to our communities. Matt Joseph has passed on a couple of ideas from a friend of his.

As tinkerers with old machinery, we have expertise that can be useful to our local governments. Every city and town has old equipment in its inventory. Such equipment is often disabled for want of an obsolete part, or by the inability of today's mechanics to fix it. So, machinery that is still usable is discarded and replaced, at great cost to the taxpayer. Car clubs, or individual restorers, can offer their services to their local government. Make them aware that you're ready to help them with the rebuilding or repair of aging equipment. You'll save money for yourself and fellow citizens. You'll get a kick out of making something work that might otherwise have been junked. *And* you'll help change our image with local officials from antienvironmental cranks to good guys.

Local governments regularly sponsor clean-up campaigns of various kinds. Local car clubs should participate in projects like collecting and disposing/recycling of old batteries, crankcase oil, tires and antifreeze. Activities like this will help officials and the public recognize the concern for the environment that we share with them, too often obscured by loud voices and finger-pointing.

Offer your club's services to local civic organizations for parades and festivals. Suggest exhibits of old cars to local museums. Historical organizations always look for speakers for meetings; so do service organizations such as Rotary. Get your most articulate members to offer their services. Include in your message the fact that old cars are not the enemy, and that we're all in the good fight together.

It's important to remember that what we are organizing against is not the issue of the danger to our environment, but rather our government's potentially misguided approaches to dealing with a genuine problem. Only you and I can make certain that our hobby has a future. Give it some thought, and take some action.

Getting our points across will make it possible for us to leave to our grandchildren not only our precious collector cars, but a safe and beautiful country through which they can drive them.

CHAPTER 7
NEW FUELS AND OLD CARS

In 1970 General Motors announced that it intended to meet federal emissions standards by the use of catalytic converters. The platinum alloy used in these devices is incompatible with lead compounds, and the eventual elimination of tetraethyl lead (TEL) from gasoline became inevitable. The Clean Air Act of 1970 led to the introduction of the necessary unleaded fuels in 1974, and to the beginning of the phase-out of TEL as a gasoline additive. It should be noted that when these decisions were made there was little concern about toxic emissions of lead fumes from automobile exhaust pipes. Lead had to go simply because it clogged up the catalytic converters.

When the federal government first announced its intention to eventually ban the use of tetraethyl lead in automobile gasoline, loud were the cries of the gloom-and-doomers in the car hobbies. Magazines carried editorials and articles condemning the move. Many predicted the demise of older internal combustion engines, suggesting that remedies would be expensive or impractical. At meets and shows, knots of enthusiasts (me among them) discussed in somber tones a nondriving future.

As always, the free market responded. Companies manufacturing fuel and oil additives added a lead substitute to their lines. Some drivers of collector cars use one, some don't. But nearly everyone worries.

My advice is . . . relax. Having to use unleaded gas should not stop you from fully enjoying most collector cars. Nor is likely to cause the prompt demise of the typical collector car engine. And, it will keep us all much healthier. To understand why, it's helpful to know something about the history of TEL in motor fuels.

In 1922 Dr. Thomas Midgley Jr. was working with Charles Kettering at the General Motors Research Corporation. (This company was a descendant of Kettering's own Dayton Engineering Laboratories Company, later abbreviated Delco.) The limited octane of existing commercial gasolines was stifling development of the performance potential of passenger cars, as experimental higher-compression ratios

The Ethyl sign found on gas pumps until the mid-1970s was not an ad—it was a warning label.

triggered knocking. Kettering and Midgley theorized that knock was the sound of *pre*-ignition, or fuel igniting before the spark plug fired.

An uncontrolled knock can quickly destroy an engine. Midgley and Kettering fitted a quartz window to the combustion chamber of a running engine, so they could actually watch preignition occur. They found that the knock was caused by a rapid rise in combustion chamber pressure *after* ignition, and not by preignition as had been assumed. Knock is often erroneously called preignition to this day.

Thus began the long search for antiknock agents. They experimented with various chemical compounds mixed into gasoline; the most practical was tetraethyl lead, first synthesized by a young chemist named Carroll A. Hochwalt in 1921.

In 1924, General Motors and Standard Oil of New Jersey formed the Ethyl Gasoline Corporation, to develop and market TEL as an additive to fuels.

By increasing the octane rating of gasoline, TEL reduced the tendency of high compression, heavily loaded engines to knock. That was its function. Period. Although gasoline refining methods continued to improve, it was

WHAT A POWERFUL DIFFERENCE THIS HIGH-OCTANE GASOLINE MAKES!

You'll always find driving more enjoyable when your car has plenty of pep and power. And the best way to get full power is to use high-octane gasoline. You see, the amount of power gasoline can deliver depends on its octane rating. So, no matter what other qualities you want in your fuel ...be sure you get a *high-octane* gasoline. Look for the yellow-and-black "Ethyl" emblem when you buy gasoline. Enjoy the powerful difference!

ETHYL CORPORATION
New York 17, N. Y.

Enjoy full power— use high-octane "ETHYL" gasoline!

An Ethyl ad from the 1950s, urging drivers to choose gas with TEL in it. Not all gasoline contained the additive. If it did, why would the Ethyl Corporation spend money on advertising?

far less expensive for refiners to further increase the octane of the gasoline by adding this compound than by more costly improved refining techniques.

Originally, the Ethyl Corporation intended to market ethyl as an additive to be poured into the tank by service station customers. A dispenser was to be provided near the gas pumps, and the motorist would attempt to guess how much ethyl fluid was needed to quiet his engine's knock. (That's not unlike the way lead substitutes are sold today.) That method wouldn't have been very effective. Most important, it wouldn't have sold much ethyl product. In a deal with Standard Oil of Indiana to premix the antiknock agent into its gasoline, Ethyl Corporation began its leap into the big time.

Lead's toxic nature was brought dramatically to light in 1924 and 1925 when 15 employees at Ethyl's three plants and experimental laboratories died of lead poisoning. Some of the fatally ill workers became insane before their deaths, prompting journalists of the time to label leaded gasoline "looney gas." Production was halted in May 1925, and the Surgeon General of the United States

appointed an investigating committee. A year later the committee reported that there were "no good grounds for prohibiting the use of ethyl gasoline," "provided that its distribution and use are controlled by proper regulation." The Ethyl Corporation promptly resumed production. The government would ban its product 50 years later.

Most gasoline marketers used Ethyl's TEL only in what became known as premium gasolines. On these pumps, The Ethyl Corporation's logo was prominently displayed. The regular gasolines supplied to service stations by most oil companies used no TEL at all for a decade. Not until 1933 was lead first used in a regular grade gasoline, and even then not in all brands.

The notion of a role for lead as a cushion or lubricant for exhaust valves was not even considered by engineers during the first 30 years of TEL's use as a gasoline additive. Quite the contrary. Most of the engineering time related to the use of TEL in motor fuels was devoted to getting rid of the lead deposits that TEL left behind! Dozens of papers at SAE conferences in the 1940s and 1950s dealt with methods of eliminating lead deposits from automobile engines. Lead was such a known nuisance that some brands advertised for decades that they obtained their higher octane without resorting to harmful additives like TEL. Blue Sunoco and Amoco White were two of these. As late as 1970, Amoco still advertised its premium product as containing no lead.

The pesky lead deposits built up on piston heads, valve guides and valve seats. Even spark plugs were found shorted out by lead accumulation. Midgley and his colleagues discovered and developed the chlorine and bromine scavengers that, added to the TEL mix, would help eliminate the buildup. Ethyl Corporation engineers teamed up with auto manufacturers on engine design changes as part of the assault on the deposits TEL left behind. Valve guides were counterbored. Valve grinding angles were arranged to narrow the contact surface of valve and seat. The contact itself was changed to an interference angle. These changes produced a narrow line contact between valve and seat that cut through the lead buildup. Valve rotators were developed by Thompson and Eaton, and saw increasing use in original engines and in the aftermarket. These devices caused the valve to rotate 10 to 15 degrees each time it opened and closed, eliminating local hot spots on the exhaust valve and seat. In the process, they also wiped away the unwanted lead deposits.

The worry today about the dangers of lead-free gasolines to older engines is based on concern about excessive wear of the exhaust valve seat, referred to as "exhaust valve

KEEPING YOUR HIGH-COMPRESSION CAR HAPPY

Snick Quicker has done some extensive studies of the performance of the high-compression cars of the late 1950s through 1970, and their operation on today's fuels. (The 1959 Cadillac, for example, had a compression ration of 10.5-1 and was designed for 94 octane gasoline.) Here is a greatly condensed version of his findings.

Based on his studies and on experience with his own high-compression cars, Quicker offers useful advice to prevent the knock, or "detonation" that would be caused by insufficient octane. He calls his solution "Smart Driving."

Of the several factors that influence detonation, the density of the air-fuel mixture and the engine speed are the only ones that can be controlled by the driver. When high-compression cars are driven at slow road speeds, they often "lug down" and knock. When driving in a lower gear with enough throttle to maintain the required road speed, the air-fuel density is reduced and engine revolutions increase. These conditions permit the engine to operate smoothly without detonation.

These huge high-compression engines were never intended to put out a great deal of power at low engine speeds. The key is keeping revolutions up. So shift down when driving at lower speeds or under heavy load. That means shifting your Hydra-Matic to a lower range too. The engine won't labor, and if it doesn't labor it won't detonate.

recession." This causes the valve clearance to steadily diminish. Hydraulic valve lifters will compensate, until their operating range is exceeded. If clearance reaches zero, the valve will not seat fully, and will burn.

Serious research on the effects of unleaded gasoline was not even begun until the late 1960s. American muscle cars of this era were reaching new levels of horsepower and performance. Recreational vehicles were growing in popularity. Highway speeds of 70 and 80 miles per hour were legal in many parts of the country. Engines had to be designed for reliability under such conditions, so testing was done to severe standards of speed and load. And valve recession *under these conditions* was found to be much greater with unleaded fuels.

The research found that valve recession starts with the transfer of material from the valve seat to the exhaust valve. The hard particles become embedded in the valve. They act as an abrasive, grinding away at the seat as the valve opens and closes. As the seat is ground away, the valve recesses into the cylinder head or engine block, upsetting the clearances.

The tetraethyl lead deposits that engineers had so diligently worked to wipe away in earlier decades had the completely unintended effect of acting as a solid lubricant, preventing metal to metal contact between the valve and its seat. Many papers dealing with the effects of unleaded fuel were presented at SAE conferences. All that I have seen date to 1970 or later. In nearly every case, test engines were run at high speeds and heavy loads. Road testing was done at 70 mph for long periods of time, under very hot engine temperature conditions. Bench testing was done at engine speeds as high as 4400 rpm, with coolant temperatures of 230 degrees. Under these conditions, exhaust valve recession in pre-1971 engines running on unleaded gasoline was measurable, and seriously affected engine performance.

The same tests found that engines run at moderate speeds and moderate loads did not suffer serious valve recession as a result of using unleaded gasoline. A 1971 paper presented by TRW engineers suggested that ". . . the average driver, who seldom exceeds 70 mph, should not experience significant engine deterioration." Ethyl Corporation engineers found that ". . . Operation at 60 mph instead of 70 mph reduced valve seat wear . . . by about two-thirds." Union Oil people stated that ". . . exhaust valve seat wear with zero-lead gasoline is responsive to engine speed . . . at 2300 rpm and 16.0-inch vacuum, exhaust valve seat wear was very low."

Some guidelines for driving all collector cars with unleaded fuel are suggested by the findings.

1. Stay within the highway speed limits.
2. Keep your cooling system in shape.
3. Don't pull trailers or haul heavy loads.

Those who own cars built between the 1930s and the 1950s are driving vehicles that spent their early years running on gasoline with little or no lead in it. It's unlikely, therefore, that the engine in a collector car of those eras will be damaged by the lack of a substance that it wasn't designed to use in the first place.

Muscle cars and the very high-compression cars of the late 1950s and the 1960s were intended to run on gasoline of a higher octane than is available at the pump today. If you drive one of these cars, you will want to read suggestions for modification of your driving habits on page 48. These simple changes to the way you drive can protect your engine.

Recent studies also indicate that there may be some benefit from using some of the additives sold as lead substitutes. If you want extra insurance, or just want to feel better, use them until the day that you need a valve job.

One fuel additive about which the author has received uniformly upbeat reviews is 85-year-old Marvel Mystery Oil. Users lace their gasoline with it at each fill-up. The military bought it during and after World War II in 55-gallon drums. Some drivers have installed top oilers, a device popular in the 1950s, which injects MMO (as its fans call it) or a similar fluid into the intake manifold to reduce carbon and help lubricate valve guides. Another use for MMO is described in Chapter 20.

If your collector car is running well, there's no need to overhaul your engine just to protect it from unleaded gas. Eventually, the regular driving that I hope you do will create the need for valve work. That's the time to invest in modern technology and metallurgy. Good machine shops now have considerable experience in fitting hardened valve seats. This will resolve the unleaded gas issue permanently. (All American car engines have boasted hardened valve seats since 1974.)

Two more points for when you have that valve job done. Back in 1971 TRW engineers found that in engines without hardened valve seats, changing the valve face angle from 45 degrees to 30 degrees reduced recession by 75 percent. And recent studies seem to indicate that the valve rotators that helped remove lead deposits in the TEL years can actually increase wear on valve seats with today's fuels. If your car is so equipped, consider having them removed.

Finally, celebrate the good things that lead-free gasolines have brought us. Studies have shown that combustion chamber deposits have been reduced, used oils contain fewer acids, and internal engine rusting has been reduced. See, there *is* a silver lining after all.

THE ETHANOL QUANDARY

For more than 30 years now, gasoline has been regularly reformulated to meet environmental concerns. Governmental pressures mandated changes in automotive gasoline beginning in the 1990s. With little real-world experience to guide them, refiners introduced oxygenates to meet the new standards. The two most widely used were methyl tertiary-butyl ether (MTBE) and ethanol. Within 10 years it was discovered that MTBE was leaching out of underground gasoline storage tanks and contaminating ground water. Its use has dramatically dropped since then.

The most widely used reformulated gasoline today is a blend of gasoline and ethanol. At this writing, an ethanol blend is mandatory during at least some part of the year in Minnesota, Montana, and Hawaii, as well as California, the Chicago area and most Northeastern states. Credit this to a combination of science and politics. There is substantial controversy regarding whether ethanol delivers more energy than it takes to produce, and over the huge government subsidies going to certain states and certain companies. Still, ethanol blends are a fact of life, so we need to know something about them.

Ethanol fuel (ethyl alcohol), the same type of alcohol found in alcoholic beverages, is made from such common materials as corn and sugar cane. It can be blended with gasoline in varying quantities. Pure ethanol is labeled E100; 10 percent ethanol is E10. Most internal combustion engines will tolerate mixtures of 10 percent ethanol. (Most cars currently being manufactured in the United States can use up to E85.) E10 is what we used to call gasohol.

What effect will these new fuels have on our older cars?

Anecdotal evidence seems to indicate that rubber components such as fuel hoses, carburetor seals and gaskets, and fuel pump diaphragms and seals may be hardened, dissolved or distorted by contact with ethanol. This may lead to fuel leaks.

Motorists in many parts of the country see the ethanol label on their gas pumps.

INSTALLING AN ELECTRIC FUEL PUMP

An electric fuel pump may be installed by cutting into the fuel line at a convenient location near the gas tank. That will put electric and original mechanical pumps in series. This is the easiest way to do it, but not the safest. That's because if the diaphragm in the mechanical pump should leak, the electric pump can pump gasoline directly into the crankcase. That's a potentially explosive situation.

The best way to install an electric fuel pump while retaining the mechanical pump is as a *parallel* system. The diagram on page 51 shows where to tee into the existing line to pick up fuel for the electric pump, and where another tee should be put in just before the carburetor. Provide a toggle switch to turn the pump on and off. Be sure to run the supply wire from the ignition switch, so the electric fuel pump cannot run with the ignition off. Now the electric pump can be used to fill the carburetor bowl before starting or as a supplementary pump on hot days or long hills, or shut off completely.

General aviation (noncommercial) propeller-driven airplanes use automotive gasolines. A 2006 FAA Airworthiness Information Bulletin stated: "The addition of alcohol (ethanol) to automobile gasoline adversely affects the volatility of the fuel, which could cause vapor lock. Alcohol present in automobile gasoline is corrosive and not compatible with the rubber seals and other materials used in aircraft, which could lead to fuel system deterioration and malfunction."

Galvanic corrosion of components of the fuel system where dissimilar materials are in contact may also increase. Metal parts, such as in-tank fuel pumps and carburetor floats, may be subject to pitting, rust or corrosion. Ethanol also corrodes cork, used as floats on the sender unit in the gas tanks of some older cars.

And, since ethanol holds water, it can expose fuel system components and steel gas tanks to rust.

What can you do to prevent such harm? Very little, if you drive your car regularly. Some states require that gasoline containing ethanol be so labeled at the pump so you can avoid them. Others don't. You will no doubt eventually wind up replacing some elastomers with new materials resistant to ethanol.

Since E10 gasoline has been in use in most states for years, you may have already had to replace some of the rubber parts in your fuel system. Until all parts, including hoses, have been converted to the latest materials keep a sharp out for gasoline leaks.

A small bright spot—with E10 in the tank you will never need a winter-time gas line antifreeze again.

MODERN GAS AND VAPOR LOCK

Your collector car starts to stutter and buck during a pleasant summer drive. You can keep it running with the throttle, but it jerks and stumbles and feels like it's about to stall. And restarting it may require a cool-down period with the hood up.

Vapor lock, which used to be a problem only for we drivers of older cars, is now back on the public agenda. The reason is that ethanol increases the vapor pressure of gasoline, which lowers its boiling point. This is a special problem on hot days at higher altitudes. Refineries change the mix of gasoline during summer and winter seasons; the summer recipe is less volatile and less likely to vapor lock. So the worst time of year is the early spring, when the weather suddenly turns warm but the gas stations are still peddling winter gas. And that's just when you want to drive your car!

State and federal regulations mandate continually lowering vapor pressures, so the gasoline component of the vapor lock problem should diminish. (Unless they change the formulas and regulations again.)

If your car vapor locks regularly, you'll have to deal with the three main causes: hot fuel, low fuel pressure and gasoline chemistry.

First check for originality. If your engine originally had insulation on the fuel lines and exhaust pipes, be sure that it's there. (Original insulation was often asbestos; today you'll have to use a replacement material, which usually abandons authentic appearance.) See that any original heat shields are in place around the fuel pump, fuel lines, and carburetor.

Examine the routing of the fuel lines. You want them far away from exhaust pipes and exhaust manifolds. If a line must cross an exhaust manifold, keep the crossing as close to right angles as possible, for the least heat transfer. If you can't reroute the copper fuel lines, consider insulating them.

Next, be certain that your fuel is under pressure for as much of the run of the fuel line as possible, especially in warm under-hood areas. Since the mechanical fuel pump is often located close to the carburetor, its action

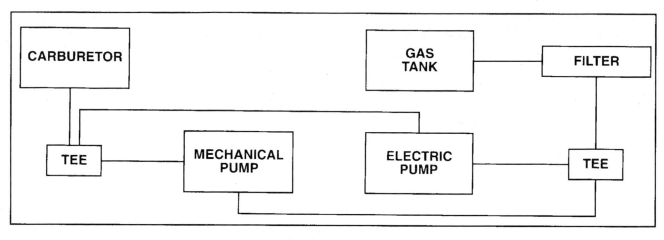

The preferred piping diagram for installation of an auxiliary electric fuel pump.

creates a mild vacuum in the fuel line all the way back to the gas tank. That's the least desirable condition. To put your fuel lines under pressure, you'll have to install an electric fuel pump. There is a way to do this while retaining the use of the mechanical pump (see below).

Percolation feels like vapor lock, but has a different cause. It's a result of gasoline actually boiling in the carburetor float bowl. When the gasoline boils, it creates pressure and expands. Since the pressure can't return down the line to the fuel pump, it forces gasoline out through the jets. The resultant flooding stalls the engine, and makes it difficult to restart immediately. Some carburetors have an antipercolation valve that automatically vents the float chamber to the intake manifold when the throttle is closed. If your car isn't blessed with this design, you can relieve the situation by decreasing the temperature of the bowl. One method is to increase the insulation between the carburetor and the intake manifold by adding more gaskets. If there's sufficient clearance between the top of the air cleaner and the underside of the hood, you can add two or three gaskets to improve this condition.

The mechanical fuel pump in many cars is located at the top of the engine, where it provides another opportunity for heat to be exchanged between the engine block and the fuel, making percolation problems even worse. In some cars with chronic problems, relief has been obtained by running the fuel line directly from a rear-mounted electric fuel pump to the carburetor. The original fuel pump may be left in place to preserve the illusion of authenticity, and to supply vacuum for windshield wipers.

The carburetor's needle valve shuts off the flow of fuel to the bowl when the float signals that the bowl is full. It's exactly the same action that takes place in the toilet tanks in your home. If you install an electric fuel pump, you may need a pressure regulator to reduce the output of the pump to a pressure that the needle valve can handle. Many electric pumps put out enough pressure to push the valve open even though the float bowl is full.

If your car chronically vapor locks no matter what you do, the installation of a modern vapor-recovery system may solve the problem. You'll have to install a three-outlet fuel filter near the carburetor. Like an ordinary filter, one line carries fuel in from the fuel pump, another carries fuel out to the carburetor. The third outlet carries vapor back to the gas tank. You'll need an additional line for this purpose. Such a system is best installed by a knowledgeable mechanic, preferably one who's done it before. The reasons are several. The outlet size on the three-outlet filter is engineered to work with the engine on which it was originally installed. Getting one to work correctly on your engine may take some experimentation. Even more important, the return vapor line must enter the gas tank through a hole that must be added for this purpose. Gasoline and its vapors are not to be trifled with. Drilling holes in any part of a gas tank that's in place in the car is not suggested practice for the neophyte. If you need this modification, ask your club members for referrals to a competent mechanic.

If your ride is vapor-locking on a hot day, make it a habit to lift the hood whenever you stop. I know this doesn't look "cool," but it helps the fuel system cool down much more quickly.

Your car ran within its normal temperature range once, and it can again. Once the system is in good shape, reasonable regular maintenance will keep it so. Stay cool!

CHAPTER 8
HOT AND COLD

The warm months of the year are the most popular ones for touring in collector cars. The higher ambient temperatures, though, lead to some of the most irritating of collector car problems: the multiple specters of overheating and vapor lock.

Vapor lock and percolation were discussed in Chapter 7. I define overheating as a condition in which engine temperatures rise steadily until a point is reached where the coolant is lost or the coolant boils. Just running at a high temperature is not in itself an overheating condition if coolant is not being lost.

Production cars of the collector car era had cooling systems that were capable of handling ordinary driving conditions while maintaining engine temperatures in an acceptable range. Some systems on older cars, though, were marginal when new. Years and miles now go by. Scale and chemical residues build up inside the cast iron block, insulating the coolant from the cylinder walls. Deposits in the radiator passages reduce the core's ability to transfer heat to the air. So do several layers of paint on the core. Add in a long grade and a hot day and the fun drive becomes a steaming nightmare.

Happily, many hot-weather problems are avoidable through maintenance. Others may require judicious modifications. And before you begin to dismantle your car's cooling system, consider some of the other factors that can cause an engine to run hot.

ORIGINALITY

Since your collector car did not overheat when it was brand new, the first step is to be sure that its parts and specifications are as they were when it was new. Unless you're the car's original owner, you can't be sure that some critical part was not changed during the vehicle's earlier life. Experience with old cars will soon convince you that it is impossible to imagine all the things that people will do to machinery, or even to comprehend why they did it. So you'll find water pumps with the wrong impellers, fan drive pulleys in incorrect diameters, belts that don't fit and slip, incorrect carburetor jets (or complete carburetors), distributors with incorrect spark advance parts, missing insulation, fans that are smaller or with fewer blades than the original, and other abominations.

To begin to solve cooling problems, start by restoring the car to its original design. Many problems solve themselves just like that.

IGNITION TIMING

Determine that the basic timing setting is correct. Check the distributor's centrifugal and vacuum advance mechanisms to be sure both are working. To be certain that they are maintaining the advance curve to original specifications, seek out a shop with a distributor machine. For a collector car, you'll probably have to supply the shop with the specs for spark advance and dwell. You'll find these in your car's service manual.

MIXTURE

An old car may run quite well on a mixture that's leaner than specifications called for. But lean gas mixtures increase the heat that the cooling system has to carry away from the combustion chambers. The result can be overheating, and even burned exhaust valves.

Besides checking carburetor specifications, look for vacuum leaks. The entry of additional air through a point other than the carburetor will lean out the mixture. The old method of finding leaks involved squirting gasoline at suspected leak points and listening for the engine to speed up as the gasoline was drawn in by vacuum. This method is messy and dangerous. A safer method using the same principle involves a propane torch. Install a nozzle with a 12-inch flexible hose on it. (The long nozzle is so you can keep your face and the rest of you far back from the test area.) Run the engine at idle. Crack the torch's valve, but *do not light it!* Play the end of the nozzle around suspected leak areas, including the base of the carburetor, the end of the throttle valve shaft, and the intake manifold gaskets. The engine will speed up when the propane enters a leak.

THERMOSTATS

Thermostats permit your engine to warm up quickly, and to maintain temperature in the optimum range. If your engine takes a very long time to warm up, there is a good chance that a thermostat is stuck open. If the temperature keeps rising, the thermostat may be stuck partially or completely closed.

One way to *not* solve an overheating problem is to run the car without a thermostat. Some cars will run too cool as a result, creating problems with sludge and acid corrosion. Others may actually overheat without the thermostat doing its part in the hydraulic design of the coolant flow.

The thermostat designed for your engine is the one you should be using. The engineers balanced many factors when they specified the thermostat. Unless you fancy yourself a better automotive engineer than they were, don't tamper with thermostat temperature specifications. Do make certain that the thermostat is opening fully, and at the specified temperature.

RADIATOR CAP

Modern cooling systems are kept under pressure by a specially designed radiator cap with matching neck. Most collector cars had pressurized systems too. Be sure that the cap is holding pressure, and that coolant is not being lost through the overflow pipe. A properly maintained pressurized system should rarely need water added. A radiator shop has the testing device to check the cap. If your cooling system isn't pressurized, check the gasket on the radiator cap. Much water can be lost through a leaky gasket here.

HEAD GASKETS

Exhaust gas entering the cooling system will increase its temperature rapidly. Exhaust gas or oil can get in through a blown head gasket or through a crack in the block or heads. While there are several home tests to determine whether this is happening, the best is an inexpensive leak test conducted by your radiator shop.

THE RADIATOR

Despite all the sophisticated analyses, the most common cause of an overheating car is still a dirty radiator core. If you suspect this is the problem, have a flow check performed at the radiator shop. If plugging is extensive, the shop can tell you whether they can rod it out. Boiling, a caustic process, will not remove the dried accumulation of gunk in narrow radiator tubes. Some core designs don't lend themselves to

Most postwar collector cars have fin-and-tube radiators. To ensure the best performance, the fins must be kept straight. This tool for straightening them is called a fin rake and works with most common fins-per-inch. It is made by the Eastwood Company. The Eastwood Company

rodding. In other cases, the tubes are deteriorated too far to save. If a new core is recommended, find out first from your car club's technicians what other owners have done to restore the radiator's cooling capacity while maintaining original appearance.

If you do need a new core, there are specialty shops that can create cores that closely resemble original designs. Such shops include The Brassworks and Independent Radiator Manufacturing.

SHROUDS AND BAFFLES

The radiator's ability to transfer heat is more dependent on air flow than on water flow. Be sure that the radiator's fins are clean, and that some previous owner did not put a coat of heavy paint on the fins.

Most collector car-era cars used baffles to direct all of the incoming air through the radiator core. Shrouds around the fan assured that the fan drew air only through the core, and not from the engine compartment. All of

Be sure all original baffles, shrouds, and fan rings are in place.

these sheet metal devices were carefully engineered to make the cooling system function efficiently. Be sure they're all in place, fastened tightly, and that they retain their correct original shape.

LEAKS

While most of us are concerned about coolant leaks that leave drips on the floor of the garage, the less noticeable leaks are often the more dangerous kind. When the engine is running, these leaks aren't letting coolant out; they're letting air in.

Air in the cooling system reduces the heat transfer capability of the coolant. It forces water out of the overflow, reducing coolant capacity. Worst of all, it provides the final component needed for rust: water, iron and air.

How to reduce the amount of air? Keep your cooling system filled to the maximum. (This is more important for early, nonpressurized systems. A pressurized cooling system with an overflow tank is always full of water, keeping air out.) Fill the radiator when the engine is warm *and running*. (Pouring cold water into a stationary hot engine could crack the block!) When the engine is cold the thermostat is closed, and may not permit complete filling.

Your radiator shop can check your car's cooling system for air leaks. They can also tell you whether the leaks are caused by loose hose connections or by exhaust gases from a leaking head gasket.

HOSES

The rubber hose in a cooling system has always been the system's weakest point, structurally. It had long been assumed that hose failure was due to cracking of the rubber caused by heat, or to failures of the yarn with which the hose was reinforced. Research done by The

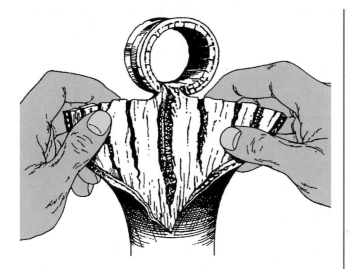

The effects of electro-chemical corrosion on the inside of a radiator hose.

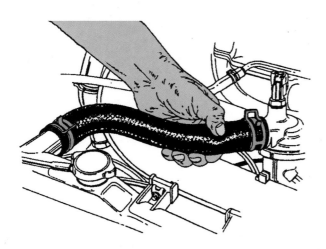

Squeeze a hose to diagnose what's happening inside it.

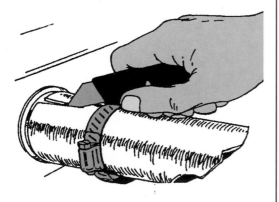

Remove an old hose by slicing it carefully.

Gates Rubber Company eventually discovered that the real culprit was in the same family as the cause of rusting chrome, corroded brake lines, rusty fenders and damaged engine bearings. It's our old enemy, the electro-chemical reaction caused by dissimilar metals in the presence of a weak electrolyte. When it affects rubber hoses, Gates calls it ECD, for electro-chemical degradation. The rubber is assaulted by the electrical charge and develops tiny cracks, or striations. Coolant seeps through and weakens the reinforcing fiber. It wicks along the fiber until it finds a weak spot, which is where the hose eventually bursts.

The damage continues whether the car is in use or not. Since it's done from the inside out, a hose that looks just fine may be about to go. Damage usually occurs one or two inches from where the hose is connected to a pipe or nipple, not in the middle. Check hoses by squeezing near the ends with your thumb and forefinger. Squeeze the middle too. If the ends feel significantly softer than the middle, replace the hoses. You may also detect a cracking sort of feeling near the ends, as the weakened hose splits under the pressure of your fingers. If hoses appear hardened, or are cracked on the outside, or bulging, replace them immediately. If they're oil-soaked on the inside, find out how the oil is getting into the cooling system. A leaking head gasket is a good bet.

Smaller hoses on your engine carry coolant to the heater or to the carburetor or other heated components. It's hard to tell the condition of these hoses by squeezing, so replace them regularly.

All the hoses on your collector car should probably be replaced every four or five years, no matter how nice they look. ECD is attacking from the inside. Murphy's Law will make certain that the rupture occurs while you're on a tour.

When replacing a hose, drain the cooling system down below the level at which you're working. (If you wish to capture the coolant for reuse, use a funnel to guide the flow into a clean container. Put a paper coffee filter into the funnel to catch the inevitable junk that'll come out when you drain coolant. No point putting that stuff back in the engine.)

Loosen the hose clamp, and slide the old hose off the fitting. If it's stuck, as it often will be, do not pry it off with a screwdriver. You risk damage to the radiator nipple or other component to which the hose is attached. Use a new blade in a utility knife to cut the hose off. Be sure the blade is new; a dull blade is much more difficult to control. Make light cuts in one direction until you've

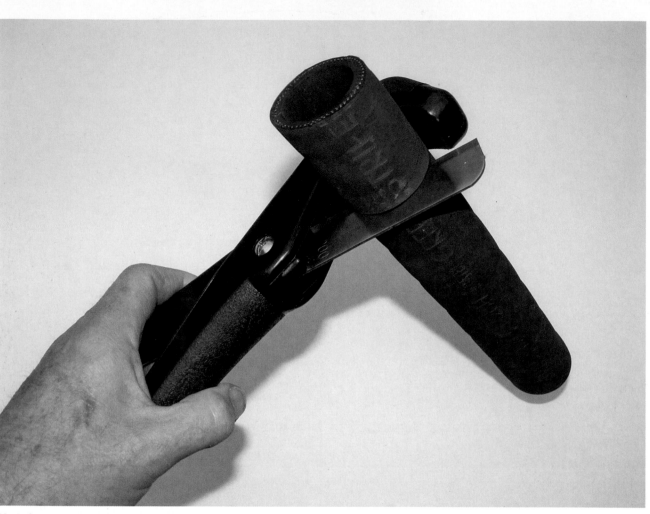

Most of us can't make a perfectly straight cut in a radiator hose with a knife. The easy way is with a tool like this one by Goodyear.

cut through the hose. Avoid deep cuts in the nipple, which can provide a leakage path later.

Make certain that the nipple is clean and smooth. Use a wire brush to remove old stuck rubber. File smooth any sharp or ragged edges that could cut the new hose.

Dip the end of the new hose in coolant, to lubricate it for easy installation. Most radiator nipples have a raised bead at the end. When you install the new hose and replace the clamp, be sure that it's positioned between the bead and the end of the hose. A clamp tightened on top of the bead will eventually cut through the hose. Tighten the clamp snugly, but not with all the force you can muster on the screwdriver. The inside surface of most radiator hoses is of a softer rubber than the outside. It conforms well to the nipple, and seals against leaks.

Refill with coolant to the correct level. Start the engine and check all hoses for leaks. If you find any, tighten down on the clamp a bit. Leave some turns for a final tightening after you've had the car out on the road, and given all the components the opportunity to warm up and cool down.

HOSE CLAMPS

Collector cars were delivered from the factory with an evolving variety of hose clamps. Some of the early ones did not exert as much clamping force as later ones did. While it is possible to get a leak-free system with older clamps, regular attention is required on trips to be sure a clamped joint has not begun to leak.

You are understandably reluctant to replace your early hose clamps with modern worm-gear types. But a solution is now available that offers the ultimate in modern clamping while not offending the purist (too much). It's the Gates Powergrip thermoplastic clamp. You slide this plastic band over the hose and push the hose onto the nipple. Now you apply a heat gun,

Gates' Powergrip hose clamp comes on a cardboard tube.

and the band shrinks to apply optimum clamping force. The device's clamping force adjusts as hose temperature changes. It actually gets tighter as temperature drops, to eliminate cold leaks. It's available in all radiator hose sizes.

The black band is not very noticeable against black radiator hoses. Now put your old-style hose clamp over it and tighten just enough to hold it on, and the Powergrip clamp becomes even less obtrusive.

Gates sells a fancy and expensive heat tool to remove the clamps. You really don't need it, though; a soldering gun, carefully applied, will melt the plastic material just as well.

SACRIFICIAL ANODES

There is an inexpensive component you can install in your radiator that will reduce corrosion in the radiator, engine block, and cylinder heads. It's called a sacrificial anode. Read about it in Chapter 17.

WATER PUMP

It seems reasonable and logical that the longer the water stays in the radiator while it's passing through, the more time there will be for heat exchanging, and the cooler the engine will run. This has led to suggestions for modifying the water pump to decrease its output, by reducing the number of vanes on its impeller. Bad mistake. Thermodynamic analyses make it clear that the *more* water you can push through the radiator and block, and the *faster* it moves, the more heat exchanging will take place. And heat exchanging, after all, is what a cooling system does.

A rebuilt water pump provided by a reputable vendor of parts for your make of car should move all the water you need. Still, for those stubborn cases like flathead Ford V-8s, vendors can supply high-performance pumps that move a good deal more water and will further lower cooling system temperatures.

HEAD BOLTS

Torquing cylinder head bolts evenly is vital to leak-free, long-lived head gaskets. Follow the torquing sequence given in your service manual, and use an accurate torque wrench. The design of some engines is such that the cylinder head bolts actually enter the cooling system passages of the engine block. This creates the

THE EVANS COOLANT

For about 15 years, Evans Cooling Systems has marketed a product called NPG (Nonaqueous propylene glycol). It is 100 percent propylene glycol, with some additives to inhibit reactions with certain metals. You fill your radiator with this; no water is used. No pressure need be applied to the system, so later collector cars with pressurized cooling systems may discard the radiator cap in favor of a nonpressurized one.

Propylene glycol boils at about 370 degrees F. That means that with this coolant your engine can never boil, even after you turn the engine off after climbing a long hill on a hot day. But since PG is a poorer heat transfer medium that water, your engine's internal and external temperatures may run somewhat higher than with the typical water/antifreeze mixtures.

Evans claims that the absence of water eliminates the vapor boiling that causes hot spots, especially around exhaust valves, and encourages nucleate boiling, which improves heat transfer. Evans also claims dramatic decreases in cooling system corrosion, since there is no water in the system.

A problem with NPG was that it was many times more viscous than water, especially at lower temperatures. Water pumps in some cars using this coolant had to be replaced with units designed to pump the thicker fluid when starting up in cold weather. Evans' current product is called NPG+. It incorporates some ethylene glycol, which helps reduce viscosity by half in colder temperatures. An expansion tank must be fitted to prevent loss of coolant as it warms.

Evans NPG+ is in use in a number of collector cars, including two that have successfully run The Great Race. (One, a 1917 Hudson, won.) Owners of these cars appear pleased with the results. Neither of the cars ever overheated under heavy load or at high speeds.

The characteristic of Evans NPG+ that will be of most interest to collector car owners is that it offers increased cooling system longevity. NPG+ is a very poor electrolyte, so it does not degrade radiator hoses and gaskets. And because the coolant contains no water, it does not have to be replaced.

Converting your system to Evans NPG+ is a tedious procedure, although it's not difficult. They key is that all vestiges of water must be removed from the system. Evans sells a product called Prep Fluid, which is a waterless flush to be used in engines that cannot be completely drained. Two other downsides are that the materials are expensive, and that when in use, the coolant turns a frightening black color, which has startled some new users!

Evans makes no outlandish claims for this product. NPG+ will not make your collector car run smoother or faster, nor will it make you more attractive to the opposite sex. But adventurous owners who are seeking long lives for the innards of their collector car engines may want to try this stuff. And if your car currently runs on the ragged edge of overheating during the summer, this may be a solution to that too.

Many thanks to author and columnist Ray Bohacz for sharing his extensive experience with the Evans coolant with me.

---

opportunity for leakage around the bolt threads. And, rusting of the threads of the bolts or the block makes it difficult to apply uniform torque.

To permit accurate torquing and prevent leakage in engine designs of this type, you need to apply a compound designed to seal as well as lubricate. You also need a product that will not set up too quickly, since it takes a while to torque all the bolts in the pattern recommended by the car manufacturer, and early set will seriously distort torque values. Loctite's engineers recommend their Gasket Eliminator 518, applied to the end threads. It provides some lubricity, gives you four hours of working time and seals the threads against coolant seepage.

COOLANT

Here's a list of coolant choices for collector cars:

Straight Water

Don't even consider it.

Water with Anticorrosion Compound Added

This choice has the advantage of the best possible heat-transfer ability. Consider it if you live where the temperature of your car storage space will never drop as low as 32 degrees. Or use this coolant in the warmer months of the year, but be scrupulous about changing to an antifreeze mixture in the fall. Actually, this was standard procedure when some of our older collector cars were new.

In those days, the corrosion inhibitor would have been a variety of soluble oil. There are better products available today. I've used No-Rosion Cooling System Corrosion Inhibitor. Originally developed for stationary cooling towers, it is very effective at keeping automotive cooling systems clean. Red Line sells a product called WaterWetter. It's promoted as a means of dropping engine temperature and as an anticorrosion additive. A surfactant, or surface tension reducer, it is supposed to reduce cavitation and permit the coolant to maintain closer contact with the walls of the passages of the engine cooling system, thereby minimizing local hot spots. Red Line shows impressive charts in its literature. While anecdotal evidence is mixed as to its effectiveness in dropping cooling system temperatures, most users seem satisfied. And it is a very effective anticorrosion additive. Try it if you want to defend your cooling system against corrosion, and don't harbor unrealistically high hopes for improved cooling system effectiveness. Neither anticorrosion additive affects the 212 degree F boiling point of water.

Water and Antifreeze in a 50-50 Mixture

Back in the 1940s, ethylene glycol used as an antifreeze was referred to as permanent. Prestone was the best-known brand name. Its permanence was by comparison with methanol antifreezes, which

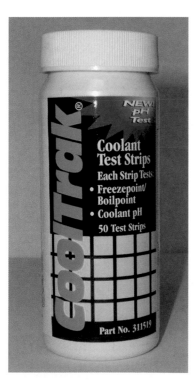

With Cooltrak dip strips you can quickly determine the freezing and boiling points of your coolant, as well as its alkalinity.

boiled away if the engine's temperature rose too high. Now the last thing that Union Carbide, Prestone's manufacturer, wanted was for people to believe that once they'd installed Prestone it was good for the life of the car. That dramatically reduced potential antifreeze sales. They outsmarted themselves, though, because believe it people did. Prestone solutions often stayed in cooling systems for years. After the corrosion inhibitors were used up, untold damage was done to engines and radiators.

If you live in an area where temperatures drop below freezing in some months of the year, a 50-50 water-antifreeze mixture is what you'll need to use. Plan to drain the cooling system and replace the coolant once a year. You'll start with fresh inhibitors, and do your engine a real favor.

Until recently, the glycol-based antifreeze available to collector car owners would have been based on ethylene glycol, or EG. This is a chemical that by itself boils at a lower temperature than water. But when mixed with water it undergoes a magical change, becoming a coolant that boils at a higher temperature than plain water. EG has been the basis of antifreeze for over 60 years. It does have a serious flaw, unrelated to its use in the car. It's highly poisonous. Even a small puddle of spilled antifreeze, lapped up by a thirsty pet, can be deadly. Worse yet, it has a sweet smell and taste that encourage such a tragedy. Colorado State University Veterinary Hospital reports that 50 percent of all poisonings of dogs and cats involve ethylene glycol antifreeze.

There is a safer alternative. Antifreeze formulations are now available based on *propylene* glycol. PG, for

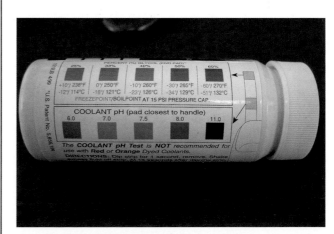

You check the dip strip against this chart on the bottle.

short, has been used for years as an ingredient in foods, cosmetics and medicinal products. Because of its lack of toxicity, the regulations regarding disposal of PG are less stringent in some states than those for the disposal of toxic EG. Check on this locally; these rules have a habit of changing suddenly.

In corrosion protection and stability, you'll find little difference between the two types of antifreeze. There are areas where the differences are more substantial, and they explain why ethylene glycol so dominates the antifreeze market.

PG's freeze protection is 5 to 6 degrees less effective than EG's. PG boils at 3 to 4 degrees lower temperature, too. Of more concern is that PG is more viscous than EG, especially at very low temperatures. At -20 degrees F, PG's consistency is about that of SAE 20 oil at room temperature. This reduces its heat transfer ability, especially at very low temperatures. And if you switch to PG, your old hydrometer won't work anymore. That's a small loss. The makers of PG antifreeze now provide simple dip strips that will tell you the freeze point and other useful information.

Bottom line: Ethylene glycol is a marginally better antifreeze than is propylene glycol. This can be an issue if you live in a very cold climate, or if your cooling system needs every break it can get. If the toxicity issue is an important one to you, then PG is the way to go. Just be aware of the downside.

Any antifreeze in your cooling system will cause your car to run a bit warmer than it will with water in it. Ethylene and propylene glycol have only about 60 percent the heat transfer ability of water. Mixing the two results in heat transfer characteristics that are proportional to the mix. So, a 50-50 mixture of antifreeze and water has about 80 percent of the heat transfer ability of water.

The tradeoff is that in an unpressurized cooling system, 50-50 EG antifreeze boils at 227 degrees F, PG at 223 degrees F (at sea level). That's 11 to 15 degrees higher than plain water. That can be an important margin on a very hot day. The engineers tell us that this margin makes a 50-50 antifreeze coolant the best one to use. Some experienced collector car drivers swear by a plain water-inhibitor mix. You may want to experiment.

Electrolytic corrosion occurs inside your cooling system, too. All the ingredients are there: dissimilar metals (like an aluminum head and iron block), and immersion in a conducting electrolyte (the coolant). The battery action causes the transfer of material from one surface to the other. Interfere with this process by keeping the corrosion inhibitors fresh. That means changing the coolant no less often than once a year. A sacrificial anode can help here too. See Chapter 17.

When it comes to your cooling system, there's water and there's water. Where I live, tap water is so hard that any spillage on the outside of the radiator dries to a crusty white film. I don't even want to think about what that leaves on the inside surfaces of the engine block and radiator. Distilled water that you buy in jugs at the supermarket makes a good basic coolant, but remember that it *must* be mixed with antifreeze or an anticorrosion chemical. Never use deionized water. It is mineral hungry, and will look to your engine block and other cooling system components to try and absorb those minerals. And avoid tap water. Even the softest tap water contains unwanted minerals.

CHAPTER 9
BRAKES

Combustion in your car's cylinders turns heat into rotating motion to make the car go. Your brakes turn rotating motion back into heat to make your car stop. In fact, when it comes to energy conversion, brakes actually out-produce most engines. The engine in your fast collector car may accelerate it from zero to 60 in, say, 10 seconds. Your brakes, in a panic stop, can probably decelerate it from 60 to zero in less than half that time. Since horsepower is a measure of work accomplished in a given time, your brakes can produce double the horsepower of your engine! (See below for a discussion of how much heat your brakes produce.)

Our collector cars, with a few rare exceptions, used drum brakes in the front and rear. A few basic designs covered nearly every make of American car. Lockheed brakes were manufactured by the Wagner Electric Company under Lockheed patents. The basic design called for brake shoes pivoted at their bottom end on one or two anchors. The primary shoe provided most of the braking power, and was leading. This means that its brake cylinder end pushed it into the direction of drum travel. The trailing shoe provided much less braking power. Shoes were adjusted using cams. Some later versions used a special design with two single-ended wheel cylinders. Each operated a single brake shoe, both of which were leading. That resulted in very powerful brakes. However, with the car in reverse, brake power would be inadequate because both shoes would become trailing when the drum turned in the opposite direction. So the two-leading-shoe design was used only on the front. Conventional Lockheed brakes were used at the rear. Two-leading-shoe brakes were particularly popular in England. In the United States, a modified version was used on Chrysler cars from 1956 to 1962. Chrysler called them Center-Plane brakes. Ford hydraulic brakes, before they switched to the Bendix design, were similar in design to Lockheed.

Bendix brakes were based on designs patented by the Bendix Aviation Corporation between 1929 and 1950. They had come into widespread use by

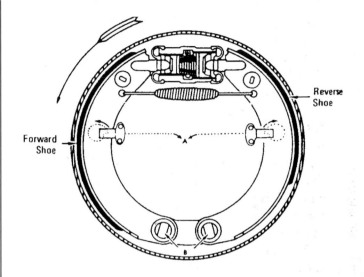

The Lockheed brake design used on many cars through the 1950s. Ford used a similar brake until they switched to the Bendix design.

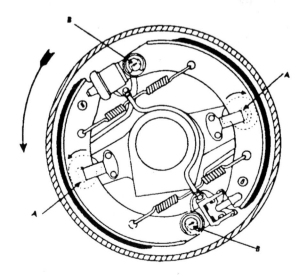

The British call this a "two-leading shoe" brake. Chrysler cars used it on their front wheels in the 1950s.

This is the nearly immortal Bendix duo-servo design, seen here on a 1957 Buick.

the late 1930s. By 1955 all American cars used the Bendix "duo-servo" design front and rear. The Bendix design permits the two shoes to float on the backing plate, connected at the bottom by an adjustable link. When the primary shoe contacts the drum, it moves with the drum, and transfers this movement to the secondary shoe through the link. In effect, the shoes wrap around the inside of the drum. The result is a significant increase in braking effectiveness.

The Bendix brake was one of the most successful and long-lasting designs in American automobile history. It's safe to say that because of the Bendix brake, there have been fewer revolutionary changes in drum brake design than any other automobile part. While there have been minor improvements in details over the first 60 years of the use of this brake in production cars, the only significant change was the addition of self-adjusting linkage in 1960. Parts for Bendix brakes of

The 1950 Crosley Hotshot, the first American car with disc brakes.

This spoon is used to turn the star wheel on the adjusting screw of the Bendix brake. Lockheed designs adjust with cams, turned by a box or socket wrench.

BRAKING ENERGY

Bill Kennedy wrote this copyrighted piece to help us understand how much heat brakes generate. I reprint it here with his permission:

There is an interesting characteristic of kinetic energy that plays heavily into the nature of brakes. The kinetic energy of an object is directly proportional to the square of its speed. That means that for a two-fold increase in speed, the kinetic energy will increase by a factor of four; for a three-fold increase in speed, the kinetic energy will increase by a factor of nine; and for a four-fold increase in speed, the kinetic energy will increase by a factor of 16.

Say your 1946 Pontiac sedan weighs 3,400 pounds and it is moving at 20 miles per hour when the light suddenly turns red just in front of you. You've got to stop. How much heat are you going to create?

There's a convenient formula that will tell us how many British thermal units (BTUs) must be created to keep you from running the light.

$$\text{BTUs} = \frac{.0004739085 \times P \times (\text{mph} \times .447)^2}{2.204622}$$

Where:

    BTUs is heat in British thermal units
    P is the mass of the moving object (the car, in this case) in pounds
    mph is the speed of the object in miles per hour

If you work the formula with the above numbers in mind, it will tell you that the heat generated to stop is about 60 BTUs. If you were going 60 mph, the result would have been about 540 BTUs. (Remember the square law mentioned above: three times as fast equals nine times the energy.)

How much heat is that? At 20 miles per hour, you might be expected to stop your Pontiac in about two seconds. If you did that, the heat production of 60 BTUs in two seconds seems like a relatively small amount. But consider this: A normal-sized house in the Midwestern United States might be heated with a 100,000-BTU per-hour furnace. If your Pontiac stopped in two seconds and generated 60 BTUs, it would be producing heat at the rate of 108,000 BTUs per hour. (60 BTUs for 2 seconds x 30 = 1,800 BTUs per minute x 60 minutes = 108,000 BTUs per hour.) That's more than the fire in your furnace! We're talking about some serious heat here, even at 20 mph.

Now suppose you were driving your 1970 Cadillac convertible. This 4,900-pound car, by the same formula, would generate about 85 BTUs to stop from 20 mph. That's 153,000 BTUs per hour!

If we scale that up to a panic stop from 60 mph in six seconds, we're up to about 315,000 BTUs per hour for the Pontiac and 455,000 for the Cadillac. If you kept that up, you could heat a small school on a cold day. The brakes on your collector car do a lot of work, no matter how you look at it.

Now remember that braking can be *continuous* under some conditions—descending long grades, for instance. So while your car is descending a western mountain, for example, your brakes may have to dissipate enough heat to warm a schoolhouse in North Dakota in the winter!

All that heat can cause brakes to fade, or lose their effectiveness. All the more reason to pay careful attention to your braking system.

Use the formula to figure out how much heat *your* collector car's brakes are producing.

the 1930s can be purchased off the shelf at your local auto supply store.

Among American production cars of our collector car era, there have been only a few other deviations in brake design. Chevrolet used the Huck brake for some years, then switched to Bendix. The other exceptional designs were the caliper brakes made by Goodyear for the Crosley Hotshot in 1949. This was the first use of disc brakes on an American production car. The Chrysler Imperial of 1949–1951 featured a Kelsey-Hayes disc brake.

Parking brakes (or emergency brakes, as we used to call them) operate the rear shoes by cables attached to a mechanical linkage. For many years, Chrysler cars used a small supplementary drum brake behind the transmission as a parking brake.

BRAKE MAINTENANCE

For the typical collector car owner, the most important brake maintenance chores will be inspecting the lining for wear, adjusting the brakes, and keeping brake fluid clean and up to the correct level.

You can learn to do much of your own brake service work. Be sure to consult one of the texts on the subject as well as your car's service manual. Brake-adjusting procedures are covered there too.

Every time you apply the brakes, you wear the brake linings a little bit thinner. That's why mileage driven is a poor gauge of lining wear. A car that commutes 50 highway miles per day will still have plenty of lining left at the end of a year. A car that spends 50 miles a day delivering pizza could need new linings long before the year is up.

The method by which the lining is attached to the brake shoe makes a difference too. Since World War II most makers have attached the lining to the shoe by a bonding process that involves adhesives and heat. This makes nearly the full thickness of the lining usable. Older cars used rivets to attach lining to shoes. This limits the useable thickness by the height of the rivet in its counterbored hole in the lining.

If you've never seen your car's brake linings, you'll have to remove each drum to verify the remaining lining thickness. Removing one drum won't do; brakes on different wheels may wear at different rates. While in theory 1/32 of an inch of thickness is the minimum, you should never let your lining get as thin as 1/16 of an inch. Drums on some makes of cars are easily removed. Others require a wheel puller. Consult your service manual.

A note of caution: Many old brake linings are made of asbestos, a material that is known to cause lung cancer. While asbestos is no longer used in OEM automobile brake linings, it is not illegal. Some aftermarket brake reliners still use asbestos, so unless you were the last person to reline the brakes there is no way to know for certain what your linings are made of. So treat every brake lining as if it were made of a hazardous material.

Asbestos encapsulated in a brake lining is not dangerous. The problem is the dust that you'll find covering the brake components and the inside of the drum. That dust is largely asbestos. *Don't blow it away, either with your breath or with an air gun.* Once it's in the air, it can easily find its way into your lungs.

Instead, try this OSHA-approved method for dealing with the dust. Place a catch basin under the brake you're working on. Thoroughly wet the outside of the brake drum using a spray bottle filled with water and a few drops of detergent. Wipe the drum with a clean cloth, and discard the cloth in a sealed plastic bag. Remove the drum. Using a rag soaked in a bucket of plain water, wash the brake backing plate, cylinder and springs. Use a fresh wet cloth on the shoes. The asbestos dust will become muddy dirt. Wash the inside of the brake drums the same way. Discard the rags in your plastic bag, and rinse out the buckets. Now you can use a can of brake cleaner to clean off the brake parts and the inside of the drum. Wipe with clean shop towels. Take the bag of asbestos-contaminated rags to the local agency that deals with hazardous wastes.

Your life depends on those brakes. No grease can be permitted to contaminate the lining. Even a greasy fingerprint can make a brake grab. If you're working on brakes with the drum off, wrap the clean shoes in plastic food wrap. That'll keep errant fingers and tools from transferring grease to the linings. It's a good idea to wear latex gloves while you're reassembling your clean new brake parts.

BRAKE LINES

Until recently, American car collectors had only a few choices for replacement brake lines—steel, stainless steel, or copper. Many cars of the 1930s used heavy copper. The only copper tubing produced today that is strong enough to withstand the hydraulic pressures of braking is made for air conditioning use. It is difficult to find a brake shop that will even consider using this copper because of perceived liability issues. Worse yet, copper "work hardens." That is, bending back and forth a few times causes it to become brittle. Think of a paper clip.

For those who want to replace their own brake lines, steel is a difficult material to work with. It requires specialized tools that most hobbyists don't own. And, steel can be damaged by corrosion—from the outside by salt on wintry roads and from the inside by water in the brake fluid. Stainless steel solves the corrosion problem, but is even less practical for hobbyists to fabricate.

Happily, a material called Cunifer has recently become available in the United States. For years available only in Europe, Cunifer is an alloy of copper and nickel, with a bit of iron and manganese. It was first used by production cars in the 1976 Volvo, and has since been adopted by Rolls-Royce, Aston Martin, Porsche, and

Audi. It is highly corrosion-resistant, and easy to bend and flare as needed.

Since Cunifer is mostly copper, some sources have raised concerns about work hardening. Bill Cannon and Neil Maken, past and present editors of *Skinned Knuckles* magazine, brought this material to my attention and did some bending tests. You'd have to do a lot of bending, straightening, and rebending to create a problem. By that time, Neil says, you should have decided to let a pro do the job for you!

Cunifer tubing is now stocked in coils by Brake & Equipment Warehouse under the name Ezi-Bend. You can buy exactly the lengths you need so there will be no joints in the lines, and no feet of expensive extra tubing left over. Cunifer sounds like the material of choice if you need to replace brake lines.

CHAPTER 10
THE LEAST-CHANGED FLUID

Every collector car owner changes his or her car's motor oil regularly. Most dump the transmission periodically. Some even replace the coolant once in a while. But almost no one pays much attention to the one fluid in the car on which your life may depend—the liquid that makes your hydraulic brakes work.

Hydraulic brakes work on a simple principle. In a closed system, pressure applied (usually by your foot) through a linkage to a piston in a cylinder (generally called the master cylinder) is transmitted by an incompressible fluid (brake fluid) to slave cylinders (wheel cylinders), fixed to the car's suspension. The fluid's movement causes pistons in those cylinders to press a high-friction material against a member that rotates with the wheels. As a result, the car slows,

then stops. The actual implementation is a bit more complex than that, but the principle has not changed since the introduction of hydraulic brakes on the 1921 Duesenberg Model A.

As we've seen, the design of the components changed some over the collector car years. While caliper disc brakes were installed on some American cars in the mid-1960s, most collector cars through the early 1970s still were stopped by drum brakes on all four wheels. Dual master cylinders arrived later in the decade.

But drum or disc, calipers or cylinders, single or dual master cylinders, all hydraulic brake systems have one thing in common—the fluid that transmits pressure from your foot to the wheels.

While all liquids are virtually incompressible, only two materials are approved by the United States Department of Transportation for use in automobile brake systems. They are identified by their numbers. DOT 3, DOT 4, and DOT 5.1 are based on glycol. DOT 5 is based on silicone. The brake systems of our collector cars all came filled at the factory with what is now called DOT 3. Collectors in recent years have experimented with the other numbers. And therein lies some controversy.

GLYCOL VS. SILICONE

The brake fluid used by our fathers and our grandfathers had no DOT number. (Actually, the Department of Transportation only began operations in 1967, and didn't assign numbers to brake fluid until 1972.) Basically, though, it was what we today call DOT 3. This fluid is mostly triethylene glycol with an admixture of other glycol compounds and a sprinkling of anticorrosion additives. It has been successfully used for more than 80 years because it does its job well. It is incompressible; it swells rubber predictably to affect a good seal in master and wheel cylinders; it is inexpensive to manufacture; and its boiling point is sufficiently high to provide safe braking in normal passenger car and truck use. DOT 3's downside is that

The 1921 Duesenberg Model A, the first American car with four-wheel hydraulic brakes.

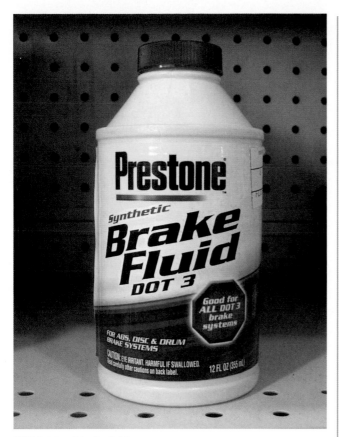

DOT 3 (glycol) brake fluid.

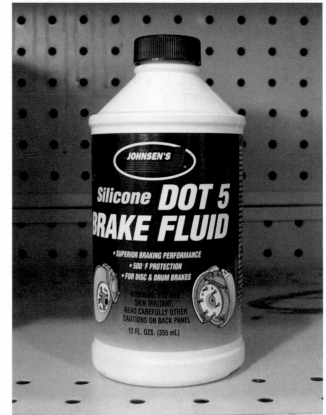

DOT 5 (silicone) brake fluid.

it is a modestly effective paint remover if not promptly flushed from the contacted surface with water.

After DOT 3 came DOT 4 and DOT 5.1. The newer fluids have the same chemistry, full compatibility with each other, and ever-higher boiling points. Since we have noted that brakes turn rolling energy into heat, a lot of it is generated. The lineup of brake fluid numbers is mostly related to the boiling points of the fluids. Brand new DOT 3 brake fluid must have a dry (no moisture) boiling point of at least 401 degrees F, and a wet (moisture-saturated) boiling point of no less than 284 degrees F. DOT 4 fluid has higher minimum boiling temperature requirements (446 degrees F dry and 311 degrees F wet). The figures for the more expensive DOT 5.1 are 509 and 356. To complicate matters further, respected European manufacturer ATE has developed a DOT 4 fluid with boiling points that match DOT 5.1 and silicone fluids.

The reason for the concern with "wet" boiling points is that DOT 3, 4, and 5.1 brake fluids are hygroscopic. That means they can attract water molecules from the surrounding environment, absorb such moisture, and

mix with it. And this is where the controversy lies.

Silicone brake fluid was first developed for military and off-road vehicles; the Department of Transportation blessed it for road use in the 1980s, designating it DOT 5. (DOT 5.1, which is a glycol-based fluid, was later given its confusing number because its boiling points are about the same as silicone fluid—500 degrees F dry, 365 wet.) While many collector car owners began using silicone brake fluid even before it was recognized for road use, today it is available in any auto supply store and online.

A major reason for the early preference for DOT 5 fluid by collector car enthusiasts was one that had also appealed to the military. Silicone brake fluid is not hygroscopic; it does not absorb any water that enters the brake system. It was believed to be more stable during long-term storage. Both army tanks and 1953 Corvettes tend to sit a lot more than they run. And, of course, the fact that DOT 5 fluid is harmless to paint is no small issue to a show car owner whose master cylinder is accessible only through contortions and a long funnel.

Many collector car owners have used silicone brake fluid for years, and are delighted with it. Others have had less happy experiences, claiming that DOT 5's inconsistent effect on brake system rubber leaves wheel cylinders oozing. And silicone fluid entrains air more easily than glycol fluids too. (Technically, its molecules are spaced farther apart.) So pedal feel is often spongier with DOT 5. That bothers some people; others don't care.

Restorers and collector car owners have reported a disproportionate number of failures of hydraulic brake switches in DOT 5 systems. In a typical switch, the contacts are separated from the brake fluid by a rubber diaphragm. It seems that silicone brake fluid may seep through the diaphragm and contaminate the switch contacts. The technical experts at Echlin, one of the makers of these switches, have stated, "Our brake light switches are manufactured in accordance with SAE J1703. These units are designed for use with DOT 3 brake fluids . . . . Some silicone oils do have great penetrating properties and if these oils penetrate the seal into the contact area, contamination of the contacts would result."

If you want to use silicone brake fluid, and if your car uses hydraulic brake switches, be sure to check the operation of your brake lights regularly. One possible cure is the installation of a hydraulic brake switch that claims compatibility with DOT 5. They are available from Bob Drake Reproductions. As a permanent cure you can rig a mechanical brake switch. These are available from restoration supply houses, and have adjustable actuating arms. Depending on the configuration of your brake pedal linkage, such a switch will be more or less visible, and a departure from authenticity.

DOT 5's inconsistent performance in different makes of cars and with different brands of rubber parts have resulted in little support for its use by major auto manufacturers, by the suppliers of brake system parts, by component rebuilders, and by collector car aftermarket suppliers. (While this is not a factor with our collector cars, manufacturers warn against its use in cars with ABS brake systems. The rapid pulsations of those designs cause foaming in the easily aerated silicone fluid. Indeed, the only vehicles that come new from a major factory with DOT 5 brake fluid are Harley-Davidson motorcycles.)

Water enters a brake system through a variety of places. Master cylinders in many collector cars have a vent to atmosphere. Even if they don't, moisture-laden air enters every time you remove the master cylinder cap to check the fluid level. Water molecules even enter the system through the microscopic pores of the brake hoses! Glycol fluids absorb this water. Some studies indicate that the absorption rate is about 1 percent per year. Three percent water will bring the boiling point of DOT 3 fluid down very close to the minimum permissible. DOT 4's boiling point, while higher to begin with, drops even faster as it absorbs moisture. And water in the fluid would seem to promote corrosion.

It is surprising, therefore, that DOT 5's celebrated inability to absorb water is not necessarily a good thing. Water still enters a DOT 5-charged system. Since it does not mix with the fluid, it remains separate as globules of water. These will settle in the low points of the lines, and may contribute to rust at those points and to corrosion where they come into contact with air.

If you are converting to DOT 5 for the first time, you will have to learn some new techniques for installing and bleeding the brake fluid. Basically, you want to agitate the fluid as little as possible. Pour it slowly into the master cylinder reservoir. Leave the reservoir cap off at least overnight to let air bubbles work their way out of the fluid.

One last cautionary note regarding DOT 5: Bob Adler advises that silicone brake fluid, when it burns, is reduced to silica sand. If it is sucked into your engine through a leaking vacuum brake booster, the result can be rapid and serious wear. Be prudent; if your collector car has a vacuum booster, don't use DOT 5.

In summary, there is no clear answer about which type of brake fluid you should use in your collector car. Most engineering and professional literature I have read urges you to stay with the glycol fluids. My own informal surveys indicate that the majority of collector car drivers prefer the DOT 3 glycol family, although there is a vocal minority that praises DOT 5 silicone. For cars that are seldom driven, DOT 5 may be the way to go. For those that are driven regularly, tried-and-true DOT 3 is probably the answer. Just be aware that it is difficult and expensive to change from one type to the other.

CONVERTING FROM ONE TYPE OF BRAKE FLUID TO ANOTHER

Although your collector car came with DOT 3 fluid, you may decide to convert to DOT 5. Or, if your particular car doesn't like DOT 5, you may want to go back to DOT 3. (For simplicity, I'm using DOT 3 here to refer to the family of glycol-based fluids.) The conversion process should be pretty much the same, although there

Corrosion has frozen this wheel cylinder.

are those who warn against going back from DOT 5 to DOT 3. Silicone, they say, is very tenacious stuff and once in the lines, it can never be entirely purged. While I have seen no definitive studies on this point, it is offered here as a caution.

Simply put, the chemistries of the two types of fluid are incompatible. Any mixture of one with the other can result in jelling and gunk formation, the last thing you want in your brake system. Ideally, to convert from one type of brake fluid to the other, you should replace everything in the system including steel brake lines and aluminum pistons. Since that probably isn't practical, the minimum you must do is replace every single piece of elastomer that comes in contact with the fluid.

That means removing and rebuilding master and wheel cylinders. This is an ideal time to carefully inspect the cast iron bores of these components. If they need to be sleeved, have it done now. Several vendors offer sleeving. Most use stainless steel, but a few use brass. Neither of these materials will ever rust. But an engineer friend of mine, the late Tom Pendergast, once warned me that brass on automobiles should be used only decoratively. I pass that on for what it's worth.

You cannot successfully switch fluid types by simply flushing the system with the new fluid. This flush-fill method was advocated in the early days of conversions from DOT 3 to DOT 5. The procedure involves emptying the brake system by opening all the bleeder screws at the wheel cylinders, then pumping the brake pedal until all the DOT 3 fluid appears to have been removed. The master cylinder was then refilled with DOT 5, and this too was flushed out. Then the system was refilled with fresh DOT 5. This procedure proved unsatisfactory. Some remnants of the replaced fluid type always remained in the system, with potentially unpleasant ramifications.

So if you change the type of fluid in your car you must replace all the rubber parts. Brake parts are among the most standardized of all the pieces in your car, and you should be able to replace every part with a brand new one. If your car is very old or an orphan you may not be able to purchase the part by car make. But a specialized brake shop will be able to help you match your original parts to a current Raybestos or NAPA or other number. (Even elderly step-bore wheel cylinders can be fitted. Just use different kits for the two ends.) Once you have recorded the correct numbers—I usually tear off and file the end flaps from the parts boxes—you will not have to go through that process again.

SHOULD YOU FLUSH YOUR BRAKE FLUID? AND, IF SO, HOW OFTEN?

The answer to the first question is "yes." The answer to the second is "it depends."

A good rule of thumb is to flush your brake system with clean fresh fluid of the same type every two years. *This is true for both glycol and silicone fluids.* While there is anecdotal evidence of silicone fluid staying clear for much longer periods, there is no way to know the conditions under which these particular cars were operated. So flush every two years. It's not that onerous a task, and it should keep your brake fluid relatively free of moisture and the system's components free of corrosion.

If you are obsessive about accuracy, though, you can now determine rather precisely when your fluid needs changing. In 2002 the Automotive Maintenance and Repair Association (AMRA) examined the issue of brake fluid testing as an aid to determining when and if fluid should be changed.

Most of the literature advocating regular brake fluid changes had focused on the issues of moisture in the brake system. This resulted in corrosion and the lowering of the fluid's boiling point. While the boiling point is of little concern to collector car owners who do not race their cars, corrosion is. To their surprise, the AMRA task force found that in their own and other learned studies it did not appear that a high level of moisture was a marker, or early indicator of impending corrosion.

The marker, it turned out, was copper.

Brake fluid chemistry includes corrosion inhibitors, pH stabilizers, and antioxidants. With time these inhibitors become depleted and corrosion begins. And high levels of dissolved copper in the system—from brake lines, coatings and gaskets—apparently indicate that the brake system is, or soon will be, under attack.

The common test for moisture in brake fluid has been proven to be inconclusive. So if you feel you need to test your brake fluid for impending corrosion, use the best current technology—a strip that uses FASCAR technology to test for copper. The same strip tests both glycol and silicone fluids. These strips are available from several sources online. Bulk containers of 100 are expensive, intended for repair shops. Hobbyists should look for the individually packaged strips. Testing may show that your brake fluid is safe well beyond the suggested two-year

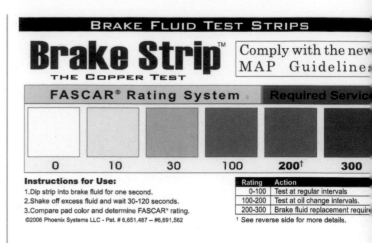

Dip a FASCAR strip into the brake fluid reservoir, then check the color against this chart on the back of the container.

period. Or, you may need to flush even sooner. In any event, as soon as the test approaches 200 ppm of copper, flush your brake system.

The safe life of all brake fluids is measured in years, not decades. Replacing yours regularly can avoid much grief.

BLEEDING BRAKES

No, that's not a British expletive. Whenever air is permitted to enter a hydraulic brake system, the system must be bled to encourage the air to leave. Unlike brake fluid, air is compressible. The effect of air in a hydraulic system is a brake pedal that feels spongy when the brakes are applied.

Air enters the system when you replace a wheel or master cylinder. It can also enter if you permit the level of brake fluid in the master cylinder reservoir to fall too low.

You're best off bleeding your own brakes. Aside from saving money, it gives you some control over this vital safety issue. Most brake shops use a pressure bleeder tank. If you're using silicone fluid, it is unlikely that the shop will have a pressure bleeder full of DOT 5 fluid. If you're using glycol, even though the better shops will keep this tool empty and only fill it before use, it is possible that the brake fluid going into your system may have been standing around for a while, busily absorbing moisture.

The traditional method of bleeding brakes involves two people. One sits behind the wheel, foot on brake pedal. The other lies under the car and cracks open the bleeder screw at each wheel cylinder in order. In

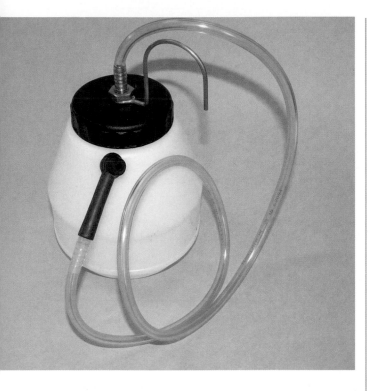

This handy Vacula brake fluid catch bottle (FAR LEFT) bolt or suspension component while you are bleeding the wheel cylinder. The unique flexible fitting (LEFT) goes over the bleeder screw and won't come off accidentally as a simple piece of tubing might. The bottle is their part number 12-018-0070.

response to commands by the under-car member of the team, the helper alternately depresses and slowly releases the brake pedal. Success of this method depends on clear communication between the parties, and good coordination on the part of both. Each time a brake is bled, the master cylinder reservoir must be checked and refilled, to be sure that the fluid level doesn't drop so low that air is drawn right back into the system. The helper is usually a spouse or significant other, often a non-car person, pressed into service. The opportunities for misunderstandings, harsh words, sulking, and poor brake bleeding are many. Still, according to brake professionals, many of whom are involved in critical racing applications, two-person brake bleeding is still the best way to get firm, air-free brakes.

HOW TO BLEED

I've tried many different devices as catch bottles for bleeding, including open jars, commercially available plastic bags, and other receptacles. Dave Zeckhausen of Zeckhausen Racing says that the one he likes best is made by Vacula. It has a sealed cover with a one-way check valve in the cap, and a rubber fitting on the cylinder end of the plastic tube that snaps in place over a wide range of bleed screw nipple sizes. It also has a stainless hook to hang the bottle from a suspension component if needed.

Dave also suggests following these steps for a quality bleed job. While these instructions may seem long, the job goes very quickly after you've developed some experience doing it.

1. Block a front wheel with chocks to prevent the car from rolling. Raise the back of the car with a floor jack, then lower it onto a pair of jack stands.
2. Remove the rear wheels.
3. Disengage the parking brake.
4. Put a wood block under the brake pedal so it cannot go all the way to the floor. Pushing the pedal past its normal range will cause the master cylinder piston to enter an area not normally used, which may have been roughened by corrosion. This will cause leaks in short order.
5. Open the brake fluid reservoir. Using a suction tool like a turkey baster or a battery filler, remove as much old brake fluid as possible. Be careful not to spill any DOT 3 fluid, as it will damage the paint on your car. Just in case fluid does spill, keep

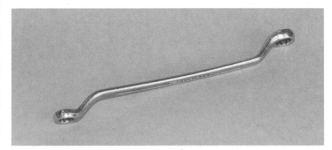

An offset wrench is required to reach many recessed bleeder screws.

71

a water-soaked rag handy to quickly wash off the painted cylinder or nearby parts.

6. Fill the brake reservoir to the top with fresh fluid.

7. Place a box-end wrench over the bleed screw on the right rear wheel cylinder. (Some cars require a special offset wrench because of the position of the bleeder.) Push the end of the tube from your catch bottle over the nipple on the bleed screw.

8. Tell your assistant to pump the brake pedal a few times until it becomes firm. Sometimes there is so much air in the system that the brake pedal will not get firm. That's OK. Just move on to the next step.

9. Tap the wheel cylinder a few times with a rubber mallet or "dead-blow" hammer. This helps to knock loose air bubbles that may be clinging to inside surfaces of the cylinder.

10. Have your assistant PUSH hard on the brake pedal and HOLD. (To avoid startling him or her, announce that the brake pedal may drop suddenly.) With a quick motion, open the bleed screw about 1/4 turn. Fluid (and probably a few air bubbles) will flow through the plastic tube and into the catch bottle. A light placed behind the tube will make it easier to see what is coming out of the cylinder.

11. Close the bleed screw when the brake pedal reaches the wood stop. Don't worry if the timing is off at first. You will quickly figure it out with feedback from your assistant.

12. Tell your assistant to slowly release the pedal.

13. Repeat steps 10 through 12 about ten times or until you no longer see any air bubbles coming out of the cylinder. NOTE: Every five pumps go to the front of the car to check the fluid level. You *must not* allow the level to fall to the point where you suck air into the master cylinder. Top off the reservoir as needed.

14. When you are done bleeding each wheel cylinder, carefully remove the tube from the bleeder screw.

15. Wash the rear of the backing plate with your wet cloth to remove any paint-eating brake fluid that might have dripped from the bleeder. Use brake cleaning spray if necessary.

16. Repeat the process for the other rear cylinder.

17. Reinstall the rear wheels. Lower car to the ground and torque the wheel nuts to factory specifications.

18. Now apply the parking brake, put the car in gear (or park) and raise the front of the car with your floor jack. Lower it onto a pair of jack stands.

A "garden-sprayer" type pressure brake bleeder.

19. Remove the front wheels.

20. Follow the exact same procedure as with the rear wheels, starting with the passenger side cylinder.

21. Reinstall the front wheels, then lower the car to the ground and torque the wheel nuts.

22. Top off the brake fluid reservoir and replace the cap.

ONE-PERSON BLEEDING TOOLS

Alternative products for one-person brake bleeding appear on the market regularly. Each new invention is touted as the solution to the problems of its predecessors. Here are Dave Zeckhausen's thoughts and my own comments on some of them:

Hand-operated Vacuum Pumps

The reservoir on these devices is too tiny to allow it to hold enough fluid to bleed the brakes. You'll find yourself emptying the reservoir every couple of minutes. And it doesn't generate enough vacuum to pull out any bubbles that need to travel any distance downhill.

One-way Valves

These permanently replace your caliper bleed screws. Speed Bleeder is the best-known brand. One problem with using them by yourself is that if you are in the car pumping the brake pedal, there's nobody watching the plastic hose between the bleeder and the catch bottle. You don't know when the air bubbles stop coming out, and you can't tell when the old rusty brake fluid has been flushed and new clean stuff is coming out. And worse, if the plastic hose should pop off, you will be pumping brake fluid all over the inside of your wheel well and possibly onto the side of your car.

Garden Sprayer-type Pressure Bleeders

I call them this because that's what they look like. They are currently very popular, presented as an inexpensive version of commercial pressure bleeders. In an earlier version of this book, I even advocated building one of these from an actual garden sprayer. The problem is, I've discovered with time and experience, that you can never

A professional brake bleeder, with a diaphragm separating air from fluid. This one is a KD 2222. K-D Tools

remove 100 percent of the air in your brake system with a device that uses air to push the fluid in, and does not separate that air from the fresh fluid. This is especially true for silicone brake fluid, which entrains air much more readily than glycol fluids do.

A variation of this type is a system that uses air pressure from one of your car's tires to push the fluid into your brake system. Same drawback.

Professional Pressure Brake Bleeders

This is a tool that requires no outside assistance from a helper, and it does work. It involves a two-chamber tank. One chamber is filled with brake fluid. The second is pressurized with compressed air. The two chambers are separated by a diaphragm, and that's the critical difference between this expensive unit and the garden sprayers. *The air and brake fluid are never permitted to mix.*

Although this tool is quite expensive, you may be able to find a used, professional-quality pressure bleeder at a swap meet or on eBay.

To use one you need a source of compressed air and an adapter for your master cylinder's lid. KD Tools makes a variety of these. The adapter is essentially a replacement for the master cylinder reservoir cover, with a standard male air hose fitting at the top. Your older car may no longer be included in KD's list, so you'll have to do some research and hunting. If you can't find an adapter for your master cylinder, you can make one out of an old cover or cap that fits your master cylinder. Drill and tap the top for a male air hose adapter. Old caps are usually vented; you must seal up the vents with brazing material or with solder.

To use the pressure bleeder, fit the adapter to the master cylinder in place of the regular cap. Put a couple of quarts of brake fluid in the pump container, snap the hose coupler onto your master cylinder adapter, and pressurize the sprayer container to the maximum recommended by the instructions. When a wheel cylinder bleeder is opened, the diaphragm under air pressure forces fluid and air out. No pumping, no trips out from under the car, no refilling of the reservoir.

FLUSHING BRAKES

Flushing your brake system is done exactly like bleeding it. The difference is that your goal is to remove the old fluid entirely and replace it with new. To detect the difference, you'll have to watch the tube that goes into the catch bottle closely.

If you decide to use ATE DOT 4 racing brake fluid, you have an advantage. It's available in two colors. Type 200 is amber, and Super Blue is (naturally) blue. Although the printing on the can seems to describe two different products, Dave Zeckhausen says that their specifications are identical. So alternating between them makes flushing brakes easier because you will know, by the color, when you have completely flushed old fluid out of the system.

After bleeding or flushing, please dispose of brake fluid properly, most likely at your local hazardous waste station. It's a poison. Do not swallow it or get it in your eyes. And remember that DOT 3, 4 and 5.1 fluid can damage the finish on your car.

ATE's fluids. Despite the different text and nomenclature, the contents of these two cans are exactly the same formula. The only difference is that the fluid in the can on the left is blue, the one on the right amber. Dave Zeckhausen points out that this causes great confusion, compounded by the text on the front of the cans, and the fact that different lots appear to be packaged in different cans. TYP 200 is DOT 4, although on the can shown it says so only in the fine print on the back. Super Blue, which says DOT 4 on the front of the can, doesn't meet DOT 4's requirement that the fluid be "clear through amber" in color. So in the legalese on the back ATE calls it DOT 3/4, only because of its color.

CHAPTER 11
RELIABLE STARTING
(WITH SIX OR TWELVE VOLTS)

According to AAA and other road service organizations, nearly 50 percent of road-service calls are due to electrical problems. Happily, an informed collector car owner can maintain his car's electrical system in a reliable state with a relatively small investment in finances and time.

If your collector car was built in the United States before 1954, it came from the factory with a six-volt electrical system. If yours is an authentic early car, you may want to retain your original system but may be concerned about its practicality. Much of this chapter is addressed to you. If you drive a later collectible with a stock 12-volt system, I hope you'll find many helpful suggestions here too.

MAKING IT ON SIX VOLTS

While six volts are authentic for American cars built before 1954, let no one suggest that those who drive cars with their original six-volt system do so because it's the preferred voltage. There's good reason for the fact that every production car in the world today uses 12-volt power, with even higher voltages in the offing. A 12-volt system suffers less voltage drop for equivalent wire size, provides more reserve in battery starting power, and is more forgiving of minor problems like dirty terminals. There is no reason, though, that a six-volt system cannot power your car reliably. You just have to pay more attention to its maintenance, and understand its potential shortcomings.

Most collectible cars served as everyday transportation when they were new. There are several reasons they have starting and other electrical problems now that they're older.

First, batteries don't always supply the full voltage that's demanded of them. The ability of a lead-acid battery to accept a full charge diminishes with time and many cycles of charge and discharge. It's also adversely affected by long periods of sitting without

cycling at all. Also, authentic antique battery cases are often made of hard rubber, and are thicker than modern plastic cases. This reduces the interior space available for plates and electrolyte. The maximum current output of these batteries may suffice under the best of conditions, but leaves little reserve in case of other starting issues.

Second, the cable that carries battery voltage to the starter can introduce voltage drop. To keep costs down, original cables were frequently sized at the smallest that the manufacturer could get away with. Most batteries were grounded to the chassis or to the body at a point near the battery. The body and frame were expected to supply the return route for current. This was not good practice to start with, and a recipe for failure as years corroded the connections.

Third, most of us take the starter itself for granted. We assume that if it turns when voltage is applied to it, it's ready to do its job. Not necessarily so. Starters begin to crank more slowly as their components age and wear. The design of a starter requires an air gap between the armature and the field coil pole shoes. A worn bushing allows the armature to move closer to the field coils. The intense magnetism of the field tries to hold on to the armature, and reduces the power available. (With enough bushing wear, the armature can actually drag on the field coils.) In addition to slowing the starter, the drag increases the current requirement, which causes the voltage to drop, which makes it more difficult for the coil to provide spark for starting! Even more . . . brushes wear, brush springs lose tension, internal insulation frays, and wires to commutator segments short or break.

Lastly, I think that standards have changed. It's hard to recollect accurately, but folks I talk to who were there remember that engines did indeed turn over more slowly when cars of the 1930s, 1940s, and 1950s were new. In most cases the engine started right up. But there was much less margin for error.

Nevertheless, your collectible car did start and run well on six volts when it was new. If you want to keep your car drivable and authentic, it can continue to do so. You'll have to address some potential problems and perhaps make some minor modifications.

There are many fine books that describe basic automotive electrical components and theory. Others deal with testing and repair. I won't repeat this material here, except as needed for clarity. With that in mind, here are some ways to put your six-volt machine in reliable touring shape.

STEPS TO A SUPER STARTING SYSTEM

The Battery

Your car battery's major function is starting the engine. That may seem elementary, but not all batteries are designed for the same purpose. Traction batteries, for example, operate forklift trucks, electric wheelchairs and electric cars. They're also known as deep-cycle batteries. They put out their energy at low rates over long periods of time. Standby batteries, as used in emergency lighting systems, are constantly being charged. Our auto batteries are best described as starter-lighting-ignition (S-L-I) batteries, with the emphasis on starter. They must put out huge quantities of power for a brief period of time, while maintaining high voltage. The chemistry is the same in all of these batteries, but the internal construction is different.

When our collector cars were new, battery power was rated by ampere-hours. This meant that a certain current could be obtained from a battery for a certain number of hours—for example, to keep a lamp lit for a certain length of time. Since we're talking about starter batteries, this is not a very useful standard of comparison. Today's automobile S-L-I batteries are rated by a standardized SAE measure of cold cranking amps (CCA). A six-volt battery, fully charged, should deliver its CCA rating for 30 seconds at a temperature of zero degrees F without falling below 3.6 volts. (Double that voltage for a 12-volt battery.) The more CCAs, the better.

The battery's ability to start your car reliably is a primary component in the enjoyment you'll get from your collector vehicle. So, since the battery is a unit that's easy to replace for shows, consider equipping your collector car with the most powerful modern battery you can find, while using an authentic-appearing battery for shows.

A six-volt Optima battery. Optima Batteries

Basically, a lead-acid battery consists of two different types of lead compounds formed into positive and negative plates, separated by insulators, and immersed in a weak sulfuric acid solution. The old open batteries permitted oxygen and hydrogen to escape during charging. They had filler caps so the electrolyte could be kept topped off. Newer maintenance-free batteries have plates made of a purer material to reduce gassing rates. During manufacturing, they're often filled with more acid than open batteries were. They still lose liquid through gassing, and usually can't be refilled. Recombinant batteries are constructed so they can convert hydrogen and oxygen back into water. They have no provision for refilling or adding water.

The typical automotive battery doesn't like sitting around. But of course, this is what the battery in a collector car does much of the time. A technology called AGM (for absorbed glass mat) does much better at this. The electrolyte is absorbed in the thin porous glass separators, so there is no free liquid in the battery case. The thin separators permit a smaller gap between the positive and negative plates, permitting the release of large quantities of current quickly. (This is not what is commonly referred to as a gel cell. Such batteries use a gelling agent to turn the electrolyte into a Jell-O-like consistency.

Cutaway of a 12-volt AGM Optima battery. The six-volt version contains only three spirals. Optima Batteries

That technology is gradually being phased out in favor of AGMs.)

The AGM battery's design also makes it better able to withstand vibration and impact. It won't crack if it freezes, and it won't leak acid if the case breaks. Perhaps more important is that it neither builds up nor releases explosive hydrogen gas.

The most popular brand of automotive recombinant-technology AGM battery is the Optima. It is available at most auto supply stores, usually in both six- and 12-volt models.

The Optima is very different in appearance from the usual battery. It resembles three large cylinders stuck together—six cylinders for the 12-volt unit. That's because that's what it is, internally. Its major differences compared with other AGM batteries lie in its construction. Its positive and negative plates are wrapped in a spiral in a manner resembling a condenser.

The six-volt Optima is rated at an impressive 850 CCA, but is only about one-half the size of an ordinary battery of that capacity. It's completely sealed, so water never needs to be checked or added. It doesn't even

A reproduction "tar-top" battery by Antique Auto Battery. The sealant is a modern plastic that looks just like the old tar. They even make this model for the 1938–1952 Buick, the only car it was ever used on. Antique Auto Battery

This tool, from Lisle, permits one-handed lifting of a heavy battery. Lifting a battery by the terminals is not advised. Lisle Corporation

Don't use a screwdriver to pry the cables off the battery terminals. The connections inside can be damaged. Use a quality tool like this one from Lisle. Cheap versions don't work very well. Lisle Corporation

have any caps to do so. That's a special virtue if your car's battery is in a less-than-accessible position.

AGM batteries like to be at 100 percent charge. For long battery life, be sure that your car's charging system is operating at full capacity. When your car is inactive, keep the battery fully charged with a modern float charger like the Battery Tender. (See Chapter 20.) If the battery discharges—because you left a light on, for example—recharge it with an electronically regulated battery charger that states specifically that it's for use with AGM batteries.

Choose a battery, Optima or any other, with the highest CCA rating that you can fit into the space available. This is Vital Step Number 1 in effective starting. And for convenience in installation, look for a battery whose terminal locations match those of the authentic battery.

The Optima doesn't look anything like the original battery, so you'll probably want to switch to an authentic-case unit for shows. Those offered by Antique Auto Battery are early, open technology but they do look right. If your car uses 12 volts, AGM batteries are available from CarMan's Garage that mimic GM, Ford and Mopar batteries of mid-1950s to mid-1970s era.

Cables

Twelve-volt users should pay attention here too. As already noted, original battery cables were sized at the minimum the manufacturer could get by with. For long cables, like the ones to under-seat or other remotely located batteries, the temptation to skimp was even greater. Typical stock cables that ran from the hot battery terminal to the starter solenoid ranged from 0 gauge to 2 gauge for six-volt cars, and 3 gauge to 4 gauge for 12-volt systems. Some were even smaller. (The higher the number, the smaller the cable cross-section.)

The return path, or ground, was usually provided by an uninsulated strap from the battery ground terminal to a nearby point on the chassis or body. Sometimes an additional smaller strap was used to ground the engine block to the chassis. In either case, the return path to the battery depended on metal-to-metal contact through frame and body joints.

Enormous pressure is needed to crimp the battery cable and terminal into an air-free mass. This hydraulic machine develops 80 tons of pressure. The Solar Biz

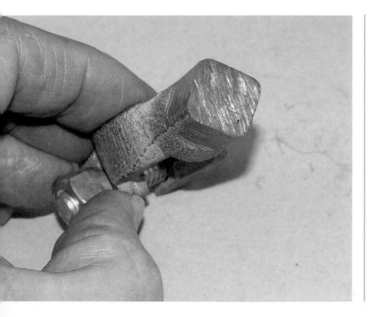

Here's the result—a single block of metal, with no voids. Solar power vendors like The Solar Biz and Solar Pals can make such cables for you.

To get reliable starting with six volts (and even better starting with 12) you must reduce the resistance loss in the battery cables to as near zero as practical, and maintain it that way. For reliable regular use, replace your old cables and terminals. The cost isn't great, and the results of this one improvement will often surprise you.

For six-volt systems, use 2/0 or larger welding cable; for 12-volt systems, use #1 or #2. Welding cable needs to be flexible, so while the diameter of the copper conductor is about the same as in automotive cable of the same gauge, welding cable has many more, smaller

Don't use one of these bolt-on battery terminals except as an emergency temporary repair.

Some makers of custom battery cables use a solder pellet to solder the cables into the terminal. Soldered joints will probably not be as permanent or as resistance-free as hydraulically crimped ones.

strands. The additional flexibility makes it easier to place the wire where you want it to go.

The method by which terminals and lugs are attached to the cables is important. The choices boil down to crimping or soldering. Crimping squeezes or pounds the cable-terminal joint into virtually a block of metal, to reduce the possibility of air and moisture later entering and causing corrosion. Fans of the solder method feel that only solder, which flows into any gaps, can keep the joint corrosion-free.

I favor crimping battery cable terminals, as do the purveyors of solar-energy equipment, who cannot afford to lose any voltage at connectors, and whose products are often in remote locations where they cannot be regularly serviced. The caveat is that the crimps must be made with professional equipment. Since few of us have these tools, solar-equipment vendors like The Solar Biz and Solar PALS can create custom-length battery and ground cables for you.

Soldering terminals can be done at home. The only tools required are a vise and an ordinary propane torch. Kits are available that include terminals and a solder pellet that is dropped into the terminal barrel and melted by application of the torch to the terminal. That seems easy, but in my opinion it is less likely to produce a minimum-resistance, last-forever joint.

Auto hobby vendors make custom cables too. Ask the company making your custom cables what method of attachment they use. Crimped or soldered terminals are both likely to outlast us. The kind you use depends on how compulsive you are about preserving every fraction of a volt and making your collector car last forever.

Stay away from bolt-on battery terminals. They cause needless resistance even when they're brand new, and they corrode very rapidly. About the only legitimate use for one of these is if neglect finds you on the road with a cable terminal that needs replacing. Have a new terminal properly crimped on as soon as you get home.

To assure reliable low-resistance current for the starter, you must run a second cable from the battery ground terminal to a mounting bolt on the starter. To plan out the path for this cable, use a length of mechanic's wire or stiff electrical wire. To minimize the damage to authenticity, look for the shortest cable path that you can conceal from normal viewing angles. The welding cable is flexible, but plan carefully for any sharp 90-degree turns. Large cross-section cables to both starter solenoid and starter ground is Vital Step Number 2.

Small welding shops and some custom auto battery cable makers use this tool with a vise or hydraulic press. It's not as effective as a hydraulic crimper. *The Solar Biz*

The Starter

Certain six-volt starters were intended for use under conditions that required frequent starts. They also needed the ability to turn over a very powerful engine. Such starters were often equipped with field coil windings, which, compared with automobile starters, contained fewer turns of heavier wire. These are often called high-torque windings. Essentially, they are wound for a lower voltage. So with the application of six volts, they'll make a starter motor turn faster. The flip side is that they draw greater current. Since you've now equipped your collector car with the most powerful—that means highest amperage—battery that will fit, you're ready to have your starter rebuilt using high-torque windings. That's Vital Step Number 3 for reliable starting.

One caveat: The greater current drawn by the starter will cause some drop in the voltage available to the coil. If you convert to high-torque windings, be sure that your coil is fresh and in good condition.

Specialized test equipment and tools are needed to rebuild a starter. The cost of having a knowledgeable professional do this for you is a lot cheaper than the tools.

SOME TIPS FOR ALL VOLTAGES

Master Switches

These switches go by a variety of names such as battery master switch, battery disconnect switch, battery cutoff switch. All refer to a heavy-duty device that is cut into a battery cable that allows all power to be disconnected.

A heavy-duty master switch.

Mount your master switch where you can reach it quickly in an emergency. This one is for an underseat battery. For an underhood battery, a point low on the firewall or on the footboard will work. Be sure you can reach the handle easily.

A remote master switch from Hotronics.

This remote switch is of the "latching" type. It uses a pushbutton instead of a toggle, and uses no current when it's on. Perfect Performance Products LLC

This switch, which should be on your collector car, has several useful purposes. First, it reduces the likelihood of dead batteries after idle time (for example, if you mistakenly leave on components for a long period of time). And it virtually eliminates the risk of fire during storage. It is also a valuable antitheft device.

Master switches have an even more important function—as emergency cutoffs. When you first sniff burning rubber or see that wisp of smoke, you want to disconnect the battery from the electrical system *immediately*. To do that, you must be able to turn off the battery master switch *from the driver's seat*.

Master switch installation is a fairly simple process. In older cars with the battery under the seat, you can break the ground cable to install the switch. For cars with the battery under the hood, you can install a remote master switch. This uses an easy-to-reach toggle under the dash to energize a solenoid that switches the ground cable on and off at the battery. To my knowledge these are only available for 12-volt systems, but I have friends who say that the same unit works fine in their six-volt cars too. If you want to try that, be sure you can return it if it doesn't meet your needs.

IF YOU HAVE 6 VOLTS AND WANT 12

If you're not comfortable driving a collector car operating on six volts, then convert the car's entire electrical system to 12 volts. No, that won't make you beloved by the purists. (I suspect that I won't be either, for even suggesting this alternative.) But if, for you, the greater reliability of a more modern electrical system is an important factor in your regular use of your collector car, then perhaps it's the right course of action.

A 12-volt electrical system may be no less authentic than the use of modern paints, gas tank sealants, stainless steel hardware, or modern wire disguised by a cotton-braided cover. Does such a conversion do violence to another small piece of auto history? It's your call. Instructions for converting your six-volt system to 12 volts are offered in books, magazines, and online. I'll try to condense here the advantage of 12 volts over six volts into one paragraph, without diagrams.

Given the same amount of work to do, like turning a starter, the current (amperage) draw in a 12-volt system will be one-half that in a six-volt system. Professor Ohm's well-known law says that voltage is equal to current times resistance. As a result, the same resistance loss in a 12-volt system will result in only half the voltage loss experienced by a six-volt system—halving the current halves the voltage loss too. Since we're dealing with very small voltages, we're talking about a big difference.

So higher voltages are more efficient simply because of our inability to completely control resistance. Wires have resistance; corrosion increases resistance in switch contacts; fuse holders corrode; starter brushes glaze; ground paths

deteriorate. The effect of all of these cumulative resistances is far less in a 12-volt system than in a six-volt one.

Twelve-volt systems arrived in cars long after they were already in use in heavy equipment, railroad cars, and trucks. The reason was that until the 1950s, 12-volt batteries were about twice the physical size and weight of six-volt batteries. There just wasn't enough room for them under the hood. In the 1950s, plastic began to be used for plate separators and battery cases, saving size and weight. Increased knowledge about the chemistry of lead acid batteries permitted the use of smaller components. Twelve-volt batteries shrank to a practical size. By the end of the 1950s, nearly every vehicle used on land, sea, or air used voltages of 12 and higher.

To convert your electrical system to 12 volts, you will not have to change wires, fuses, lamp sockets, or switches. Indeed, some of these components will be subjected to less load and heat than they were with six volts. You will have to change the battery, voltage regulator, starter solenoid, coil, light bulbs, and turn signal flasher. You won't have to change the generator; the generator puts out whatever voltage the regulator limits it to.

You'll also have to reduce the voltage to the radio and the heater motor, and to other accessories. A practical way to do this is with a 12/6 volt battery. This is a 12-volt battery that has a six-volt center tap for those components—radio and some gauges—that must be limited to six volts. As far as I know the "6/12" and "12/6" batteries are only available in early technology, with caps for keeping them filled with water.

If you convert to 12 volts, starter concerns will be the same as those described on page 89 for the Orpin switch.

A brush tool designed to keep battery cable ends free of corrosion. A wire brush on the inside cleans the battery terminals.

Why install the switch in the ground cable? That way it's fail-safe. In the unlikely event of an internal short in the switch, all you'll have is a normal ground connection. If the switch were installed in the hot cable, you might have a fire.

Mechanical master switches from which the handle can be removed are an effective antitheft measure. Just be sure that you leave the handle in the switch while you're driving. An emergency is not the time you want to be hunting for the handle.

Incidentally, most car clubs do not deduct points in judging for neat installations of safety equipment like a battery cutoff switch.

ALTERNATORS FOR SIX VOLTS, TOO

Before 1960, all American cars, whether six- or 12-volt, were equipped with a generator. The generator's purpose, of course, was to replace the current used by the car in normal operation, and to keep the battery charged. (This isn't precisely correct chemically, but it's the end result.) External regulators were required, since a typical generator will simply keep increasing its voltage output as its rotational speed increases.

Generator design progressed from the third-brush designs of the late 1920s and early 1930s to the "shunt" (two-brush) designs of the mid-1930s. At the same time, regulator design progressed from simple cutouts to two-charge regulators to vibrating voltage and current regulators. By the late 1930s most American cars were so equipped. With minor exceptions, and aside from a continuing increase in output, there was really no further improvement in the basic engineering of automobile generators and regulators until their replacement by alternators beginning in 1960. (For most collector cars made between 1954 and 1960, the 12-volt generator functions satisfactorily. Today's enormous electrical loads of power-everything were not yet upon us.)

Your car's specifications will usually give the rated output of the generator in amperes. In most cases, the figure is the maximum that you can expect from that generator, in new condition and at its maximum permissible rpm. At highway driving speeds, expect about 75 percent of that figure.

There are good reasons why every new car in the world is equipped with an alternator. Its voltage curve is far more suited to the way cars are driven than is that of a generator—alternators begin to charge at not much more than idle speed. This becomes important in a car that may not be driven for long periods, and then only for relatively short distances.

For years I used an alternator made by Fifth Avenue Auto Supply on my 1930s collector car. It installed easily and worked beautifully. Its only problem was that it looked . . . well, like an alternator. A large anachronism right where everyone can see it.

I recently replaced this unit with one that is essentially an alternator built into a generator case. The maker, Don Allen of Don's Starters & Alternators, calls it a Gener-Nator. It is created from an existing generator by removing all the internal and external parts from the housing. A proprietary alternator subcomponent assembly—rotor, stator, rectifier, and electronic voltage regulator—is then installed in the case shell. Allen claims that the Gener-Nator is not an alternator machined down and stuffed inside a generator case. He describes it, instead, as "a sophisticated piece of electrical artwork." I cannot comment on the internal art, but it does look good and

A Gener-Nator conversion for a 1957 Cadillac. Don's Starters & Alternators

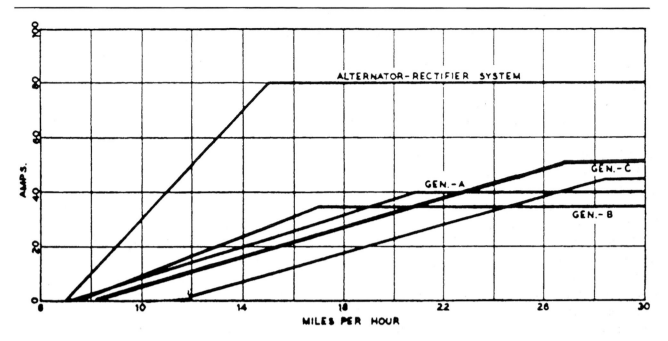

ALTERNATOR-RECTIFIER SYSTEM

GEN.-A

GEN.-C

GEN.-B

AMPS.

MILES PER HOUR

A chart made in the 1950s showing the comparative output of the then new automotive alternator with several contemporary generators.

Wire and Terminals

A loss of 1/2 volt in a six-volt system means the loss of about eight percent of the total available voltage. It affects 12-volt systems, too, just not as badly. To appreciate the effects, consider that headlights lose about 30 percent of their brightness for every 10 percent of reduced voltage.

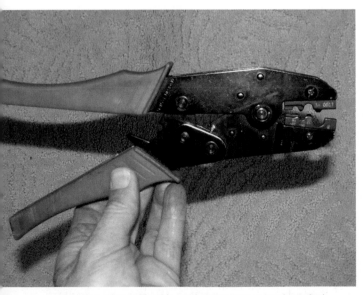

A ratcheting crimper like this one helps assure a good terminal connection. The jaws won't release until the crimp is complete.

Wherever resistance occurs, voltage in the system is reduced. There is resistance in the wire leading to each load. Proper sizing keeps this to a minimum. There's resistance at every connection, so clean and tight are the watchwords here.

New wiring harnesses, made to factory dimensions, are available for nearly every popular collector car. The wires have color codes that are close to the original. For earlier cars they even look like the original lacquered cotton. Underneath though, they boast modern insulation. Terminals are usually crimped, often soldered as well. Installing a new harness can be a chore, but if you're experiencing intermittent problems that are traceable to old wires, the new harness can make your driving a happier experience.

Inevitably you will have to make up some additions to the original wiring, or replace only a portion of a damaged or worn one. This is not the place to scrimp.

Wires with vintage appearance and color-codes are available from several sources. Vendors can supply braiding services too, for when you need to create a new short harness.

Ordinary terminals and crimping tools are available at every hardware store. I suggest you can do better.

The standard color scheme of red (22 to 18 gauge wire), blue (16 to 14) and yellow (12 to 10) was not used by the manufacturer of your car. And the quality of the terminal inside the sleeve varies from brand to brand. I buy uninsulated terminals. That way I can check the thickness of the terminal stock—they do vary by brand, and I don't have to yank off and discard the plastic. Before you crimp the terminal, slide a short piece of heatshrink tubing on the wire. After the terminal is attached, apply a heat gun to the tubing. Use the heat gun sparingly; you don't want to shrink the tubing tightly to the terminal. The result looks much like an older rubber-insulated OEM connection.

For a proper crimp, you need a better tool than the hardware store variety. A ratcheting crimper assures that full pressure is applied to the crimp before the handles will release.

Some recommend flowing solder into a properly crimped terminal. I don't. Solder wicks up the stranded wire, making the end stiff. If it is bent sharply just after that point it is more liable to break.

Grounds

Mentioned earlier was the need to ground the starter directly to the battery with a second cable. The grounding issue applies to every electrical circuit in your car. My engineer friends often lecture me on the importance of good electrical grounds, especially in older machinery that depends on potentially rusty points of connection. Most cars were originally grounded through a single ground strap from the battery to the nearest point on the frame or body. It was expected that the steel body and frame would provide the return path from headlights, taillights, horns, and other electrical devices. Classic car collector Buck Varnon calls this the invisible battery cable.

This arrangement worked adequately when the car was new. But both deterioration and restoration disrupt the invisible battery cable. The return electrical path must pass through body-frame connections, joints between lamp housings and fenders, and panel-to-panel connections. In many cases, rubber gaskets or antisqueak materials are interposed between units, and the only ground path is through bolts or sheet metal screws. As these connections corrode over time, resistance grows. There is no difference, electrically, between resistance in a supply wire and resistance in the ground path. The result is the same: flickering lights and sputtering horns.

Here's the Catch-22: Restoration of the car often will make the problem worse. In our zeal to restore Plymouths and Fords to Rolls-Royce standards, we often diligently paint every surface of every part. Rust, a poor conductor, is replaced by paint, a very good insulator. Freshly installed horns may not blow if their brackets are painted. Nor may headlights light if their connections to sheet metal are thus insulated.

The first part of the solution is to be certain that there's a metal-to-metal path for the ground return from each electrical device. In some cases, to get a good connection between body panels, and between panels and frame, you'd have to break the paint film; that would contribute to future rust. Furthermore, current flow between adjacent metal panels is thought to contribute to accelerated electrolytic corrosion. If the wires can be concealed, consider grounding headlights and taillights directly back to the starter ground or the battery. Use a wire of the same size as the supply wire. If you're making up new harnesses, you might want to build the ground wires in. You may be pleasantly surprised by brighter lamps and more reliable operation.

Coils

A coil has no moving parts, so it would seem to be no cause for concern until it suddenly stops working. Not so. The coils made in the earlier years of our collector car era used shellac and similar substances as internal insulation. Many years ago, classic car owner Pat McCarthy tested the internal circuits and resistances of NOS coils. (NOS stands for new old stock, or new original stock. Either way, what's meant is a part manufactured during the era of the original car, and never used.) Pat used very sensitive instruments available to him at his work. He found that time was breaking down these early coils, even though they had never left their boxes. The coil would still work, but produced lower output voltage. When the current draw of the starter reduced the voltage available to the coil, hard starting resulted. Take a pass on those NOS coils at swap meets or on eBay.

If the coil's polarity is incorrect with respect to the sparkplugs, your car will usually run but it will not run as well as it could (and sometimes will start poorly). If your coil terminals are marked plus and minus, the hookup seems simple. That is, coil plus to battery plus and minus to minus. This will usually result in the correct polarity at the plugs. But some coils are marked DIST and BAT instead of plus and minus. And what happens if you convert from six to 12 volts and/or from positive to negative ground?

Battery Tender can be kept constantly connected to your car when it's garaged, but add a timer. It is available in six- and 12-volt versions.

A 6/12 battery, for "mugging" the starter. The Orpin switch may be seen at the top. Antique Auto Battery

A 12/6 volt battery, for cars that have been converted to 12 volts. Six volts is available at the center tap. If your battery is hidden, two six-volt Optima batteries can be hooked up to provide the same function. Antique Auto Battery

Well, oddly enough, regardless of voltage or system polarity, it takes approximately 15 percent less voltage to form an arc at the sparkplug if the center electrode is negative and the ground electrode is positive with respect to the coil. (Don't confuse this with battery polarity—we are discussing only the polarity of the coil vis-à-vis the plug.)

We've all seen diagrams of this test: Place a pencil lead between the spark plug wire terminal and top terminal of the plug; then watch to see on which side the spark flares. Besides the possibility that you'll be knocked on your backside by 20,000 volts, you probably will not be able to figure out which side the flare is on anyway!

The answer is a device called Sparklite. It's about the size of your index finger and has no moving parts. Just two terminals and two LEDs. Sparklite indicates the presence of a spark and, most important, coil polarity, while the engine is cranking or running. It makes no difference whether your system is six or 12 volts, positive or negative ground. When placed anywhere in the high-tension wires between the coil and the sparkplug, the Sparklite's high-intensity flashing lights show whether spark is or is not present and whether polarity is correct or reversed. It works with all types of ignition systems—points, magneto, electronic, capacitor discharge, etc.

I took my Sparklite to some local car shows recently. Of eight cars that the owners asked me to test, two were hooked up backward.

ALTERNATIVES TO A SIX-VOLT SYSTEM

The major perceived problem with six-volt systems is their starting ability. Some makeshift arrangements have been used to deal with these problems. One is the use of an eight-volt battery. In my opinion, this brute force response creates more problems than it solves. For one thing, you'll need to install solid-state voltage—dropping devices or dropping resistors to avoid damaging voltage-sensitive instruments, radios, and other accessories. There aren't any eight-volt accessories available, and six-volt equipment used on eight-volts will have a short life. Headlights will be much brighter, but very short-lived.

Another solution to the problem of starting on six volts is the automatic 6/12 volt battery. Basically, this is a six-cell battery divided into two six-volt sections of three cells each. A solenoid-operated series-parallel switch is mounted on specially cast terminals on the battery. All car wiring is supplied from a center tap on the switch, so only six volts go to the car wiring, regardless of the position of the switch.

This switch originally was patented and manufactured by the Orpin Company, and still often is referred to by this name. (The Orpin switch also can be mounted remotely, and used to connect two ordinary six-volt batteries.) In its normal position, the Orpin switch connects the two batteries in parallel, creating one large six-volt battery. When energized by the car's starter button, the Orpin switch reconnects the two six-volt batteries in series, creating a single 12-volt battery. Twelve volts go only to the starter; six volts go to every other circuit from the center tap.

As far as starting goes, this works very well. The six-volt starter spins merrily on 12 volts, and starting is usually quick. My friend Matt Joseph refers to the use of 12 volts to spin six-volt starters as "mugging the starter." Before I discovered the three secrets to six-volt starting, I used Orpin-switched batteries for many years. Never once did I burn out a starter. However, when I examined the Bendix drive in my car afterward, I found that the pinion was becoming loose. I'm not positive that the substantially greater impact of the pinion hitting the flywheel ring gear was responsible, but it certainly seems possible.

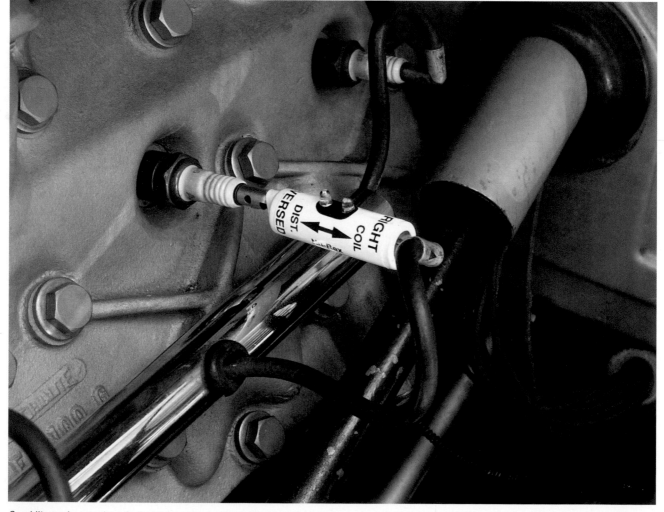

Sparklite works anywhere in the high tension wiring between the coil and any sparkplug, as long as the "Dist" arrow points toward the plug.

The solenoid in the Orpin switch has a heavy amperage draw. If your battery is not fully charged, the switch's contacts may not close. In that case, you'll get only six volts at the starter, just when you most need 12. If you get your six-volt starting system into tiptop condition and still don't have reliable starting, and if you don't want to convert your car's entire electrical system to 12 volts, the Orpin switch may be your last resort.

If you use a 6/12-volt battery with an Orpin series/parallel switch, you'll need two battery cutoff switches for safety. Strange as it may seem, lights and horn will work just fine with one terminal of the battery disconnected! The electrical system is still connected through the other terminal and the center tap on the battery. You have to disconnect both terminals to be safe.

Orpin switches have been out of production for many years. But they show up on eBay from time to time.

CHAPTER 12
LIGHTING FOR THE OLDER ONES

Standardized 7-inch-diameter six-volt sealed-beam headlamps were introduced in the United States with the 1940 automobile models. They superseded headlights of a variety of shapes, sizes and effectiveness. After 1954, all headlamps on American cars were sealed beams operating on 12 volts. In 1957, Chrysler, Cadillac, and Nash introduced four-lamp systems in some states. The following year, all American makes featured them.

Post-1954 cars can upgrade their lighting systems by using modern, greatly improved sealed-beam units, available in any auto supply store or online. This chapter therefore addresses itself primarily to the six-volt cars built between 1940 and 1953 with sealed beams, and those built prior to 1940 without them.

With the fine brakes with which modern cars are equipped, today's motorist drives well within the capabilities of his lighting system. That isn't always true for collector cars. As a general rule, the less effective your brakes, the brighter your headlights need to be; at night you'll want to see objects from as far away as possible. You may not intend to drive your collector car at night. But the occasion will occur when, like Cinderella, you'll stay too long at the ball. It's for those occasions that you must pay attention to your car's lighting systems.

For adequate lighting, you must be sure that full voltage is reaching your lights. The process of searching for voltage losses is explained in detail in publications dealing with general or collector car electrical systems. The tools used are simple: a digital multimeter, and a selection of test probes and jumper cables. Owning them will pay dividends.

FOR DRIVERS OF ALL PRE-1940 CARS, AND SOME LATER ONES

Adding Headlight Relays
Most cars built before 1940 did not use headlight relays. Those came into general use with the advent

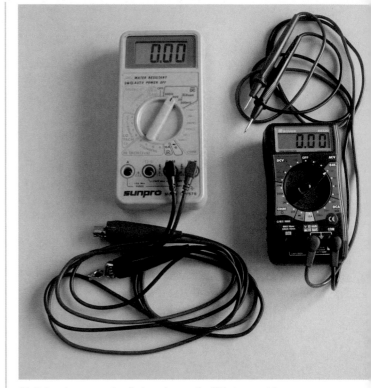

Digital meters come in all sizes. I carry the little one on trips.

of sealed-beam headlamps. (Some makes took even more years to implement their use.) The purpose of a relay was to shorten the length of the wire run, and to reduce voltage drop. To enable owners of older cars to gain these advantages, headlight relays were widely sold by auto supply stores. If your car is of the earlier era, consider installing a headlight relay. If you've installed a sealed-beam conversion, a relay is imperative. Six-volt single- or double-headlight relays aren't made anymore. But they can still be found at automotive swap meets and from some Internet vendors. Installing a relay does more than just reduce the effective length of the wire run; it also saves the headlight switch. Many older switches

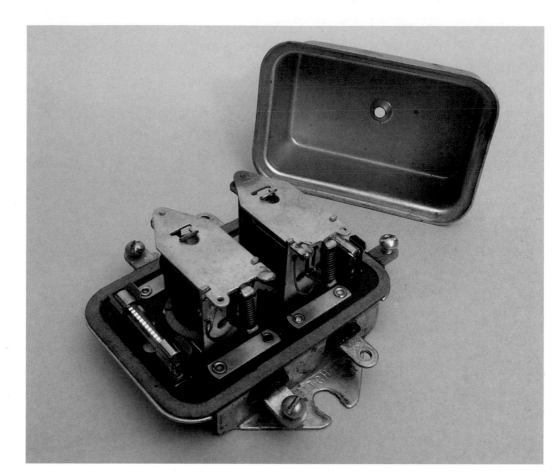

*A six-volt dual
headlight relay. Some
online vendors still
carry them.*

were barely capable of handling the full load of the headlights when they were new. Age and wear have further reduced this ability. Feel the switch after you've had the headlights on for a few minutes. You may be surprised by how warm it is. An aging switch also contributes substantially to voltage drop to the headlights. And remember how dependent bulb brightness is on voltage; using a relay means that the switch only needs to handle the load of a relay coil, greatly prolonging the life of the switch. The relay also minimizes voltage drop through the switch.

Typically, the relay is intended to be installed close to the headlights. Considerations of authenticity may force you to seek alternatives. Wherever you put the relay, run a #10 wire directly from the battery or ammeter to supply power.

Sealed Beams

Improved sealed-beam units were introduced in 1954, coincident with the conversion of American cars to 12 volts. The units delivered a 25 percent wattage increase

and some minor internal changes. In 1956 aim tips or aim pads were added to sealed-beam units. These made aiming much more precise, for both the shop and the do-it-yourself car owner. Modern sealed-beam units use halogen technology, offering even brighter lamps. These install in place of your existing sealed-beam units.

For six-volt cars with round headlamps built before 1940, sealed-beam conversions are available from vendors specializing in the various makes. In addition to the relay, consider increasing your headlamp output by such a conversion. This damages authenticity, of course.

But if you've already taken this step, you can go to the next level with halogen lighting. So can the owners of 1940–1953 six-volt cars with factory-sealed beams. While you may see these halogen units described as sealed beams, they really are not. The unit is a combined lens-reflector-socket unit that accepts a six- or 12-volt H-4 halogen lamp installed from the rear. The reflector does have a long life, and the lamp puts lots of light on the road.

GETTING THE BEST FROM BULB-REFLECTOR HEADLIGHTS

If you choose not to convert your pre-1940 car to sealed beams, you'll have to make sure that your original headlamps give you everything they've got. 1930s-era headlamps included three basic elements: a lens, a reflector, and a bulb. Like those of today, headlamps had to be adjusted to determine where the beam pointed. (Before 1934 the bulb also had to be focused to place the filaments at the most effective point in relation to the reflector. With the introduction of the prefocused bulb, this variable was removed.) While the bulbs were standardized after this date, lenses and their accompanying reflectors came in a variety of shapes.

It should be noted that the reason for the introduction of sealed beam lamps in 1940 was not

An aiming pad on a six-volt sealed beam headlamp.

A reflector converted to use an H-4 halogen bulb, available in six or 12 volts. Be sure that the bulb focus is unaffected.

A silvered headlamp reflector will eventually tarnish to this degree.

necessarily an inability of the lens-reflector-bulb arrangement to put enough light on the road. The main problem was the difficulty of keeping the light output consistent, with the reflector the worst culprit. The coating that gives the highest reflectance is silver; about 94 percent of the light gathered from the bulb is returned. Despite efforts to seal the unit with gaskets, the silvered reflector tarnished quickly. Light output began dropping at the same time. It was not unusual for light output to diminish by half within six months of the installation of new reflectors. (The silver surface is so delicate that fingerprints accelerate the tarnishing process, and ordinary silver polishes are too harsh to use on it.) By contrast, the disposable sealed beam unit had a reflector that lasted the life of the bulb, and was renewed each time the bulb was changed.

The UVIRA coating is aluminum coated with glass. It gives nearly the same reflectance as new silver, and lasts for years.

The reflectors are key to the successful use of original headlamps. To effectively concentrate the available light from the bulb, the reflectors must be free of dents and highly reflective. Most reflectors are badly tarnished. In an attempt to solve this problem some owners chrome-plate the reflectors. Bad mistake. True, they don't tarnish anymore, but they don't reflect much light either. Shiny as chrome looks, it's very dark compared with silver. Its reflectance is only about 65 percent, compared with new silver's 94 percent.

Several decades ago space technology came to our rescue. The proprietor of a company called Uvira, Inc. in Merlin, Oregon, was a car collector. His company made mirrors that were used to reflect laser beams; he adapted this process to the headlight reflectors on pre-1940 cars. He still offers this service to discriminating drivers. The reflectors you send him must go first to an electroplater who will buff them down to brass, then plate them with nickel and polish them. Then Uvira's vacuum process will deposit a pure aluminum coating, with a microthin layer of glass over it to protect it. Voila: an original reflector with a reflectance of 92 percent that's guaranteed not to fall below 90 percent for five years.

If you still choose to have your reflectors silver-plated, and have to store them for a while before they're installed in the car, here's a tip: Seal them in a box with unscented mothballs (pure paradichlorbenzene). The evaporating mothballs turn to a heavier-than-air gas that drives out air and keeps the reflectors from tarnishing.

Newly refinished reflectors deserve new sockets. Brand-new units are available. They're of more modern designs, but are identical in appearance and function where it counts—on the reflector side. The original headlight bulb in most pre-war cars was rated 32-32; that's 32 candlepower on the high beam, and 32 on the low. (All that's different is the direction of each beam.) Replacements for the prefocused headlamp bulbs of the mid-1930s are available with 50 candlepower on the high beam, 32 on the low.

Prefocused halogen bulbs are available as direct replacements for the incandescent originals. Their filaments are in exactly the same spot as the originals, so focus is maintained. (I have seen adapters intended to permit the installation of six- or 12-volt H-4 halogen bulbs in original reflectors where this placement was not that accurate. Be cautious about these.) Remember too

that halogen bulbs are much hotter, and many of the old headlight lenses were not Pyrex. The possibility of cracking exists.

Don't even consider a halogen conversion unless you're using new wiring harnesses, direct grounds, and a headlight relay. Halogen bulbs draw considerably more current than the bulbs they replace. Any wiring problems can quickly turn into disasters.

AIMING HEADLAMPS

Your headlights can be bright as anything, but if they are not putting the light exactly where it needs to go, you will either be seeing dimly or blinding oncoming drivers. The headlights need to be aimed correctly.

For many decades the DIY collector car owner aimed headlights using the time-honored aiming screen. This procedure typically requires a level driveway at least 35 feet long with a vertical surface at the end of it at least 8 feet wide and 5 feet high. Markings are made on the wall, or on a screen in front of it, indicating where

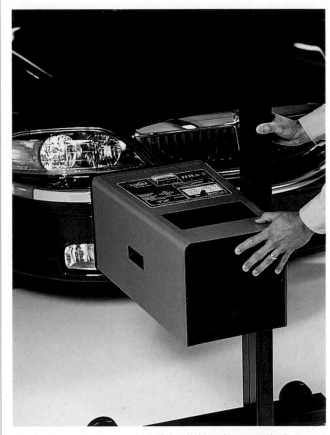

The best way to aim your headlights is by using an optical headlight aimers. Many good body shops have them. This one is made by Symtech. Symtech Corporation

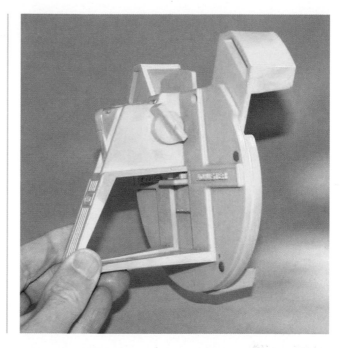

the hot spot of the low beams is to fall. This is a time-consuming process, though, and not everyone has the real estate for it.

Considering how seldom headlights need to be aimed, you should take advantage of the latest technology. The optical headlight aligners, sometimes called headlight aimers, used by many auto body shops will correctly aim any headlight, on any car, of any year. If your headlights are anything but the standard round sealed-beam, you will need to explain to the shop in advance that you will do the actual adjusting yourself. Work out the fee arrangement in advance too. Some places will not want to bother under those

LIGHTING FOR THE OLDER ONES

They may be beautiful, but older taillights are hard to see compared to newer taillights.

A third brake light from L & N Enterprises is adaptable to many collector cars. L & N Enterprises

Stock incandescent and replacement halogen bulbs for taillights.

circumstances. Look for a shop that will do it happily, or the experience could get uncomfortable.

Taillamp Improvements

By today's standards, the taillights in pre-mid-1950s cars are rather small and dim. Drivers today expect more, and might not notice your taillights or brake lights until too late.

Many early taillamp housings used painted interiors as reflectors. As the surfaces rusted the output got dimmer and dimmer. If you repaint the inside of your housing, use gloss white. Aluminized paints are actually less reflective.

Halogen lamps are now available in dual-filament configurations for use as taillamp/stop lights. They come in base designs to replace the original bulbs. Some care is needed, however. Halogen bulbs draw much more current than do the incandescent filaments you're replacing. Be sure your brake light wires are in good condition. Also, be prepared for the possibility of more frequent brake switch replacement.

Most important, halogen bulbs produce much more heat. Be cautious when using a halogen bulb as a replacement in a taillamp that's fitted with plastic lenses.

Several vendors who sell halogen conversions also supply an LED "third brake light" that mounts in the rear window of your collector car. Only one that I know of, from L & N Enterprises, is available in both six- and 12-volt versions. It's quite slim, so it doesn't affect vision. It puts a brake light where modern drivers are accustomed to seeing one, a useful safety modification. You'll have to add the wiring, but with some ingenuity the device can be made removable for shows.

CHAPTER 13
LIFTING YOUR CAR

I don't know about you, but it just isn't as easy for me to slide under my car and slither around as it used to be. Must be that the car is sagging closer to the ground. I also find that I can't see things that are only three inches from my nose as easily as I used to. Maybe it's getting darker under there too.

The answer, my friends, is to get the car off the ground a bit. It's not that difficult to do, but a few safety admonitions are in order.

You've heard it before, so hear it once more. Never (that means N-E-V-E-R) get under a car that's supported only by a hydraulic jack. We do not have so many collector car enthusiasts that we can afford to lose any. Every time I'm tempted just to take a quick dive under the car without setting the jack stands, I use a technique that works for me. By neglecting the stands I can save about 120 seconds, right? Now how long would it take, after the car falls on me, to have it lifted off, wait for the paramedics, ride to the ER in the ambulance, lie on a gurney in the corridor till they get to me . . . ? Anyway, you get the idea. I do the same when I'm too lazy to walk over and get my safety goggles before getting underneath to look up at a dirty frame crossmember. It works for me.

There are multiple ways to get your car up and keep it there while you work. They are limited only by your pocketbook and the configuration of your workspace.

Rhino Ramps at work.

FOR BRIEF LIFTING

To grease your car, or to check for a leak or for a loose part or wire—or for any job that requires just a few extra inches of ground clearance and does not require the removal of the wheels, the safest and most cost-effective way to provide more working clearance is with ramps. Ramps are made of steel and high-strength plastics. The plastic ones are much easier to carry around, and light enough to hang on the wall for easy storage. And, they won't rust. Typically, a plastic ramp will lift your wheels about six inches. You can put a car on four ramps, which will give you uniform clearance from front to back of the car. Need a bit more height? A steel ramp will go about eight inches, but steel ramps are much heavier and harder to store. With ramps under your tires, the bottom of your car will be 14 to 16 inches above the ground.

You can drive forward or back onto two ramps on the same end of the car. If I'm lifting four wheels, or two on the same side of the car, I prefer to lift the car with a hydraulic jack, then lower it onto the ramps.

GOING HIGHER

If you need the wheels to hang free, you'll want to put the chassis on jackstands. These simple devices are indispensable for the collector car owner. Check workmanship on the jackstands; neat welds usually

From the left: three-ton and six-ton jack stands from the auto supply store, and my 12-ton BendPak/Ranger truck stands.

indicate greater potential strength than sloppy ones do. If the stands are of the ratcheting type, be sure the ratchet has substantial bearing on the toothed post. The pin type of jackstand is not as easily adjustable, but engagement is absolutely positive.

Remember that the weight capacity on the box is, unless otherwise stated, for *both* stands. Get stands with the highest weight-carrying ability you can afford. Spring for three-ton units in preference to two-ton ones; six-tonners are better yet. Stands with these weight-carrying capacities all have, within a few inches, the same range of maximum and minimum heights. Heavier stands have a safer, wider base, and give more margin of protection. And don't be misled by the seeming logic of four legs being better than

If needed, the Acme screw on top permits fine adjustments. The removable handle adds leverage for doing this with the car's weight on the stands.

With legs collapsed, the four huge jack stands store in less than two square feet of floor space.

KwikLift in a private garage. The ramps are in position for a car to be driven on and off. The black "bridge" holding the jackstands and bottle jack is for lifting the car if the wheels must be removed.

three. A device standing on three legs always has all three legs firmly contacting the surface, even when that surface is a bit uneven. A four-legged stand can rock if the surface is not flat. Why do you think milking stools have three legs?

Good auto supply stores and website tool companies sell quality jackstands. The price difference between sizes is very small; consider that your life is on the line here.

While it may be unlikely, I have always had a scary fantasy of being under the car while it's supported on *four* jackstands at their maximum height, having a friend show up to see what I'm doing, having him lean on the car, and . . . . Yeah, it's never happened, but I still was never happy under my car while it was supported on four jackstands. Until I discovered truck stands.

These are the big brothers of the stands you can buy in your local chain store. They are rated for 12 tons (24,000 pounds). While they are only two to four inches higher than six-ton stands, all their dimensions are beefier—especially, and most important, their bases. A typical six-ton jackstand's base covers 90 square inches; a twelve-tonner may stand on a 130-square-inch rectangle—nearly 50 percent larger.

I tend to be cautious, especially when my survival is at stake. So I bought stands that, while also rated for 12 tons, appear to be capable of supporting those 12 tons *each*. They are made by BendPak/Ranger, and their height range is similar to other 12-tonners. But they stand on three very widely spaced legs with floor pads, they have Acme screws that permit fine height adjustments, and their welded saddles make the cast ones look like toys. The legs fold by removing three bolts on each—an important feature for those of us with small garages. When my car goes up in the air for its annual checkup, or when I do a brake job or longer-term project underneath, four of these are what it stands on. Keep in mind that they weigh three times what six-ton jacks do, and are priced to match. I get them out only when I really need them.

EVEN HIGHER

If you need even more ground clearance, or if you are working on an extensive or long-term project, there are

two more ways to get your car in the air and hold it there safely. Both are made in the United States.

One is a unique product called KwikLift. Basically, it's a pair of ramps that sit on a pair of pedestals at the front and two swing-down legs at the rear. You raise and lower it with a garage jack. That may sound awfully simplistic, but a great deal of engineering and experience has gone into this product.

KwikLift has a very large base of satisfied owners, and a very few who feel that the space it takes and some of its inconveniences make it not worthwhile for them. Especially useful for long-term projects, KwikLift does provide a safe

Easy Access stands provide just that. Backyard Buddy Automotive Lifts

Disassembled when not in use, Easy Access' many parts can store reasonably compactly. Backyard Buddy Automotive Lifts

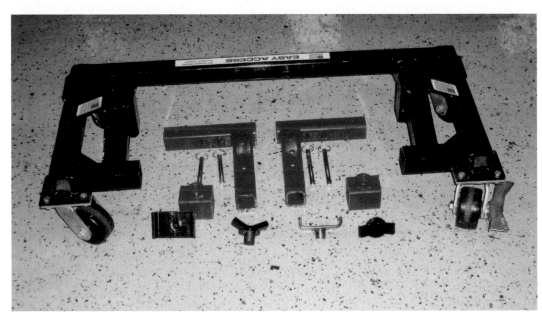

method of setting your car's chassis 30 inches from the ground. Owners swear by their customer service, too.

Another method of achieving almost this height is an interesting set of devices called Easy Access stands. Offered by Backyard Buddy, they come in pairs—one section lifts the front end, one the rear. The front ones come with adapters to negotiate the variety of front-end chassis shapes of collector cars. Easy Access stands can sit your car even higher than six-ton jackstands, but their wide configuration makes them tip-proof.

The stands come apart, but they still take up more storage space than jackstands. A plus is that they ride on

four-inch casters, so you can even push your baby around while it's on the stands. Cool.

POWER LIFTING

The ultimate way to lift your car is with an electric or air-operated lift. The new twin-post lifts require no excavation. But, while prices have come down, they're still pretty pricey for most hobbyists. The controlling factor is garage height. To be able to lift the car (with its hood up) to a height where you can walk underneath it, you need a clear ceiling or rafter height of 12 feet or more. That's rare in home garages.

A mid-rise lift by BendPak. It can be locked at several heights. BendPak, Inc.

Consider a compromise. A mid-rise lift, used by some tire shops, only lifts the car about three feet, by pads under the frame. It is much less expensive than a two-post or four-post full-height lift. Most work on 110-volt household current. Check out the design of the lift you're interested in. Since lifts are intended to be used from the side for tire work, some have a jungle of braces on the inside that make them useless for work under the car. But if you find one that works for you and the price is right, it's much easier to work sitting up than flat on your back!

As tire shops expand into other service areas, they're purchasing twin-post asymmetrical lifts. As a result, they are known to sell off old mid-rise lifts for reasonable prices. Ask shops in your area that use mid-rise lifts to let you know when they upgrade. What's obsolete to them may be just right for you. Call some local lift suppliers, too, and ask about used lifts.

WHERE TO PUT THEM

Jacks and lifts have to live someplace when they are not in use. Jackstands are, of course, the least burden. They wind up against a wall or under the bench. Bigger lifts vary in convenience. Unless you have a garage with multiple bays, large units like the KwikLift and mid-rise power lifts will spend their idle time under your car. They will be in the way of some small tasks for which you just wanted to reach under the car—changing the oil, for example. And they are trip hazards when the car is not sitting over them. Nothing is perfect.

CHAPTER 14
WHEELS AND TIRES

If it doesn't perform acceptably on the road, even the handsomest collector car will find itself left in the garage. A large measure of responsibility for the quality of that performance rests with the wheels and tires. So does your safety.

Your car may be equipped with its original steel or wire wheels, or may wear aftermarket alloy units. All need attention and care, albeit of different types.

Check your wheels visually at least once a year. The older your car, the more vital this procedure is. With steel disc wheels, you'll be looking for cracks in the wheel and rim. With wire wheels, you'll be looking for loose spokes as well. Cracks can start as a result of metal fatigue caused by thousands of blows from bumps, curbs and potholes, and millions of cycles of rotation.

The openings in the wheel include the bolt holes, and may also include other apertures. Look for hairline cracks from any hole to any other, and from any hole to the rim or wheel center. Also look for rust or corrosion in corners and crevices. If you find cracks or serious corrosion, you should probably discard the wheel. The only possible exceptions are for a very rare or irreplaceable wheel. In these cases, consult a wheel expert. Stockton Wheel Service is a well-known one.

Examine the bolt holes. Look for holes worn large or egg-shaped. Either condition will make it difficult to properly torque the bolts or nuts, and can result in loosening while driving.

Be especially wary if the wheels on your car were rescued from what we used to call a junkyard, or if the car you restored spent part of its life immersed in mud to the hubcaps. Badly rusted wheels can sometimes be esthetically salvaged by sandblasting, but their mechanical integrity will be severely compromised. Best to look elsewhere for the wheels to which you trust your life.

Don't tighten the wheels on your collector car with an impact wrench. We're sometimes advised to run the wheels up with an impact wrench, then do the final tightening with a torque wrench. If you do this, you'll need a light touch on the impact wrench's trigger. Besides, you'll lose the feel for stripped or cross-threaded nuts or studs that you get when you install the nuts by hand. It's not that much harder to run the nuts up with a lug wrench. Besides, the interface of human and machine via lug wrench is one of those lost artifacts of the good old days. You may not want to do it too often, but it isn't such a horrible chore when done once in a while.

On wheels with an odd number of lugs, tighten every other lug around the wheel. On wheels with an even number, tighten opposite pairs all around. Do the final tightening, in the same pattern, with a torque wrench.

Your wheel rims have probably hit many a curb in their lifetime. They may look fine to the eye, but only a dial indicator at a good tire and wheel shop will tell you the truth. To give acceptable performance on the road, wheels and tires must be round and within acceptable tolerances for radial (up and down) and axial (side to side) runout. (Many old-line tire shops use the equally valid and more descriptive terms hop and wobble.) Good standards to follow for your older original wheels—1930s to 1950s—are a maximum of .020 axial runout, .050 radial. After those years, go for no more than .020 in either direction.

An impressive selection of reproduction tires is available for collector cars, going back to the classic and antique eras, American and foreign. Few of these tires are made in the original molds. In most cases, new molds have been made to closely reproduce original sidewall and tread patterns. Since the steel molds are expensive, there are a few sizes and patterns that it's not financially practical to reproduce. Collectors of most cars, though, will be able to choose from several brands and several tread designs.

RADIALS VS. BIAS-PLYS

If your older collector car is intended primarily for show, then you probably aren't reading this book in the first place. Since you plan to drive your car, you should become familiar with some tire history and technology.

Your 1930s through mid-1960s American collector car came with bias-ply tires. (A few European cars used radials earlier.) Later collector cars may have been equipped with radials at the factory.

Basic tire maintenance involves inspecting your tires regularly. Learn to read patterns; they are warning signs of trouble. Tires should be inspected three ways. First, visually examine all four tires; second, feel the tread by hand to detect wear patterns; and third, check all tires with a quality pressure gauge. The "eyeball" method of estimating pressure can be misleading, especially with radial tires.

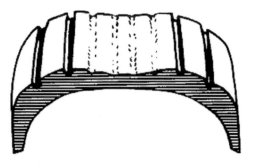

OVER INFLATION

Excessive wear at the center of the tread indicates that the air pressure in the tire is consistently too high. The tire is riding on the center of the tread and wearing it out prematurely.

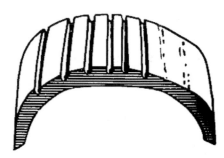

ONE SIDE WEAR

When an inner or outer rib wears faster than the rest of the tire, the need for wheel alignment is indicated. Misalignment could also be due to sagging springs, worn kingpins or ball joints, or worn control arm bushings.

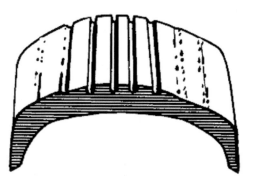

UNDER INFLATION

When a tire is under inflated, there is too much contact with the road by the outer treads, which wear prematurely. When this type of wear occurs even though tire pressure is known to be consistently correct, a bent or worn steering component or the need for wheel alignment could be indicated.

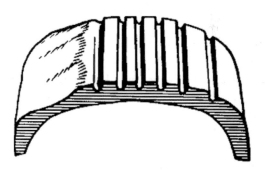

CUPPING

Cups or scalloped dips appearing around the edge of the tread on one side or the other almost always indicate worn (sometimes bent) suspension parts. Any worn component that connects the wheel to the car (kingpin, ball joint, wheel bearing, shock absorber, springs, bushings, etc.) can cause this condition. Occasionally, wheels that are out of balance will wear like this, but wheel imbalance usually shows up as bald spots between the outside edges and center of the tread.

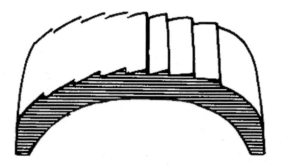

FEATHERING (LEFT)

Feathering is a condition when the edge of each tread rib develops a slightly rounded edge on one side and a sharp edge on the other. By running your hand over the tire, you can usually feel the sharper edges before you'll be able to see them. The most common cause of feathering is incorrect toe-in setting. Occasionally toe-in will be set correctly and this wear pattern still occurs. This is usually due to deteriorated bushings in the front suspension, causing the wheel alignment to shift as the car moves down the road.

WHEELS AND TIRES

Graphics and adapted text courtesy of Autozone's ProCare

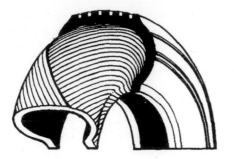

Bias-ply tire construction.

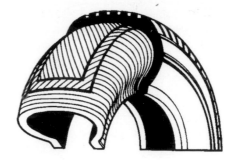

Radial tire construction.

Bias-ply tires were constructed of between two and eight rubber-coated corded fabric plies that ran diagonally down one sidewall, across the width of the tread and up the other sidewall. Alternate plies ran in opposite directions diagonally, so the plies crisscrossed each other for strength. The more plies, the stronger (and usually stiffer) the tire. Tire cord material improved from cotton to rayon to nylon to polyester over the decades, but the design remained essentially the same.

Radial tires use a totally different architecture. They too contain fabric corded plies, but the cords run straight across from bead to bead. Usually only one or two plies are used. In addition, several belts—plies with diagonal steel or fabric cords—wrap around the circumference of the tire.

Because the plies of the bias-ply tire solidly connect the tread and the sidewall, every element of the bias-ply tire distorts as the tire revolves under load. The scissoring action between the diagonal plies of bias-ply tires causes interply friction and generates much heat. In the area near the tread contact with the road, deflection of the sidewall causes a sideways wiping movement of the tread against the road. This is one of the main reasons for tread wear.

In the radial design, the sidewall of the tire operates independently of the tread. Interply friction is virtually eliminated. The firm circumferential belts keep the tread of the radial flat on the pavement without the wiping motion characteristic of bias-plys. This dramatically increases traction, especially laterally, and eliminates the bias-ply tire's tendency to wander. (This problem is especially noticeable in the relatively narrow original equipment tires used on cars of the 1930s and 1940s.) The reduction of heat and the elimination of the wiping are the main

reasons for the radial tire's substantially increased longevity. And because the belts restrain the tread's ability to squirm, the rolling resistance of radial tires is about 10 percent less than equivalent bias-plys. This helps increase gas mileage a bit.

A BRIEF HISTORY OF RADIALS

In the 1930s, Michelin of France began to investigate ways to reduce interply friction and tread movement. Its first production radial tire for passenger cars was on the market in 1948, aimed primarily at sports cars and sporty sedans. For some years Michelin was the major producer of radial tires, and provided them only for European cars. In 1965 Goodyear, Firestone, and U.S. Rubber began selling radial tires in limited areas, primarily in sizes to fit European cars. In 1966, Sears Roebuck stunned the tire industry by introducing radials made in sizes for American cars, to be sold as aftermarket replacements. (At that time only 1 percent of American cars rode on radials, as compared with 70 percent of the cars in France and 25 percent of the vehicles in the United Kingdom.) A year earlier, Sears and Michelin had signed an agreement under the terms of which Michelin would supply its radial tires to Sears, branded with the Allstate name.

The Michelin/Allstate tires used steel belts, as opposed to the fabric belts used by American manufacturers. As radials grew in popularity, some manufacturers offered radial-tuned shocks or suspensions. These may have been intended to counter the reported harsher ride of the steel-belted radials.

Ford offered American-made radials on some of its 1967 models. Within 10 years every production car offered radials, first as an option and later as standard equipment.

ABOUT RIMS AND TUBES

As noted previously, the radials that Sears introduced to the American market in 1966 were aftermarket tires. They were installed on rims designed for bias-ply tires. By 1970 Sears was selling a million radial tires a year, all to the aftermarket, and nearly all of them mounted on wheels designed for bias-ply tires. Before Sears, Michelin had been mounting radial tires on bias-ply rims in Europe for nearly 20 years. Millions of miles of experience showed that mounting radial tires on rims originally designed for bias-plys was practical and safe.

Nevertheless, scare stories have been spread in print and online regarding the wisdom of mounting tubeless radials on rims not designed for them. Some remember incidents of wheel breakage in the late 1960s and attribute this to the conversion to radials that was taking place then. Others have offered the notion that the alloy used for wheel rims was changed when tubeless tires were introduced and again with the advent of radials. Metallurgical engineer Joseph Tunick Strauss clarifies this history. Until the late 1960s wheel rims were made of rimmed steel. This term has nothing to do with what was fabricated from them, but rather refers to the process of removing the top surface of a steel ingot at the mill so the oxides and impurities that rise to the top as it cools do not become entrained in the steel as it is rolled into sheets. During the late 1960s some rimming was done improperly at one mill, and some fatigue failures of automobile wheel rims resulted. Changing the process of fabrication to continuous cast steel ended the problem. The fact that these metallurgical failures occurred during the period of changeover from bias-ply to radial tires was purely coincidental. And there has been no substantive change in the steel alloy used to make wheel rims from the 1930s to the 1980s. Frank Mauro of Stockton Wheel Service also states that rumors of rim failures caused by the use of radial tires are baseless. Mauro says, "There were no changes to rim design or material in the late '50s when the tubeless tire came on the scene. In fact the idea was for backward compatibility to shift people with older cars to the new tubeless tires. So those tires had to be safe on the old rims."

The cautions voiced earlier about using rusted, cracked, or restored wheels and rims certainly apply to their use with radial tires. Don't do it.

Tubes are another issue. Goodyear introduced the tubeless tire in 1947. By the mid-1950s, they had become standard equipment on American passenger cars. The new tires reduced heat buildup caused by friction between the tube and the tire; they also reduced the danger of sudden blowouts when the tube was punctured. But Michelin was not certain that new radials on old American rims would hold air properly. So Sears initially sold the Allstate radial as a tube-type tire. A special tube was used to cope with the flexing of the radial sidewalls. Within six months it became clear that the tube was not needed, and from that point on Sears sold and installed the same tire as a tubeless.

MEASURING TIRES

The size of bias-ply tires is measured in inches. The two figures represent the height of the tire (usually omitting the decimal point) and the diameter of the wheel on which it is mounted. The approximate diameter of each mounted tire can be easily calculated. A 650-16 tire is approximately 29 inches uninstalled. This is calculated as (6.50 x 2) + 16. A 600-15 tire is about 27 inches—(6.00 x 2) + 15.

Radial tire measurements are an odd mix of standard (English) and metric figures. They show the tire section width in millimeters and the wheel diameter in inches. An inch is 25.4 millimeters. (They also include the aspect ratio—the sidewall height divided by the section width. The larger this number, the taller the tire.) The formula for the diameter of the mounted tire is: ((section width/25.4) x (aspect ratio/100) x 2) + wheel diameter. So the diameter in inches of a 225/70R16 radial is ((225 / 25.4) x (70/100) x 2) + 16. That's about 28.4 inches.

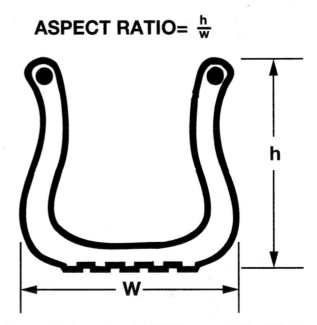

ASPECT RATIO = $\frac{h}{w}$

Aspect ratio is the maximum height of the unmounted tire divided by the maximum width.

In the bad old days, collector car tires were often made in worn molds by off-shore suppliers, and delivered out-of-round. This machine shaved rubber off to make them round!

BUYING TIRES

You can purchase collector car tires by phone or online, and have them delivered by one of the common carriers. They're usually shipped wrapped in clear plastic. It's important to examine your tires, especially if they are whitewalls, while the delivery person is present. Look for damage done by conveyor belts or rubbing against another parcel. It is normally the responsibility of the consignee or customer to determine if the parcel is damaged and to so advise the delivery person. If the damage occurred in transit, claims are made to the carrier, not the vendor.

Tires are highly complex products. They're manufactured from an array of chemicals including chlorobutyl rubber, natural rubber, carbon black and calendared fabric made of polyester, rayon or nylon. With time all of these chemicals will break down or oxidize from exposure to the atmosphere. It is best to put off purchasing tires until the final weeks of a restoration project, so you're sure of purchasing fresh ones.

NOTHING LASTS FOREVER. . . . AND TIRES ARE NO EXCEPTION.

The Tire Rack (www.tirerack.com) is a major online source of accurate information about tires. Some of the information below is adapted from its site.

Information on the sidewall tells you when the tire was manufactured. Since tires age, this is important knowledge. The last four digits of the 12-digit code that begins with "DOT" are the date code. It's often enclosed by an oval, as in this example. The four digits do not mean month and year. They identify the week of the year in which the tire was manufactured. In this example, "0103" means that the tire was made in the first week of 2003.

In the 1970s, bias-ply tires wore out after about 15,000 miles during two years of service. In the 1980s, early radial-ply tires wore out after about 40,000 miles during four years of service. And by the turn of the century, radial tires lasting 60,000 to 80,000 miles were providing four or more years of service on vehicles averaging about 15,000 miles per year. In all of these examples, the tire treads wore out before the rest of the tire aged out.

Your collector car almost certainly doesn't average 15,000 miles per year. So you may have 10-year-old tires with significant remaining tread depth because they've been driven fewer than 1,000 miles a year! The growing realization that tires are perishable means that the tires on some of our vehicles will actually age out before they wear out.

How long will tires last before aging out? The U.S. National Highway Traffic Safety Administration and tire manufacturers are currently studying the many variables. Current industry recommendations on the subject originate outside the United States. The British Rubber Manufacturers Association (BRMA) recommended practice, issued June 2001, states "BRMA members strongly recommend that unused tyres should not be put into service if they are over six years old and that all tyres should be replaced 10 years from the date of their manufacture.

"Environmental conditions like exposure to sunlight and coastal climates, as well as poor storage and *infrequent use*, accelerate the aging process. In ideal conditions, a tyre may have a life expectancy that exceeds ten years from its date of manufacture. However, such conditions are rare. Aging may not exhibit any external indications and, since there is no non-destructive test to assess the serviceability of a tyre, even an inspection carried out by a tyre expert may not reveal the extent of any deterioration."

More recently, the Japan Automobile Tire Manufacturers Association (JATMA) recommended practice, issued May 2005, states "customers are encouraged to have their vehicle tires promptly inspected after five years of use to determine if the tires can continue to be used. Furthermore, even when the tires look usable, it is recommended that all tires (including spare tires) that were made more than 10 years ago be replaced with new tires."

Several European manufacturers of high performance sports cars, coupes and sedans specify in their vehicle owner's manual that "under no circumstances should tires older than six years be used." While American driving conditions don't include the high-speed challenges of the German Autobahn, the U.S. divisions of DaimlerChrysler and Ford Motor Company joined their European colleagues in 2005 by recommending the tires installed as original equipment be replaced after six years of service. (General Motors declined to offer a recommendation until a more scientific analysis of driving conditions and tire aging could be completed).

Because many collector car tires are manufactured in Europe or Asia, it's common for the tires you buy to be six months to one year old by the time you receive them. (You can determine the date of manufacture from the data on the sidewall).

While no hard and fast lifetime can be specified yet, be aware that those 10-year-old tires on your collector car, the ones with the still-perfect tread, may be nearing the end of their safe lives.

If you must buy your tires long before they are to be mounted on your car, here are a few things you can do to limit the damage they suffer in storage. Store your tires in a cool, dry and dark environment. A basement is better than an attic or outdoors.

Many manufacturers recommend removing the clear plastic wrapping during storage. Place each tire in its own large, opaque, airtight plastic bag—a lawn-and-leaf bag works. Avoid allowing any moisture in and remove as much air as practical. Some drivers even use a shop vac to draw out as much air as possible. Close the bag tightly and tape it shut. This places the tire in its own personal miniatmosphere, helping to reduce oil evaporation.

Store tires white sidewall to white sidewall, and black sidewall to black sidewall. Make sure that no whitewall touches black rubber. Black rubber contains carbon black, which will stain any whitewall permanently. As for tubes, buy those just before you need them.

Ozone speeds the deterioration of rubber products. While ozone exists in the atmosphere, there's no need to expose your tires to more. Don't store tires near electric motors, since these emit ozone while in use.

Most cars were originally delivered with black sidewalls. This is true of every make from Dodge to Duesenberg. Today most collector car owners prefer the look of wide white sidewalls. Responding to the demand, vendors have made white whitewall radials available for the collector car market. Diamond Back Classics vulcanizes a heavy white sidewall onto major makes of radial tires, after buffing off the raised lettering

A Diamond Back employee lays on the white rubber strip. Diamond Back Classics

on one side. Their tires are available in most sizes and rim diameters, including those for the prewar classics. I have driven my 1930s classic many thousands of satisfactory miles on Diamond Back whites. Coker Tires, one of the largest distributors of tires to the collector car hobby, also offers radial sizes for collector cars. Some sizes use the bias-ply sizing, like 600-16, although they are radials. Bucking an industry standard, some of Coker's radials require tubes. Check this out carefully before buying.

KEEPING THEM WHITE . . . AND BLACK.
Wide whitewalls should be cleaned on a regular basis to keep them white. Because whitewalls on most collector tires are somewhat porous, dust and dirt can become imbedded. So it's best to keep them clean, rather than try to recover a filthy tire. My favorite cleaner is described in Chapter 16.

Diamond Back can make redlines, too. Diamond Back Classics

Bleach-type whitewall cleaners give a bright result. But bleach dries out the rubber. So if you must use a bleach product like Westley's Bleche-Wite, be sure to wash the whitewall immediately with a mild cleaner. If your whitewalls are really dirty, you're going to need some abrasive. Keep it mild. A white Scotch-Brite will work. So will a fine sanding sponge. If you use an SOS pad, remember that it contains bleach. This method for cleaning whitewalls also applies to redlines, pinstripe whitewalls or raised letters.

Rubber and vinyl treatments are also popular at auto supply stores. These products claim that they will prolong the life and enhance the beauty of the rubber on your automobile. Frankly, most result in black rubber that's too shiny for my taste. You can also buy tire dressings that make your dark gray tires look black. Tire companies generally recommend against them. In addition, whitewalls, redlines, and raised white letters will be stained by the chemicals in these treatments.

INSTALLATION

Although you can mount your own tires by hand, I recommend that you turn this job over to a qualified expert. Choose carefully, though, because not all tire shops are willing to take the care needed to mount your tires with minimal damage to the rim finish. Ask fellow collector car owners for a good shop in your area.

Tire balance is more critical on some cars, less on others, but all newly installed tires should be balanced. Today's computerized machines spin tires for just a few seconds. As with nearly every piece of machinery, the skill of the operator is important—sometimes more important—than the sophistication of the technology. If you find a good person, give him or her your business.

Many times tires wrongly take the blame for a car's other mechanical problems. If you're still experiencing vibration with round and balanced tires, check for proper front end alignment. Shocks on older cars may need filling, or rebuilding. When the steering wheel vibrates while applying brakes, the likely culprits are the drums, not the tires.

INFLATION AND EFFORT

Correct inflation is important to long tire life. The maximum pressure molded into the sidewall of every modern tire is the proper inflation when the tire is carrying its maximum load. For normal driving conditions, manufacturers generally recommend a pressure of about 90 percent of the maximum.

If you've converted your collector car from bias-plys to radials, and your car does not have power steering, you will find that steering effort when the car is standing still, or when parallel parking, is considerably increased. That's because the radial tire's contact patch with the road is much larger than on the bias-ply it replaced. The lower the pressure, the bigger the patch and the greater the effort. This puts a lot of strain on your steering gear. As a matter of practice, unless there is no alternative, be sure the car is moving just a bit before you turn the steering wheel. Effort, and strain on mechanical parts, drops significantly.

FILLING 'EM WITH NITROGEN

Environmental groups have begun to push for inflating tires with nitrogen rather than plain air. They claim that nitrogen-inflated tires hold air pressure better, avoiding the gas-eating under-inflation that many owners permit. They also claim that nitrogen will keep tires cooler, reducing wear.

All that probably is true. But consider that the air around us is 78 percent nitrogen to begin with. And collector car owners are much more scrupulous about checking and maintaining tire pressures than are the average drivers. It just doesn't seem worth the handsome fee per tire that some tire shops are charging to purge the old air and refill with nitrogen. And what if you need a few pounds of inflation while you're on a tour? Are you going to go hunting for a nitrogen station, or will you add a few pounds of that plain ol' air and dilute the fancy nitrogen gas?

I'd pass this by.

CHAPTER 15
THOUGHTS ON SOME CHASSIS COMPONENTS

FRONT END ALIGNMENT

The average collector car owner will never have occasion to do his own front-end work. Front-end alignment is a task best left to specialists who have the equipment and theoretical knowledge to do the job. However, to be sure this work is done correctly, it can be useful for owners to understand front end alignment basics.

There are good texts on wheel alignment. They'll illustrate that all alignment theory flows from one simple purpose: to keep a vehicle's four wheels rotating with a minimum of slipping, scuffing, and dragging, no matter by what amount the front wheels are turned. There are four angles that affect the handling, steering, and tire wear patterns in older cars. These are camber, caster, toe—toe-in or toe-out—and kingpin inclination. Not all of the first three are adjustable on every car. Kingpin inclination almost never is. Specifications for your car will appear in the car's service manual.

To these relatively simple concepts today's cars have added complications like all-independent suspensions, four-wheel steering, front-wheel drive and all-wheel drive. Digitized, laser emitting, beeping and blinking alignment equipment is needed to keep track of all the variables. But we are lucky. The cars that we collect, nurture, restore, and love are far simpler. They permit simpler solutions.

There are several obvious symptoms indicating that your car's wheels may be out of alignment, and a few that are more subtle. The obvious ones are excessive and uneven tire wear, the tendency for the

You can check for front-end wear quickly in your own garage.

Grasp the tire at top and bottom. Pull the top and push the bottom, then reverse. This will check for play in wheel bearings.

Grasp the tire at the sides, and repeat the test. This checks for steering system play—tie rod ends, idler arm bushings, steering gear, and pitman arm.

car to pull to one side or the other when being driven on a flat road surface, a lack of stability that causes the car to wander about on the road, lunging into turns, failure of the steering wheel to return to center, or a tendency to violently snap back. More subtle symptoms sometimes involve a handling feel that is just not right. All of these can be due to improper wheel alignment.

Wheel alignment is actually the final step in correcting these problems. That's because the problems also can be due to worn or bent steering linkage, a sloppy steering box, bad ball joints, bad shocks, worn kingpins, or worn suspension bushings. Unevenly worn tires will throw alignment settings off. A straight and square frame and correct spring height are also prerequisites for predictable road manners.

Most of our collector cars, unless they've been in a bad accident or sadly mistreated, are not heir to all the ills described above. Use your club buddies as a source for a good local shop. The shop will check these factors out as a matter of course.

The easiest component of wheel alignment to adjust is toe-in (or -out, in a few cars). For this reason there are dozens of gadgets advertised that encourage do-it-yourself toe adjustments. These include trammel bars and similar devices. There is little question that nearly all of them are capable of measuring toe pretty accurately. And they will serve the owner-mechanic well when used on cars that provide a single adjustment that sets the toe on both front wheels simultaneously. But they are not useful for setting this adjustment on cars on which the toe is set for each front wheel independently. That's because these devices measure *total* toe. Say the correct specification for your car is 1/8-inch toe-in. That's supposed to be made up of 1/16-inch toe-in on each side. The device may show that 1/8-inch toe-in is indeed the current total reading. But it offers no way of determining whether this figure is the resultant of the correct 1/16 inch on each side, or of 1/8 inch on one side and zero on the other, or even 1/4-inch toe-in on one side and 1/8-inch toe-*out* on the other! For your car to track correctly, the toe adjustment must be equal on each side. These devices can't tell you that.

Front end alignment is fussy work that requires both experience and a feel for the theory. An experienced front-end man, using 30-year-old equipment by Bee-line, Bear, Hunter, or Beam can properly align the front end of your collector car. So can the operator of the digitized, laser and diode alignment equipment in dealerships and newer shops. In every case, the key factor is a technician who understands the theory of what needs to be accomplished. Find one, then cherish him or her.

SPRINGS

Most of our collector cars were intended as family vehicles or touring cars, and were designed to ride as comfortably as possible. Truth be told, though, many of our cars ride more harshly and noisily today than they did when they were younger. Uncovered semi-elliptic springs are probably the most common rear suspension on our cars. Ford-built cars used a single transverse leaf spring at the front and at the rear through 1948. Most collector cars used coils up front.

Coils can weaken and sag, but leaf springs are prey to a host of other ailments. While primitive provisions were sometimes made to lubricate these springs, most were neglected for much of their lives. Rust, and the abrasive dirt that gets in between the leaves, creates a great deal of extra interleaf friction. Since the spring leaves have to slide on each other as the spring flexes, the car's ride may be adversely affected. In early automobiles, some interleaf friction was designed into the spring, to help damp the spring's action. As modern shock absorbers were developed, this became less necessary. In any case, it is important that interleaf friction remains constant. To accomplish this, some production cars over the years have used interleaf liners made of fabric, wax and plastic. Others used buttons of rubber or bronze, or zinc strips. Still others provided a drilled center bolt and a grease fitting, with channels in the leaves to distribute the lubricant. Studebaker, which used a transverse leaf as the front springing medium for years, ground a short channel near the ends of the leaves in which a ball-bearing rode. (Some makers covered the springs to retain a lubricant. These covers were designed to keep dirt out and lubricants in; in practice it sometimes seems like they keep water in, and make it difficult to get lubricant in.) If your original leaf springs are not sagging, you can restore the original ride quality to them.

There's a great deal of energy stored in car springs. Unless you're experienced at this, it would be best to take your project to a good spring shop. Chances are they'll be able to do it just the way you want it. If you are equipped to do this yourself, the procedures are the same.

Slip Plate #1 comes in quart and gallon cans. It is also sold as an aerosol. Superior Graphite Co.

Consult your shop manual for instructions on removing leaf springs. Then disassemble them. Clean and strip the spring leaves of paint and rust. For want of lubrication, the ends of some leaves may have worn a groove in the leaf below them. This groove may make

the leaves catch when they lengthen as the spring flexes, and makes the ride harsher. Carefully smooth any such grooves. There are several ways you can maintain the original predictable action of your rebuilt springs. Both involve a reduction of interleaf friction. One method is to insert thin polyolefin plastic between the leaves of your springs. This is slippery stuff that comes in rolls of varying widths. The plastic is black; with the spring leaves painted black too, the plastic is essentially invisible on the job.

Another way of keeping interleaf friction predictable is to paint the spring leaves with a graphite-laced finish called Slip Plate. This is basically a charcoal gray paint with very good adhesion to clean metal, and excellent lubricating properties. It's designed for an environment with extreme pressures and slow movement, which well describes a leaf spring.

If your springs—coil or leaf—are sagging, buy new ones or have them made. Forcing steel supports into sagging coil springs will simply reduce the spring's ability to flex. Some shops re-arch sagging leaf springs by laying each spring leaf over an anvil, then striking it with mighty blows from a large hammer. Others bend the spring back to its original shape with a powerful hydraulic press. The spring's arch is restored while it's off the car, but doesn't last very long after you're back on the road. Indeed, most shops admit that only the

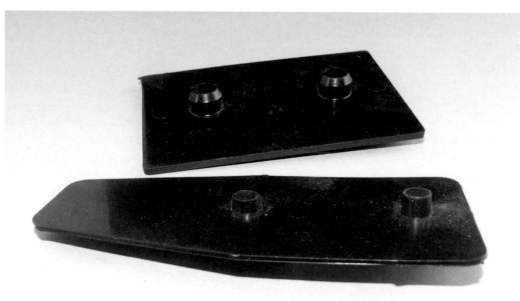

Makers of new replacement leaf springs can install plastic pads at the ends of the leaves to reduce interleaf friction. A nipple holds them in place in holes in the leaf.

A pocket for the plastic insert is created during spring manufacture. Eaton Detroit Spring, Inc.

addition of an extra leaf will give the job any longevity. That will affect the spring rate and the ride. Save your time and money; get new springs.

New coil and leaf springs are available for popular collector cars. If your vehicle does not fall into this category, check out Eaton Detroit Spring. This company has more than 24,000 original specifications for automotive coil and leaf springs, and can make you a correct set. Its leaf springs are even tapered and rolled at the ends, just like many originals. And unless otherwise requested they build plastic pads into the ends of the leaves, to keep interleaf friction consistent.

Replace all the rubber bushings when you reinstall your leaf springs. This alone will often improve the ride and restore a more precise feel to the car.

THE GAS TANK

One of the parts most vulnerable to corrosion on an old car is the gas tank. It's made of comparatively thin material, and is attacked from within and without. Any water that enters the tank with gasoline falls to the bottom. The tank is pelted from underneath by rocks and stones, and is subjected to corrosion from salt mixtures in the winter. It's amazing that some of them last as long as they do.

Rust on the inside of the tank can detach itself and be drawn into the fuel line, or block the line and cause fuel starvation. You don't know what misery is until you've driven a car with dirt and rust alternately blocking the fuel line, then falling back so the car runs again for a while giving brief hope to the owner. It's an exquisite form of automotive torture.

This problem brought gas tank sloshing sealers into the old car market. They were originally a material that had been used in airplane fuel tanks. New automotive fuel formulations, some of which are not compatible with the old sealants, have brought new formulas, especially for old cars. As often happens, the purveyor of each new formula derides the capabilities of his

The Gas Tank Renu process begins with mediablasting the tank exterior. Then a hole is drilled in a corner of the tank so the interior can be blasted. Holes uncovered by the blasting are repaired.

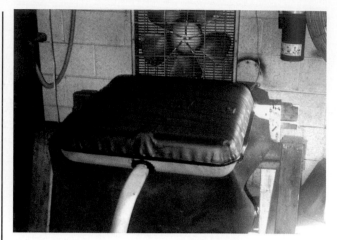

The outside of the top of the tank is coated and baked. The bottom of the tank will be done next.

The interior of the tank is filled with sealer. Adhesion is positive because the interior is bare metal. Then the sealer is poured out.

competitor's formula. We are told that certain colors are useless, and that others are frauds. It's a frightening choice for the car owner.

None of the sealers can be properly used unless the tank is removed from the car. But doing this opens another avenue. A company called Gas Tank Renu has franchises in many states. Using a process that involves bead blasting,

Gas Tank Renu will clean out your tank to bare steel. To do so, they drill a hole in a top corner of the tank to admit the blasting nozzle. After the interior of the tank is clean and the blasting media removed, a sealer is poured in and the tank is manipulated so all inside areas are covered. The rest of the sealer is poured out. (That part of the process is little different from the sloshing method, but the bare steel inside makes all the difference when it comes to sealer adhesion.) The outside of the tank is coated by brush with a black sealant. The tank is then baked at 350 degrees for 10 minutes to cure the sealants. Finished tanks are guaranteed against leakage or internal sealant separation for the life of the car. Gas Tank Renu's process is also guaranteed to resist the effects of ethanol.

The black exterior sealant has a satin finish, and closely resembles the original finish on the gas tanks of many collector cars. For show buffs, the process is offered with only the interior seal, so you can put your concours finish on the outside. The guarantee is then limited to two years.

Certainly this is more expensive than buying a quantity of sloshing sealer, but it seems to me that you buy a lot of peace of mind, too.

CHAPTER 16
EXTERIOR AND INTERIOR MAINTENANCE

There are a number of good books on the subject of cleaning and maintaining the exterior and interior of your collector car. The subject is usually referred to as "detailing". Some of these volumes do indeed go into excruciating detail on keeping the visible surfaces of your collector car beautiful and protected. This chapter, therefore, just gives an overview of this subject, and some of my thoughts on materials and methods.

Keeping your car clean and its surfaces protected is vital to its long-term survival. As with other tasks you set for yourself in the maintenance of your collector car, the level of effort will be determined by how you use your car.

I much prefer driving my car to cleaning it. So here are some of my thoughts on the subject. I won't offer instructions for using the products I like; those are amply supplied by each manufacturer.

1. Before you prepare the car, prepare yourself. Take off rings, watches, buckles, or anything else on your body, clothing, or shoes that could scratch the finish of your car. Ask yourself this question: Is there anything I'm wearing or plan to bring within one foot of the car that I wouldn't want to drag across the hood? Look at the rivets on your jeans, and at the zippers on your coveralls. If the answer is yes, then don't go near your car with that item! Murphy will sooner or later scratch the finish with it. (I wear cheap sweat clothes when I work on or clean my car.)

2. *Read the instructions for whatever product you select.* Some can be harmful to your car's finishes if improperly used. Many can even be dangerous to you: your eyes, your skin, your respiratory system. Take appropriate precautions.

3. *Use the most gentle product and technique that will do the job.*

4. Under this rule, don't wash your car more often than you need to. Some older cars are not entirely watertight. Water running down the window glass, for example, can wind up in the bottom of the doors, where it will cause rust and corrosion. A car that is garaged and covered does not need to undergo a weekly washing routine. (Unless you love washing—in that case, enjoy!)

5. When you do wash your car, make sure that it is cool and in the shade. Washing a hot car will cause the wash water to dry on the finish, causing water spots.

6. Car-washing tools make up a substantial portion of every automotive toy catalog. Here are some of mine:

a. A film of dust is not a good reason to wash your car. Instead, I use a KozaK dry wash cloth, which is a heavy flannel dusting cloth with a deep nap. I fold it in a pad, pass it lightly over the surface first to collect dust, and then pass it over a second time more firmly to polish. Be sure to unfold and "snap" the cloth periodically to release the entrapped dust. The cloth comes with a mild perfume that's very distinctive. You'll remember it years later if you smell one again. This piece of fabric has been dusting cars for over 80 years. I've tried the many brands of California car duster. The latest version uses microfiber strands. I still find them clumsy to use.

My well-used Kozak cloth. Used as directed, it cleans without damaging paint.

b. For routine washing, when needed, I use the Mr. Clean AutoDry Car Wash tool. Yes, it sounds hokey and looks clumsy, but this gadget does minimize the need to dry your car after washing. As I understand it, it filters the wash water and adds a polymer to the rinse water. The tool doesn't cost much; the manufacturer makes its profit by selling you soap and filter refills. But it does make for quick work.

The Mr. Clean gadget is klunky, but effective. This is its "drying" mode.

c. When I do wash for a show, I use a tubular nozzle. I can adjust it for a blast to knock mud and dirt off from under the fenders, or for a variety of sprays and mists. (Northerners and Midwesterners will need that to get salt off the underside, too.) The one I like best is sold by Griot's Garage. It cost more than I've ever paid for a hose nozzle. But when I add up all the inadequate ones that I've tried and thrown away, maybe the cost isn't really that high. I don't care much for trigger spray nozzles; I find them wimpy.

And here is a uniform mist.

d. The best way to rinse, before and after soaping, is to flow the water on in sheets rather than blasting it into thousands or millions of droplets. A simple shut-off valve and a 6-inch section cut from the end of an old garden hose is a good way to apply rinse water.

The other end of the spectrum in sophistication, but great for flowing on rinse water.

(LEFT) This is the Rolls Royce of hose nozzles, from Griot's Garage. The knob-type regulator lets you turn off the water while maintaining the spray pattern you like. It also permits you to adjust the volume of flow. This is the "firehose" mode. Gano Filter Company

e. I just love microfiber: cleaning cloths, polishing cloths, wash mitts, drying towels and even the upholstery of my favorite reading chair at home. It's really miracle stuff. BUT . . . not all microfiber is created equal. There are differences in nap, stitching and quality of manufacture. (The Korean stuff gets higher marks than the Chinese.) You can get microfiber products really cheap in a warehouse store, but consider coddling your car with a better-quality product that you can buy from catalog houses or online. Griot's Garage and properautocare.com are good sources. Classic Motoring Accessories Ltd. is another good supplier, and they have great detailing tips on their website.

Using a flexible squeegee leaves less water for the towel to absorb.
Griot's Garage

Microfiber makes for thirsty towels, too.

f. I've tried several brands of store-bought auto wash concentrates, and have noticed no difference between them. The one I do like is used by commercial car washes. It's known in the trade as red soap. I got a pint from my favorite auto body shop.

g. I find a flexible squeegee useful for getting most of the water off the car's horizontal and vertical surfaces before starting the toweling. It definitely reduces the amount of water to sop up. Don't think your car will be dry when you're finished blading, but it's a good start.

h. To get my paint as smooth as a baby's . . . well, you know what, I use cleaning clay before waxing. Box sizes and prices vary, so check the weight of the bar inside before buying. Use a quick-detailing spray from any reputable supplier as a lubricant.

A wringer gets your towels dryer than hand wringing. This is a shiny new one; if you can find a fugitive from an old washing machine it will work too.
Griot's Garage

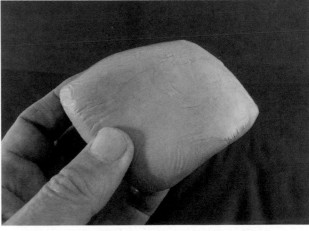
A clay bar with some of the tiny contaminants that embed themselves in your paint.

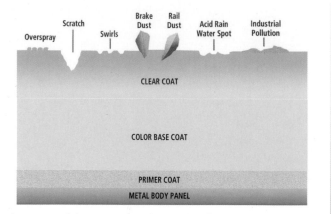

An exaggerated cross-section of your paint after washing. Classic Motoring Accessories Ltd.

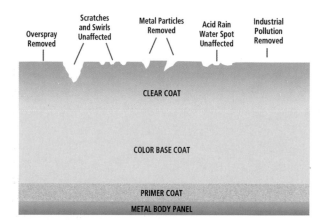

Here's what it looks like after claying. Classic Motoring Accessories Ltd.

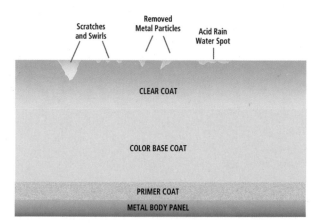

The fillers in the polish fill in the microscopic voids and hide the imperfections. Classic Motoring Accessories Ltd.

i. Like other steel parts, chromed parts are subject to electrolytic corrosion. The conducting electrolyte can be as slight as water absorbed from the air by the dirt on the surface of the parts. Despite its hard appearance and reputation, chrome plating is quite porous and very thin. I hate polishing chrome. And since I discovered ZoopSeal, I rarely have to. ZoopSeal was developed for the hot rod set that boasts acres of gleaming chrome and polished aluminum under their hoods. It's a liquid ceramic that protects aluminum and chrome from oxidation. Preparation is tedious. You must clean and polish every square inch of what you want to protect, or ZoopSeal will simply put a nice seal on a grungy part. The two-part material is very expensive, and has a short refrigerated shelf life. All ZoopSeal does is stop oxidation, but it does it so well! I have not polished my car's bumpers, hubcaps and other chrome parts for nearly two years. That's years. I probably will have to polish and ZoopSeal again soon, but it's been a great respite while it lasted.

ZoopSeal can protect your polished parts for many, many months. It's "painted" on with supplied pads, rather than rubbed. A little goes very long way.

j. For our collector cars, I divide waxes into two categories: carnauba and synthetics. Carnauba wax is harvested from the carnauba palm, which grows in South America. The raw wax is very hard, and must be dissolved with solvents in order to be usable on our cars. I have had good results with PS21 wax. It gives a beautiful gloss but only lasts a couple of months.

k. Synthetic waxes are similar to carnauba, except they are created on the designer chemist's bench. They are logically similar to synthetic oil. Just as a good synthetic oil has a number of advantages, so too does the synthetic wax. My favorite synthetic is a liquid made by a small New Jersey company called Zaino. It's available online.

l. Some owners, especially those whose cars have wire wheels, have a collection of pointed, rounded and strangely shaped brushes that they use for cleaning wheels. The major parts chains and discount stores offer a wide variety of detailing brushes. Prowl the housewares sections of your local supermarkets and home products stores. The bristles of any brush you buy should be soft enough so they don't scratch the wheel's finish.

m. I like Eagle One All Wheel & Tire Cleaner. My collector car has a full wheel chrome hubcap and wide whitewall tires with black all around. And there's a painted rim between the whitewall and the hubcap. Eagle One AW&TC leaves the chrome shiny, the painted rim clean, the whitewalls white, and the blackwalls smooth black. What more could I ask?

A little 3-finger foam wash mitt gets into places that the big ones can't. Griot's Garage

To keep tire cleaner spray off your wheels, try this mask. The Eastwood Company

ODOR

Odors can build up in older cars, especially closed vehicles. Cigarettes, mildew, food, and young children all can leave their characteristic signatures. Here's a trick shared by John Schoepke of Pine Ridge Enterprises, makers of the CarJacket. If your car has an objectionable odor inside, sprinkle freshly ground coffee on the problem area, or over the carpet and upholstery. Leave it for 24 hours, then vacuum it up. This method has been used many times, with surprisingly effective results. Commercial odor absorbents are available too; but try the ground coffee first.

LUBRICATION

After you've carefully cleaned old grease and oil off all the visible parts of your car, you'll now have to go back and apply oil and grease to many of those same parts. These include door latches and strikers, hinges, hood latches and other parts that move against each other. You'll apply clean grease to replace the dirty and contaminated stuff that you removed. You'll also apply grease stick or oil gun neatly, and wipe off any over-application. But eventually this fresh grease will be old and dirty, and will have found its way onto parts where you never put it originally. Then it'll be time to clean it off, and do it again.

CHAPTER 17
RUST AND CORROSION

According to many car collectors, rust is caused by the "tinworm." According to my dictionary, rust is "an electrochemical reaction that occurs as iron reverts to its natural state as iron oxide." Iron, and the steel that's made from it, is always trying to do that. All that's required is oxygen and water. Both are present in abundance in the air around us. And rust is permeable to air and water, allowing the metal to continue to corrode internally even after a surface layer of rust has formed. Given sufficient moisture, any ferrous mass will eventually convert entirely to rust and disintegrate. So the coatings we put on car parts are an attempt to keep the air and water away from the iron.

R. Pierce Reid of the Vintage Garage in Stowe, Vermont, (http://www.vintagegaragevt.com) tells us that rust is nine times thicker than the metal it replaces. So for every .001 inch of metal that turns to iron oxide, rust grows by .009 inches. That's why rusted parts don't want to come apart. Iron oxide is much harder than mild steel. Oxides make great lapping compounds and are a main compound of rouge and other polishing compounds. So rust rubbing against steel rapidly erodes the steel.

Cars are particularly vulnerable to rust. They're made of thin sheets of steel. They travel on roads on which more than 12 million tons of salt are poured every winter. Their shape includes pockets and crevices where dirt and salt can hold water against the steel for long periods. Some cars, sad experience has revealed, have shapes that lend themselves to trapping corrosive materials. No make, be it Chevrolet or Mercedes, is immune to such design flaws.

Modern cars make use of the latest in anticorrosion technology. Sheet steel may be galvanized on one or both surfaces. Trim fasteners are made of plastic, so as not to encourage corrosion between dissimilar metals. Parts are attached with adhesives rather than by welding. Sheet metal parts, and connecting seams, are designed not to trap water. More components are made of plastic and aluminum, which don't rust.

BOTTOMS FIRST

Your collector car lacks many of these protections, so it depends on you to help protect it from rust. The area that is most in danger is the underside. Wash it regularly, paying attention to the crevices where road dirt and salt collect. Besides the fact that they are constantly attacked by the debris thrown up when you drive, the frame and floorboards are also the most difficult to inspect. They also

Rust at the edge of a painted panel. Corrosion Doctors

Big-time rust. Rust Bullet, LLC

have the most irregular sheet metal surfaces, which can hold and conceal moisture and the dreaded road salt.

Many cars from the 1940s on, and most cars since the 1950s, were factory-undercoated. Some had this done as an extra-cost procedure. Older undercoated cars are particularly in danger today. The undercoating material was a rubberized material applied about 1/8-inch thick. Sound-deadening, not rust protection, was its major function. Decades later, this material is peeling and flaking away from the sheet metal of the car floor. In addition, typical undercoating spray patterns created pockets that did not entirely cover the metal, but provided ideal traps for moisture. About half the states in the country use salt on their roads in the winter months to melt ice. If your car was ever used in the wintertime in any of these states, chances are good that a mixture of salt and water remained trapped in some of these pockets.

So inspect the bottom of your car at least once a year. You'll probably find that some areas of the underbody are entirely rust-free. These are usually the frame members or mechanical parts that are covered with any one of the fluids that tend to leak from our old cars—motor oil, transmission fluid, grease. (That's a clue to one way we can help prevent rust.)

Examine the sheet metal floorpans. Look for flaking and peeling undercoating. Peel off large pieces and scrape off loose ones. A putty knife is a good tool for this. Look for where undercoating may still be intact, but sagging away from the sheet metal. Cut such areas open now, and scrape them clean. Check drain holes in the door bottoms and in rocker panels. Stick an ice pick carefully through any that are clogged; try not to scratch the sheet metal as this can leave a scar vulnerable to rust. Then run a pipe cleaner back and forth to finish cleaning the hole.

As for the rest of the car—the shiny parts—dust them when they are dusty and wash them when they are dirty.

EXHAUST SYSTEMS

Your exhaust system is probably rusty. Console yourself; as rusty as it may look on the outside, it's probably rustier on the inside. Not much you can do here. While there are coatings that can be applied to exhaust pipes that will stand the heat, all of them require a clean rust-free surface for initial application. The time to make your exhaust system less vulnerable is the next time you replace the pipes.

Consider stainless-steel exhaust pipes. They can be expensive, but not enough to require a second mortgage. Type 409 stainless steel has proven extremely resistant to corrosion in salt-spray tests. It's also less likely to crack

due to vibration. It does eventually get a rusty look, which can be mitigated by spraying the pipes with a heat-resistant paint before installation. You will find that 304 stainless discolors less, but for a car that's driven regularly I prefer the cheaper 409. If you're comparing prices, be sure to determine from each vendor which material was used. Some vendors also offer stainless-steel mufflers to complete the system.

Exhaust pipe rust is a greater threat to collector cars than to your everyday driver, because the water that's created by combustion must be burned away by the heat of full warmup. Less water is produced when you drive your car every day than when it may stand for weeks at a time. (There's another good reason for driving your collector car regularly.) Consider the inevitable disintegration of these pipes, the fact that prices will go up as the years go by, the potential hazard of driving a car with any leakage of exhaust fumes, and the effort or expense of complete replacement. Those stainless-steel pipes may not sound so expensive anymore.

DISSIMILAR MATERIALS

Where two different (dissimilar) metals are in contact with each other and moisture is present, the point where they meet will corrode faster than would a connecting point of two similar metals. The metal that is more

Gold	1
Platinum	4
Silver	17
Stainless Steel	21
Bronze & Copper	27
Brass	29
Tin	32
Nickel	36
Cadmium	41
Iron & Steel	44
Chromium	50
Zinc	57
Aluminum	64
Magnesium	67

This table shows the comparative vulnerability of common metals to corrosion. Where two dissimilar materials are in contact with each other in the presence of moisture, the point where they meet will corrode faster than a joint between similar metals. The wider apart two metals are on this index, the faster and greater the corrosion.

vulnerable to rust will corrode faster. Consult the Vulnerability Index on page 123. The farther apart two metals are on the index, the greater will be the galvanic corrosive action when they're in contact and damp. Most of the corrosion will attack the more vulnerable metal. For this reason, it's best to avoid placing metals with widely different vulnerabilities next to each other.

REMOVING RUST

Before any protective coating is applied to rusty components, rust must be completely and thoroughly removed. While the finishes described below are advertised as being suitable for coating parts after loose rust has been removed, you'll get the best results by removing as much rust as possible before applying.

Hard rust can serve as a base for the antirust finishes described below. Just don't count on them to last forever. Of course, if you have the right equipment, you can completely remove the rust by bead blasting. Just one tip: No matter what blasting media you use, never blast an assembly of parts. It will be very difficult and time-consuming to remove every particle of highly abrasive blasting media from assembled parts. Take everything apart first; it will save you time in the end.

DEFENDING YOUR CAR

Terry Cowan of H.C. Fasteners describes rust as light, mild and heavy. Light rust is what a piece of cleaned steel will acquire overnight. It's soft, transparent, and does not pit the surface. Mild rust is not transparent and causes some pitting. Heavy rust involves deep pitting and substantial weight loss to the metal.

Since rust is such a universal problem, makers of rust cures have their hype machines in full voice at all times. Basically, though, there only a few ways to combat rust with chemicals:

- Rust converters attempt to convert rust into a more stable material like magnetite. Examples of these are Rust Doctor, Ospho (manufactured by Skybryte), Rust Reformer (Rust-Oleum) and Extend (Loctite).
- Antirust fortified slow dry enamels include Corroless and the original Rust-Oleum. These coatings encapsulate rust and contain a material, often tiny glass flakes, that seals the pores so neither oxygen nor water can get through.
- Moisture-cured urethanes were designed to protect steel bridges from corrosion in high-humidity

climates, especially in coastal areas. They also encapsulate rust, and draw the moisture from it to stop further progress. The best-known example is POR-15, but a newer product called Rust Bullet has received some very positive referrals from users.

Formulations of these products change from time to time, so the results of tests done years ago might not apply today. The Internet provides access to the experiences of others. Search for the name of the product you're interested in; you're likely to find tests by clubs and magazines, and comments and critiques by users.

If your car was originally undercoated, you can remove any areas that have lifted from the steel and recoat them. Spray and brush materials are available for this purpose. If your car was never undercoated, you still can have it done. Some modern materials can be professionally applied over firm rust, and will protect even better than did the undercoats of yesteryear.

You've also noticed, of course, that the parts of your car's frame that are covered with oil from a leaky engine or transmission haven't rusted. This is because oil and grease seal the metal parts away from air, denying rust one of its necessary ingredients. However, spraying oil

Waxoyl kits and refills are available for DIY use. The kit includes a built-in pump. J.E. Robison Service Co., Inc.

Waxoyl can be professionally applied. J.E. Robison Service Co., Inc.

over the undercarriage of your car and into all its crevices is probably not a practical long-term rust-prevention strategy. It's also very messy.

Fortunately, there is a more practical a method for covering parts with oil. It involves a British product that has been in use in England for some years, in both military and civilian applications. It's also used on North Sea oil rigs. Essentially, it's oil and a corrosion inhibitor in a waxy carrier. It's called, understandably, Waxoyl. Rust is often doing its dirty work in enclosed places like the insides of rocker panels. It's unwise to attempt to undercoat in there through a drilled hole, because of the risk of missing spots and creating crevices where moisture will pool. Waxoyl can be effectively applied in such areas. It's available in kits for owner application, or may be professionally applied. Currently all of the authorized application centers in the continental United States are in New England.

CATHODIC RUST PROTECTION

This impressive-sounding concept surfaces regularly, each time in the form of a gadget with claims of "improved" capabilities over the previous version. Ads remind car owners that ship hulls and oil pipelines are protected by a device that impresses a low-voltage current on the vulnerable steel. Owners are told that they can now protect their precious car with a device that uses the same principle, at a cost of only a few hundred dollars.

The principle is simple, and is based on the fact that the process of corrosion is electrical. A negative voltage is applied to the car itself, making it a "cathode." A positive voltage is applied to one or more terminals that are attached to the car. These are called anodes. So, if the device works as advertised, the current that flows from cathode to anode is supposed to interfere with the corrosion process.

It should be noted that cathodic protection does work on ships and pipelines because an electrolyte is required to make this process work. Ships float in conductive salt water. Pipelines lie in moisture-soaked soil. But for application to a car on dry land, the principle is flawed.

Cathodic protection might protect your car if it were completely immersed in salt water, or if a grid of anodes spaced only a few inches apart covered the entire vehicle. Neither is practical. Save your money.

COOLANT SYSTEM ANODES

There *is* one major system in your car that can benefit from cathodic protection. It's your cooling system.

Every water heater installed in homes and businesses has a sacrificial anode (or two) built into it. The industry considers the single most important factor in whether a water heater lives or dies to be the condition of its sacrificial anode. For more than 50 years, it has been used as a key part of the rust protection of the tank, although few people know it's there. It's a rod made of magnesium or aluminum that's formed around a steel core wire, and is screwed into the top of the tank.

As we have read, dissimilar metals will experience electrolytic corrosion in the presence of moisture. Can you think of a better description of your car's cooling system? Iron, aluminum and brass, all immersed in water!

A plug of magnesium—the anode—immersed in your coolant can reduce the effects of electrolytic corrosion. Because the most vulnerable metal in the system will be attacked first, the magnesium plug sacrifices itself

This sacrificial anode has given its life for its radiator.

to save the iron, aluminum and brass. An anode alone will not fully protect your cooling system, but it's a useful supplement to your antifreeze or anticorrosion additive.

A simple method of immersing the anode in the cooling system water is to attach it to the radiator cap where it will rest in the top tank. Rad Caps are radiator caps made for most popular cars. They include a cap with an anode suspended by a spring. The anode is shielded in perforated plastic so it doesn't damage core tubes. You can buy the anode separately and attach it to your own cap.

(And the sacrificial anode in your home water heater? It should be checked and replaced regularly; you might want to go and check it right now!)

A Rad-Cap with magnesium anode attached.

CHAPTER 18
SAFETY

We spend countless hours primping our cars, and many more adjusting and repairing them. Yet most of us spend very little of our time on safety checks. On this subject we can learn much from the antique airplane folks. It's true that in the event of catastrophic failure they have farther to fall; but we car folks can get killed just as dead while sitting only 18 inches above the ground.

A SAFETY CHECKLIST

I suggest that you put together a safety checklist to be performed at least once a year. Here's my list to start you off. Knowing your car as you do, you'll no doubt have items to add.

At least once a year, preferably in the spring, get the car up off its wheels, with sufficient room to work and inspect underneath.

Use a good light. The new fluorescent worklights are far better than the old dusty 75-watt incandescent droplights. They won't burn you, either. Halogen droplights do get hot, but good ones keep the bulb well-shielded. Some have magnets for temporarily mounting the light where you need it to be.

If your vision is not all it used to be, consider a binocular headband magnifier like OptiVISOR. This product has been around relatively unchanged for more than 50 years. The LX models focus at about the correct under-car distance. A magnifying glass can be useful too.

1. Remove all four wheels with a lug wrench. While you're turning, feel for cross-threads or burrs or stripped threads on the studs, nuts or lug bolts.
2. Check the wheels for visible cracks.
3. Inspect the tires for tread wear and cracks. Look at the inside sidewalls especially; they're the ones you never get to see. Look for separations or bubbles. Check the spare too.
4. Look for any leakage at brake line fittings and at any hydraulic brake switch.
5. Bend all the brake hoses. Look for cracks that might signal the beginning of deterioration. Swing the front wheels from lock to lock and check to see that hoses aren't rubbing on any part of the suspension or frame.
6. Examine the full length of every brake line. If the metal line is dirty, wash it clean with solvent so you can see it clearly. Look for shiny spots where a line may be touching another part. Be sure clamps are tight. Look for kinks or dents in lines that may have been caused by rocks or by careless use of jacks or stands. Try to wiggle every line at its end.
7. Before you take the next step, *reread the proper procedures for working around asbestos dust* in Chapter 9.
8. Remove all four brake drums. Be sure there's a safe amount of thickness in the remaining lining.
9. Turn back all wheel cylinder boots and look for any leakage. Examine springs, anchor pins, cams, and retaining devices. Be sure everything is tight and in place.
10. Check the brake pedal linkage for free play. Be sure there is a cotter pin in every clevis pin.
11. Look for frayed wires in the parking brake cables. These can cause sticking and make the brake inoperative. The parking brake should be adjusted so there's just a little slack in the cable with the brakes released.
12. While the brake drums are off, carefully examine the spindles on which the wheel bearings turn. (That will be on the front wheels, except for front-wheel drive cars.) Clean the spindles carefully, and use your magnifiers. If there is any question in your mind about a possible crack, use one of the crack detection methods described later in this chapter.
13. Shake every pipe in the exhaust system. Look for loose joints or for pipes that don't nest together properly. Be sure that all hangars are present and tight, and that rubber mounting insulators aren't deteriorated. Examine every pipe and muffler for holes. Poke at suspicious areas with an ice pick. Use a mirror to check the top sides.
14. Examine the fuel line from gas tank to carburetor. Look for oozing at fittings and joints.
15. Go over the frame from end to end. From your marque club, you may have learned of potential weak spots or likely rust sites on your particular car. Pay special attention to these.

16. Wires and harnesses that run through holes in the firewall and frame are often located near moving parts. Look for frayed loom or insulation. Be sure there are grommets where they are supposed to be.

17. Look for looseness in the steering linkage and kingpins. Push and pull on pitman arm, drag link, idler, and steering arms and tie rods.

With the car back on the ground, do a topside check:

18. Blow the horn.

19. Wet the windshield, then turn the windshield wipers on. Be sure the wipers clean the glass smoothly.

20. Turn on the parking lights. Be sure that they and the taillights and license lights are burning. Turn the headlights on, and try both beams. (Check the taillights again; old switches can do funny tricks!)

21. Check the headlight aim. See Chapter 12.

Now you're ready to enjoy your collector car on the road!

FINDING CRACKS EARLY

Steel doesn't tire, but cyclical stress can result in tiny cracks that become bigger cracks, eventually leading to part failure. A failure in a transmission gear may result in a stalled car and perhaps an unhappy end to a tour. A failure of a front wheel spindle can have far more disastrous consequences. Try to anticipate failure before it happens. If your safety inspection turns up a questionable part, you may be able to determine whether it is about to fail by the use of one of several methods of crack detection.

Race cars and other highly stressed machinery are checked regularly for the beginning of cracks that could cause disaster on the track. Racers often use the term Magnafluxing as a generic for magnetic crack detection. That's one of the prices paid for being the first or a leader in your field. Magnaflux USA, with Xerox, Vaseline, Kleenex, and Frigidaire, continues to fight the good fight for the protection of its trademark. In deference to its efforts, we'll employ the generic term here.

The process of magnetic crack detection goes back at least to the early years of the twentieth century. It's based on the principle that magnetic lines of flux induced in a part made of a ferrous material will be distorted by any flaw on the surface of the part, or just below the surface. Several different methods are used to induce those lines of flux. Large parts like artillery gun barrels may have large currents passed thorough them. Smaller parts may be placed inside an induction coil carrying a heavy current. Or, a magnetic field may be induced by placing parts between the poles of a large permanent magnet or electromagnet. This is the method most applicable to our car parts.

The simplest way of using the magnetic field to identify cracks is to use the field to attract magnetic particles that collect around the sites of defects in the test piece. This makes the flaws visible. Magnetic detection powder, containing iron particles, may be applied to the test piece in dry or wet form.

Most machine shops routinely use magnetic crack detection to check engine blocks and cylinder heads before rebuilding. These shops can test other parts too. If you're rebuilding your collector car, consider having critical parts tested for cracks before reinstalling them. A list of such parts would include steering linkage, spindles, steering knuckles, brake parts and axle shafts. Include in this list any other parts whose failure could threaten injury to car, driver, or passengers.

It is possible for an adept amateur to build magnetic detection equipment, but it's probably more practical for most of us to bring components to a local shop. Look in your Yellow Pages or online under Magnetic Inspection Service.

There is, however, another effective method of crack detection that can be used very effectively and inexpensively in your very own garage. It's called dye penetrant inspection. It has an advantage over magnetic crack detection in that it can be used on nonferrous metals like aluminum. The limitation is that it must be used on smooth, preferably machined, surfaces. (Happily, that describes many of the parts that we might want to test.)

Dye penetrant inspection can be done by ultraviolet light using fluorescent dyes, or by visible light using a red dye. The visible method is the simplest, and thus, best method for most collector car owners. Modestly priced dye penetrant kits contain all the materials needed for inspecting dozens of parts.

Briefly, these are the steps for conducting dye penetrant inspection of a metal part. First, clean the part scrupulously. Then spray a red dye, which comes in an aerosol can, on the surface of the part. Allow a few minutes for the dye to penetrate any cracks. Then use a clean cloth and solvent to remove excess dye from the surface. Next, spray a "developer" onto the surface of the part. It dries quickly to a fine, powdery absorbent film. The film draws out the dye that has seeped down into any cracks or pores. The result is a marking on the surface that clearly shows the flaw.

Whether you do your crack detection in your own shop or take it out, it's important to know of this technology. Use it as one of the preventive weapons in your safety arsenal.

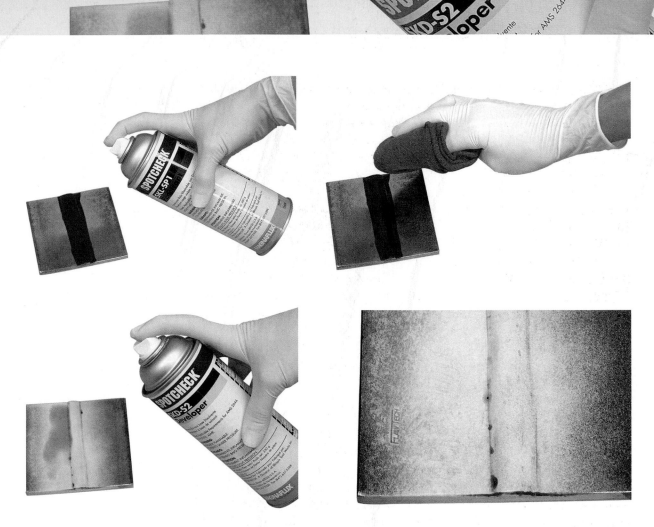

The Magnaflux Spotcheck dye penetrant system is easy to use and quite accurate. After the part is cleaned, the dye penetrant is sprayed on (TOP LEFT), *then wiped off* (TOP RIGHT). *Next, the developer is sprayed on* (LEFT). *The photo on the right shows flaws.* Magnaflux Corporation

FAMILIARITY BREEDS CONTEMPT— AND MAYBE CARELESSNESS

We've learned to be leery of asbestos and to steer clear of other dangerous materials. But it's easy to forget that plain ol' gasoline is no longer the friendly stuff that we kept around in cans to fill the lawnmower. Frankly, it never really was that friendly. But now it's downright scary! The gas you buy at the pump today is a highly toxic liquid. Remember when we'd start a siphon by sucking on a tube in the gas tank, then spitting it out when the flow started? No more. This stuff is poison! Even inhaling fumes in small quantities is dangerous. We need it to run our cars, but stay away from it for other uses.

JUMP-STARTING A BATTERY

Another death-defying act that we treat all too casually is the jump-start of one car's dead battery from another car's battery. This operation all too often takes place on the side of the road, or amidst snowdrifts, or in other unpleasant circumstances. So it's understandable that we don't don safety glasses to do it, although we should. But we can be careful not to smoke. Many batteries release explosive hydrogen gas.

To perform a jump-start safely on a negative-ground car, follow these steps in this order. Reverse the connections for a car with positive ground.

1. Clamp one end of the positive (+) booster cable to the positive post of the dead battery.
2. Clamp the other end of the same cable to the positive of the booster battery.
3. Connect the second, negative (-) booster cable to the other post of the booster battery.
4. Make the final negative booster cable connection on the engine block of the stalled vehicle, *not* to the stalled car's battery. That's because a spark sometimes occurs when the last connection is made, and you want to keep any sparks far away from the battery.

CHAPTER 19
THE OPEN ROAD

Many of today's drivers are surprised to discover that our collector cars, even those that predate the muscle car era, can comfortably cruise at today's speed limits. Moreover, they can travel at such speeds for hour upon hour, with no harm to themselves. Some of our cars are so comfortable at touring speeds that we actually forget that we're not driving modern iron. And therein lies a danger.

Many of today's drivers do not appear to have the foggiest notion of how long it takes to bring a car to a stop from 70 miles per hour. Perhaps that's why so many people drive only five feet behind other cars on the Interstate. When entering a highway behind us, they expect us to move smartly out of their way. They make no allowances for the slight drop in speed as we shift our gears; you'll see them suddenly grow larger in your rear view mirror.

When given a choice, I prefer to drive my car on secondary highways rather than interstates. It's more relaxing, you can stop whenever and wherever you please, and you meet the nicest people.

Still, we occasionally must venture onto a major highway to get where we need to go. If those who share the road with us won't drive safely, we must drive even more defensively, and deal with some of our cars' potential shortcomings too.

DIRECTIONAL SIGNALS

Many collector cars were built with directional signals or offered them as an option. If your car has them, use them. The driving public no longer understands our hand signals. If your early car has no provision for directionals, consider modifying its existing lights. A change of sockets can put double-filament bulbs in parking lights. If that's not feasible, check to see whether your state requires working parking lights. (When does one even use them?) If they don't, you can abandon the parking lights altogether and use the fixture as a directional signal. Fog lamps can be pressed into this service too. Over the years, various collector car magazines have included wiring diagrams for switches that can be installed unobtrusively, including wiring plans that cause existing lights to flash correctly.

Directional signal switches range from toggles to be mounted under the dash to electronic column-mounted switches engineered for six- and 12-volt collector cars. Ron Francis Wiring sells the former, Electro-Tech Systems the latter. Both types can convert existing lights to turn signals while maintaining their brake and other functions. They can also operate discrete directional lamps.

DRIVING IN THE RAIN

Today's radial tires have treads designed by computers, with grooves and slots and god-knows-what-else. Their rubber composition is carefully calculated to provide a reasonable balance of dry traction, wet traction and wear life. Bias-ply tires are innocent of such sophistication. Their tread designs, in most cases, are simplistic replicas of those of bygone years. Bear this in mind if it starts to rain while you're out driving your collector car. Studies have shown that highways are actually more slippery when they're a little wet than a lot. Slow down a bit, even more than in your everyday car.

An electronic directional signal switch by S/M Electro-Tech. The brains of the system are in a box mounted under the dash. This unit offers variable time delay as well as emergency four-light flashers.

Most of our collector cars include an ammeter on the instrument panel. Markings devolved from complete ampere readings, to just maximum charge and discharge figures, to no numbers at all. But at least you can see the position of the needle. The "idiot lights" of today don't even give you that minimal information.

THE AMMETER

One of the nice things about older cars is that they rarely used mere lights to indicate a malfunction. Most had meters to show engine temperature, charging rate, and oil pressure. In the 1930s, gauges carried numerical markings, even though many could not be precisely relied upon. By the 1950s most gauges had lost their numbers entirely, so the pointer positions became largely symbolic. Still, they were far better diagnostic tools than lights.

The best diagnostic gauge on your dash is the ammeter. Its scale has zero at the center. The markings to the right of or above zero show the amount of charge; to the left or below, the amount of discharge. The ammeter is wired into the car's electric circuit in a position where any electrical load except the starter must pass through it. Current from the generator to the battery goes through the ammeter too. As a result, if the current draw is greater than the amount of current

being restored by the generator, the ammeter will show a discharge. If the current draw is less than generator output, the needle will be on the "charge" side.

When a car is started, the battery is depleted. A little or a lot will depend on the amount of starter cranking you had to do. Once running, the generator will begin to recharge the battery. The needle should be well up on the charge side of the scale. If it isn't, have the generator and regulator checked. As the battery recharges, the regulator will reduce generator output, and the ammeter needle should fall back toward zero. If the ammeter reading remains high after a long period of highway driving, there's a possible regulator problem.

Keep an occasional eye on your ammeter when you're on the road. For most driving the needle should be just to the charge side. Zero is usually OK too. If the needle shows a slight discharge, the generator may not be charging. The small current draw is the coil and ignition system. If you're playing the radio or running the heater, the discharge will be greater. If the ammeter suddenly shows full discharge, that indicates a short circuit. Pull to the side of the road (if the car is still running), and turn off your battery master switch.

The short may reveal itself by smoke or odor or both. Use your eyes and ears. If the shorted circuit is not immediately evident, use the elimination process. Disconnect one circuit at a time until the short disappears. Removing fuses is the easiest way to do this. A central fuse location makes this chore convenient. If your car isn't so equipped, there'll be fuses located somewhere in most circuits—on a headlight switch, in line with the radio power wire, in a headlight relay. To disconnect those circuits or accessories that aren't fused, you'll have to remove the wire that feeds each component. Disconnect one circuit; the radio, for example. With your eyes glued to the ammeter, turn the battery master switch back on. Full discharge means that this isn't the shorted circuit. Go on to the next one. When the ammeter doesn't move, you've found the bad circuit.

If you can get back home or to a service station without the affected circuit, just leave the fuse out. If the shorted wire powered the coil, you'll have to make a temporary repair. Look for worn insulation. If you can't find the problem, try wiring around it. Note where the ends of the wire to the coil attach, at the coil and at the ignition switch or terminal block. Disconnect both ends of this wire. Now attach a jumper wire in its place. If there's no short now, this will get you home.

DAYTIME RUNNING LIGHTS

DRLs are front lamps that go on with the ignition and stay on all the time. They're required equipment on all cars in Canada, Sweden and Norway. Finland requires them outside of urban areas. They're now working their way into practice in the United States. On some cars they're separate dedicated lamps, on others they're reduced-output headlights.

Canada's DRL laws date back to 1990. In 1992, the Canadian Bureau of Standards did a study of daytime accidents. The results showed a drop of about 4 to 6 percent in multiple vehicle collisions. Skeptical? Do your own study. On a day that is anything less than totally sunny, see how many oncoming cars you can spot with their headlights on. Now notice how those cars stand out of the pack in which they're traveling.

It's true that the countries that now mandate DRLs are all closer to the Arctic Circle than any of our lower 48 states, and thus have special concerns regarding visibility during much of the year. Still, we should learn our lessons wherever we can, and there *is* one to be learned here.

In less-than-sunny weather, most cars tend to look gray. Since many of our collector cars are painted in dark colors to boot, they tend to be even more difficult to see. Do yourself and your precious car a favor; *drive with your headlight low beams on all the time.* You'll be visible to oncoming cars much earlier. Since your taillights will also be on, you'll gain an additional measure of visibility from that angle. Think this is extreme? Then at least keep the headlights on when driving on highways or roads that don't have a center median strip or barrier.

It's true that your bulbs or sealed beams will burn out more often, but they're a small expense to exchange for a major safety device. (You'll also have to be certain that your charging system can handle the higher load created by the headlights.)

TEST YOUR BRAKES

Get in the habit of testing the brakes on your collector car *every time* you take it out of the garage. In the safety of your own driveway, *stand on the pedal with everything you've got.* We usually treat our favorite cars gingerly, and try not to stress any component more than we have to. Brakes are the exception. When that little kid chases a ball into the street, you're not going to worry about your 40-year-old components. You're going to stand on the brake pedal! If anything is going to fail, you'll want it to fail in your driveway. A brake system that is safe enough to drive with will not be damaged or start to leak as a result of such a test. And if it does fail, it needed rebuilding anyway—and you may have saved yourself lots of aggravation, or even a life.

STARTING AND STOPPING YOUR ENGINE

Starting your engine is a not a terrible thing to do. *Starting your engine without keeping it running is a terrible thing to do.* Engines begin to produce water as soon as they start. We've all seen water actually dripping from the exhaust pipe of a cold engine. It's this water that combines with sulfur compounds in the engine to produce sulfonic acid in the oil. Corrosion from acids is a major cause of engine wear, particularly affecting cylinder walls and combustion chambers. To minimize this, make acid-reduction your primary concern in engine startup. So . . . .

1. Warm your engine up as quickly as possible. Don't idle a cold engine. Give it up to a minute for oil

pressure to stabilize and the intake manifold to begin to warm, then drive off slowly. Yes, the cold engine may stumble and run rough. But the light driving load is vital to rapidly bringing engine temperature up to full operating level.

2. Don't stop the engine until it has reached full operating temperature. The time and distance it takes to do this will, of course, vary from car to car. Don't run the old girl around the block thinking that this exercise is good for it. It isn't.

There's a suggested routine for stopping too. I learned it years ago from John M. Sico, and have been using it since. He developed it after years of observation of corrosion in combustion chambers and the upper part of the cylinders. The corrosion, John felt, was the result of rust. Exhaust gases condense into acidic products when the engine cools. Light rust happens. Enough rusting and there's metal loss. And this happens in the upper part of the cylinder wall, the very area where lubrication is least adequate. I have never torn down the engine in my collector car, so I can't personally prove the usefulness of this technique. But it makes sense. Here are the steps:

1. We've been through this before; be sure the engine is up to operating temperature before you shut it down for the day.
2. Gun it a few times to blow any accumulated liquid out of the combustion chambers.
3. Increase the rpms to about 1/3 of the safe maximum and hold it there for a couple of seconds. This throws more oil up on the cylinders. Higher vacuum draws some oil past the rings and valve guides.
4. With the engine running at that speed, turn off the key.
5. Release the throttle after the engine comes to a stop.

John feels that it's better to leave fresh fuel mixture in the cylinders than exhaust gases. And while there may be room for theoretical arguments, his are supported by the examination of many engines.

HOT STARTS

Nearly every collector car driver experiences just a bit of anxiety when the finger approaches the starter button after the car has been standing all day under a hot summer sun. It *is* harder to start many collector cars when they and the weather are hot. What's the best way to do it?

The starting problem is often a result of percolation. The effect is a flooded carburetor. There are several accelerator-handling techniques that can help. You can slowly depress the accelerator and hold it down. Crank the engine without releasing the pedal. The engine should pump out the over-rich mixture, and start with a roar. This works every time with many cars. An alternate method is to crank the engine for about ten seconds without touching the gas pedal. Then depress the pedal about halfway. The engine should start. In either case, run the engine at fast idle for about a minute. This will refill the carburetor bowl with fresh, relatively cool gasoline. If neither of these methods work, stop. If you keep cranking until the battery is dead, you may not get home. Leave the car's hood up. Go sit in the shade, read a bit, indulge in some ice cream. After the engine has cooled, the car will start.

DON'T LEAVE HOME WITHOUT THEM

You can't very well take every spare part you own with you. You know your car best, so you know which items might be most likely to need a spare. Besides, spares are like umbrellas; you'll never need them if you have them with you.

Here's a list of items that I carry on long trip in my collector car. If you don't have a list of your own yet, use this one and add or subtract from it to suit your own needs and those of your car:

1. Fluids: any special fluids that may not be easy to find or match on the road. Include your favorite motor oil, transmission lube, steering box lube, silicone brake fluid.
2. Tire-changing equipment: jack, lug wrench, special hub cap tools. I carry a torque wrench to tighten up wheel nuts accurately. For safety, bring wheel chocks. Carry an extra inner tube, too, if your tires use them.
3. If you have to stop for an emergency, you'll need to protect your own rear end. Set out reflective triangles. They're much safer than flares, and tests have proven that they actually can be seen from a greater distance. Many of the electronic LED gadgets found in catalogs and online are not visible from a sufficient distance for safety.
4. A copy of your car club's directory. You may need specialized help from a local club member.
5. Spare bulbs and fuses.
6. Owner's manual and service manual.
7. Your tool kit or box. I risked a hernia getting mine in and out of the trunk until I discovered that half the weight was the steel box itself. Modern plastic tool boxes are light, quite strong and inexpensive. Widemouth fabric bags are even lighter, and fit irregular spaces better.

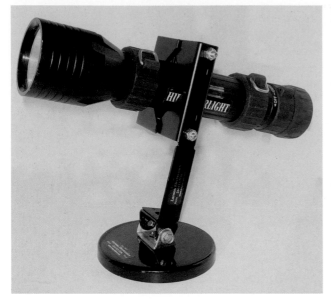

If you need light under the hood to troubleshoot a nighttime problem on the road, this magnetic-base holder from Magnalight will handle any diameter of flashlight.

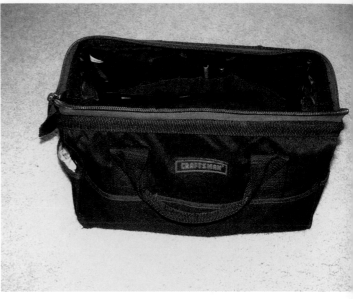

A widemouth fabric bag is much lighter than a steel box. It flexes to squeeze into smaller trunks, too.

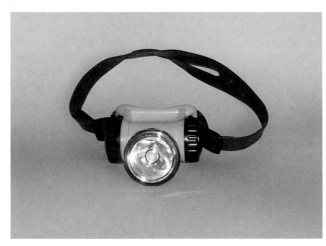

A headband light like this one makes an excellent alternative (or supplement) to a flashlight for emergency underhood repairs.

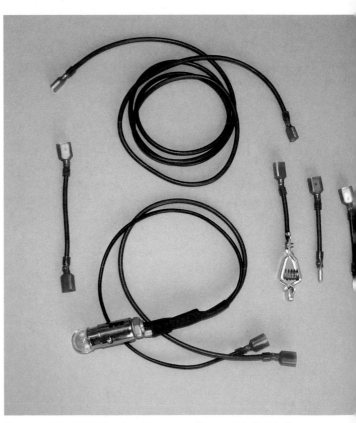

You never know what lengths of jumper cables and what ends they might require in a roadside emergency. I made up a jumper "mix-and-match system" using modern quick-disconnect terminals. I can put together several lengths and a variety of clips, adapters, and lights.

8. Flashlight. Consider one that has a magnetic or clamp-type holder for those times when there is no one to hold the light. Headband-mounted lamps can be handy too.
9. A gallon jug of the coolant you use.
10. Battery jumper cables. I carry mine in a neat circular bag.
11. Small-gauge jumper cables. In the event of a wiring problem, it's good to be able to temporarily wire around it. A couple of lengths of red and

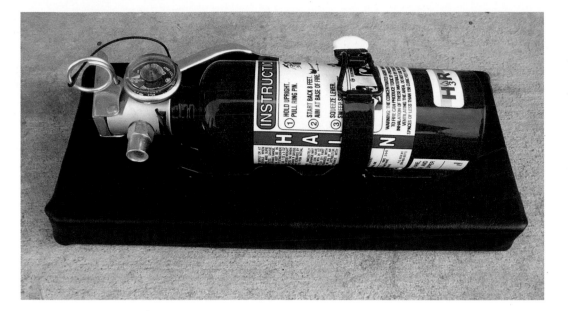

You may never need this lifesaver in all the years you drive your collector car. But if you do, you really do. I chose a halon-charged unit; it does the least damage to the car. It uses recycled halon. Carry it always, and check the charge regularly.

black wire with crocodile clips on the ends can be a godsend.

12. Tow rope. Polyethylene ropes are light and don't clank around like chains do.

13. Fire extinguisher. I know that you never even leave your driveway without this. Check the gauge regularly. Incidentally, they're of little use in the trunk. I mounted mine to a wood block, and keep it on the floor on the passenger side.

14. First aid kit.

15. A spare set of keys: ignition, door, glove box, spare tire locks, gas-cap lock.

16. Hand cleaner. Some of the new citrus-based ones work well and smell great.

17. Coveralls. Disposable ones made of Tyvek are now available. (Tyvek is the paper-like material from which tearproof envelopes are made.)

18. Latex or nitrile disposable gloves.

19. Paper funnels, for water, motor oil and gear lubes, and brake fluid. (I keep them in a dispenser in my garage, too.)

20. Paper towels.

21. Tire pressure gauge.

22. Ground cloth or tarp.

23. Rain-X, exterior and antifog. These products are very valuable for cars with less-than-perfect wipers and defrosters.

24. Duster. A KozaK takes less space than a duster. If you have to wash your car, the hotel's plastic waste basket and shampoo should work fine in a pinch.

25. Local and state maps, even if you're carrying a GPS.

26. Distilled water, battery filler, and hydrometer if your battery has removable caps.

27. Battery carrier.

28. Emergency link belt. These clever devices sure beat trying to install a new fan belt at the side of an Interstate while the 18-wheelers roar by. One size fits all, and they should get you to a service station. Practice putting them together at home first.

29. Spare wiper blades.

30. Gasket material, in several thicknesses.

31. Last but not least, small tubes of Loctite products. There's a list in Chapter 22.

CHAPTER 20
STORAGE: SHORT AND LONG

I'm fortunate enough to live in an area where my car can be driven nearly all year round. I never have to put it in storage for the winter, so I can treat it essentially the same way for 12 months of the year. Years ago I lived in New England, so I'm familiar with that side of the coin too.

Even if your car never goes "up on blocks," there are routines you should follow and materials you should consider that may help increase its aesthetic and mechanical longevity. Some of these techniques even apply to the short 'storage' period between drives.

Your car's enemies are sun, air and dirt. The ultraviolet rays of the sun fade or dull paint and cloth upholstery. They also dry the oils out of leather. Humidity is in the air everywhere, even in Arizona these days. Dirt on the car helps absorb water from the air, and holds it close against paint and chrome. It's the humidity in the air that permits electrolytic corrosion to happen. That reinforces the oxidation of your paint and helps make chrome rust.

So keep your car clean. Wash it regularly, but sparingly, during the months you use it. Dry it carefully to eliminate moisture. Store it indoors and keep it covered to protect it from sunlight and dirt. If a day or more has elapsed since the wash, or if you've driven any distance from the car wash to your home, go over the car with a duster before you put the cover on. Just lowering your garage door can shake abrasive dirt onto the car. While your soft car cover will not scratch the paint, the dirt on the surface, propelled by the cover as you move it across the body, surely will. This is especially true of flannel covers; they're great when they're clean, but they can also hold more finish-destroying dirt.

I prefer a cover that has a flannel interior—i.e., the material that touches the car is made of flannel. That's because my car is a sedan. If yours is a convertible with a fabric top, avoid flannel. Flannel creates lint, and you'll be picking fuzzballs off your top forever. If you want the soft flannel next to your paint, plan to throw a cotton sheet over the car's top before you put the car cover on.

During the flannel manufacturing process, the fabric is uniformly abraded on one or both sides to give the fibers that fuzzy feel. Some car covers are advertised as "flannel-lined." Actually, there's no lining; it just means that the material is "flanneled" on the inside. (Your pajamas, on the other hand, are flannel on both sides.) To prevent the abrasion from resulting in a too-weak fabric, material to be processed as flannel starts out much thicker. When you lift a flannel car cover for a large car, you'll feel the significant difference in weight.

Most companies now offer a variety of fabrics in their indoor car covers. In addition to flannel, stretch covers of a satin-like Lycra blend allow the cover to hug your car's curves tightly. Why anyone would want this is beyond me.

All-weather car covers are designed to protect your vehicle against harsh outdoor conditions. Evolution is a fabric made by Kimberly-Clark. (Each vendor gives it his own unique name, but the fine print will mention Evolution.) It's a multilayer fabric-like plastic that has water-repellent qualities, allowing it to be used outdoors or indoors. (Each time Kimberly-Clark improves the material or construction, the series number increments upward.)

NOAH is another multilayer fabric. Many collectors claim that it makes up the best covers for outdoor use. It protects against rain, pollution and snow, as well as dust and dirt, bird droppings, and tree sap.

Order your cover by year, make and model of your car. It should fit snugly but not tightly over the body. Be sure the supplier is aware of mirrors and radio antennas so they can provide pockets and grommet holes respectively. If your car is equipped with nonfactory mirrors, the vendor can send the pockets separately, allowing you to mark the cover and have the pockets sewn in place locally.

Wash your car cover several times a year. Be sure to follow the manufacturer's instructions, particularly for specialty fabrics. The logical times to do this would be after the winter snooze and before putting the car

The inflatable Carcoon should keep the body of this collectable Delorean stainless. This is the clear version. It's available in several sizes. Carcoon Storage Systems International

away for the season. The easiest way is to use one of the commercial washers and dryers at your local coin laundry. Warning: Don't ever put your Evolution cover in a dryer. It will melt.

Moisture is the major car-killer. It encourages mold growth on fabric and leather. The ever-present humidity in the air will condense on the surface of your car under the right atmospheric conditions. Here's how that happens. The amount of water that air can hold depends, among other things, on the air's temperature. Warmer air can hold more moisture than cool air. Warm, moist air is most often generated on fall and spring days. (Occasionally on winter days, too.) When that air comes in contact with a large cool object like your car, the temperature of the air is lowered. Now it can't hold as much water, so it releases it onto the cool object. That's condensation, less politely known as "sweating." That's how the lovely vehicle that you never took out on a rainy day during the summer months comes to be bathed several times a year in wet, corrosion-encouraging condensation.

How to prevent this? One way is to modify the environment. You could make certain that the temperature in your garage never changes. That requires an expensive heating system. You could attempt to keep

A 1956 Chevrolet being zipped into a CarJacket. It has been covered with a car cover first. Pine Ridge Enterprise

The Airchamber's end panel can be unzipped so the car can drive in and out. Copperstar Products

the humidity very low, but this requires an expensive ventilating and dehumidification system.

Actually, the only environment you're really concerned about is that of the car itself, not the rest of the garage. So a practical way to go is to create an environment for the car that seals it off from moisture-producing condensation. First get the car indoors: a garage, a barn, a warehouse or a plastic 'shelter'. Then enclose it.

There are several types of products that are designed to do this. I'll define them as zippered coveralls, cocoons, and air structures.

CarJacket is an example of a zippered coverall. It encloses the car on all sides, including the bottom. It seals with a zipper. The zipper closure makes it practical to bag a car that you use only on weekends, or only for shows and tours. Since the bag opens up completely, the car can be driven onto it under its own power. One person can then zip the bag shut in just a few minutes. Because the bag opens completely, any spills or leaks during storage can be cleaned up relatively simply. A zippered coverall does require several feet of free space on one side of the car while it is being bagged or unbagged.

Carcoon is a high-quality example of cocoon storage. It's a lightweight bubble that is inflated around the vehicle to be stored. Two low-voltage fans keep the Carcoon inflated and maintain a constant flow of filtered recirculated air around your vehicle. Much like the zippered bag, you drive your car onto the base pad, put the upper section over the car, and zipper the two together. Plug in the power supply, and Carcoon inflates in less than five minutes. It's available in clear vinyl versions (so you can admire your car) and opaque versions (to protect from UV). The power unit incorporates computer-managed circuitry to keep the car battery charged too.

Carcoon's strong point is that it completely insulates the car from the changing temperatures and humidity to which your garage is subject. Condensation is essentially eliminated, and corrosion greatly reduced as a result. Getting the car in and out is a bit tedious, but less so than you might think. The Carcoon has six loops sewn into the roof section, so the owner can tie it up to the ceiling of the garage. This handy feature keeps the bubble out of the way when it's not in use, and enables it to be dropped over the car more easily.

Airchamber is an air structure that protects your car in much the same way as Carcoon. But it also has a unique, lightweight, rigid frame. That means it takes a while to set up, and occupies a bit more space in your garage. On the other hand, it allows you to easily drive your car in and out, making it practical for use with regularly driven collector cars. The British take preservation of their collector cars very seriously; like Carcoon, Airchamber is made in the United Kingdom.

For the ultimate in indoor storage, the Motor Inn is in a class by itself. It essentially creates a custom Lexan room inside your garage. Options include heating, air conditioning, dehumidification, smoke and security alarms, gas and carbon monoxide sensors and alarms, and fire suppression. Wireless security cameras and lighting packages are also available. The cost, as you might imagine, is commensurate.

The Motor Inn pampers your car. . . at a price. The Motor Inn

Of the storage devices described, only Carcoon makes a version that can be used outdoors. Its outdoor model has heavy double walls with air space between, and an insulated base pad. Its coated skin protects the car inside from UV. Seems like practical winter storage for that extra car.

By the way: Never enclose a freshly painted car. Allow at least three months for the paint to cure and for vapors to evaporate. That's a conservative recommendation, but better safe than sorry.

Wash your car at least a day before you enclose it. Time will be needed for all the nooks and crannies to dry completely. Leave doors half-latched so water can drain out. Be sure the car is cool. Don't put it in an enclosure while the engine or exhaust is hot. Be sure there are no leaks in the car's cooling system or air conditioner. If you find oil leaks that can't be fixed immediately, place absorbent mats or trays under the car after it's in the bag. Oil and grease inside the enclosure will make cleaning it for reuse a most unpleasant chore. *If the leak is gasoline, do not enclose your car until the leak is completely repaired.*

If you're using a car jacket, bag your car during a low humidity period, if possible. The idea is to reduce the amount of moisture that you seal into the bag. Midafternoon on a dry day is best. Some air and moisture will be trapped with your car when you seal the bag. It's important to enclose the desiccant pouches that are supplied with the bag. Desiccants, such as silica gel, absorb moisture out of the air. Think of those little bags you find packed with your imported electronics to keep them dry during their long sea voyage. The desiccant eventually will become saturated with water. Before you use it the next season, dry it out in a conventional oven. Follow the instructions that come with the desiccant; it loses effectiveness if overheated. You can also buy additional desiccant from several suppliers.

Bags and cocoons help in other ways too. The opaque ones protect your paint and upholstery by keeping out sunlight and its ultraviolet rays. They also keep rubber-deteriorating ozone at bay. And, since they keep your hands off your car, it'll spare you the temptation of starting up the engine for a few minutes every so often and causing acid damage!

It should go without saying, but neither a car cover nor a bag is a substitute for a garage. Some brands of "instant garages" can do a decent job of protecting a car through the winter. But be aware that if you pitch one of these heavy plastic/canvas tents on grass or dirt, you're courting serious corrosion from the moisture coming up from the ground. All that moisture will be attacking your car's surfaces throughout all those months. Several layers of heavy-gauge plastic must go down before the car rolls inside. Even better, protect your car with a storage bag or zippered coverall inside the temporary garage. Such a combination is an effective winter storage measure.

So what about menaces of the living, breathing, kind? Some of us have found out the hard way that mice like to use original upholstery for nest material. All of the storage enclosures described above will deter mice. But if your car spends the winter unenclosed, ultrasonic technology has been touted as a way to keep the vermin away. This intriguing idea involves installing a small transmitter in your garage. The device emits sound waves in the range above that which human beings can hear. The theory is that animals *can* hear them, and that the frequency of the waves is such that they cause pain to rodents. End result: The creatures will avoid your garage and car like—pardon the cliché—the plague. Deluxe versions of these devices change frequencies at random, and remain silent for random intervals. The idea is apparently to keep the mice off balance.

The scientific concept has some validity. Unfortunately, the machines advertised for use in a full-size garage are simply inadequate as a stand-alone pest control method.

Government agencies in the United States and Denmark, as well as several American universities have conducted comprehensive tests of ultrasonic technology as a pest control. None of these studies have deemed ultrasonics to be useless for pest control. They aren't. Mice are easily frightened creatures, and will avoid unfamiliar sounds or sounds coming from new locations. The problem is that the remedy is short-lived and haphazard. Each test has shown a similar result. At first, the ultrasonics either cause rodents to leave an area or dissuade them from entering. But eventually the vermin adjust and return to stay a short time later.

When ultrasonics are advocated for pest control, it's almost always in conjunction with other pest control methods. Here's where we find solutions that actually work. They're the traditional steps, including rodent inspections, sanitation (removing food and nesting materials), rodent proofing (keeping the critters out), and population reduction (a pretty name for trapping and poisoning). Competent consultants are just a phone call away. (Usually consultation is available through state university extension services or local health departments.) In any event, check your unenclosed car for mice and other vermin during its winter sleep.

For a confident start, make sure that the battery remains fully charged. Enclosures all provide for battery chargers to be connected although it's best to remove the battery from the car entirely. If you don't do that, then each time you put the car way wipe off the top of the battery. This will make certain that electrolyte mist and dirt haven't combined to provide a leakage path for a tiny bit of current. That's enough to reduce the battery's cranking power next time you're ready to go.

Whenever you return your car to its garage, turn off the battery master switch. That will effectively eliminate any current leakage from any device that you forgot about and that may draw current. It also reduces to near zero the likelihood of a fire in the car started by a short circuit.

Over the years many of us used a trickle charger to keep our batteries at maximum charge during storage periods. These crude devices were, essentially, very small battery chargers. When the battery approached full charge, a trickle charger diminished the charging current, but not the voltage. A six-volt battery gasses at about 6.9 volts, and the trickle charger sometimes exceeded that voltage.

The modern method is to use of a device called the Battery Tender. It charges your battery at 1.25 amps until the battery is accepting only .5 amp. At that point the charger switches to a "float," or maintenance mode. Current drops to very close to zero (actually 10 milliamps). Voltage drops to 6.8 volts, just below the battery's gassing point. This is especially important for AMG batteries like the Optima, which should be kept at a 100 percent charge.

The Battery Tender protects itself from damage with solid state controls that indicate if you've hooked the polarity up backwards. It maintains constant voltage to the battery in the event of brownouts or power surges. It also compensates for ambient temperatures by lowering the voltage as it gets hotter in your garage.

There are other brands of chargers that work similarly to the Battery Tender, but this is the only one I know of that's available in both six- and 12-volt versions.

Like nearly everything in this world, the Battery Tender is not perfect. If left connected to your battery constantly, even this smart unit can eventually run an older-type battery out of water. Solution? Plug it into a simple timer like the

kind used to turn the lights on and off. Set the timer for 30 to 60 minutes a day, and forget it.

The Battery Tender comes with a two-prong polarized female miniplug attached to the output wires. A choice of two harnesses is provided, each of which has a male miniplug. The one for temporary hookups ends in two clamps; the other has ring terminals that allow permanent attachment to the battery. I recommend this. When you return from a drive, just plug the Battery Tender cable into the battery harness. The red light will go on, indicating charging. After a few hours the green light will come on. Your timer will turn it on and off. When you next want to enjoy your car, all of your voltage will be there when you turn your ignition key.

If you're planning to store your car for the long, cold winter, take some steps now that will make the spring startup more pleasant. Many of these were suggested by Neil Maken, editor and publisher of *Skinned Knuckles* magazine:

- Make a list now of the things you'll need to do in the spring, especially if you've drained fluids or taken other storage steps that will affect the car's drivability. It may easily slip your mind in April that you emptied the radiator in October. Place the list on the driver's seat so you can't miss it in the spring.
- Put the car away as clean as it can be. It's easy enough to get the top and interior clean. You'll want to get at the bottom, too. For this, consider a local self-serve car wash. (Check to be sure your locality and state permit this, because you are going to spray degreaser on the undercarriage and wash it off with the wand.)
- Overinflate the tires by 10 to 15 pounds. This helps reduce flat spots. And if you have a slow leak, chances are the tire will still have some air in the spring.
- If you are confident that your gas tank is sound, or if it has been sealed using a quality procedure like Gas Tank RENU, or if your local gas contains no ethanol, fill the tank just before you put the car away. Otherwise, consider draining the tank.
- Modern gasolines include a short-term stabilizer that counteracts the gumming tendencies of some of their components. If your tank contains gas, you'll want to be safe rather than sorry—add additional stabilizer. STA-BIL is a widely available brand. Drive the car for at least 10 miles, so the stabilizer gets all the way up to the carburetor.
- Remove the windshield wiper blades. Store them in a cool dark place. Pad the ends of the arms, and secure with a nylon tie.

- Change your engine oil. You don't want to leave that acid-contaminated oil in there all winter. Do this just before you fill the gas tank for the last time. The same drive that brings the fuel stabilizer to the carburetor will circulate the clean oil through the engine. *Be sure to drive long enough for the oil (not just the coolant) to get hot.* This is necessary to activate the rust and oxidation inhibitors in the fresh oil. If you will not be able to do this, then change the oil last and don't start the engine.

- Now also is the time for some of those annual pain-in-the-neck chores. Drain the cooling system. If you keep it dry for the winter, be sure you drain the radiator and the block. Some blocks have more than one petcock. Drain any windshield washer bottle or bag too. If you are refilling with fresh water/antifreeze make sure that it will do its job at the lowest anticipated temperature. If it's time to replace your DOT 3 brake fluid, do it now and bleed the brakes. This way, when you're impatient to get going in the spring, everything will be ready.

- Finally, drive the car halfway into the garage with the tailpipe outdoors. Remove the air cleaner and start the engine. Dribble Marvel Mystery Oil into the carburetor while you keep the engine running with the throttle on the carburetor. Eventually it will stall, but the carb, manifolds and combustion chambers will have been coated. Remove the spark plugs and dribble some MMO in there too. Don't forget to replace them. Now push the car all the way indoors.

- Remove the battery. Wipe the top with a rag dampened in a solution of baking soda, then dry it carefully. Connect the battery to your Battery Tender. Clean the terminals on both battery and cables while they are disconnected.

- Cover the car with its newly washed, dry car cover. The car will come out as clean as it went in. Make sure to put new or regenerated desiccant bags inside.

- If you're using a bag, put the car in now. Place pans or absorbent mats under the engine, or anywhere where you know leaks occur. Be sure the desiccants are regenerated, and in place. Seal the bag.

In the spring . . .

- If you used a bag, be careful when you reopen it. Crack it open a bit and sniff. (This goes for all bag storage, short or long.) Be alert for gas fumes. Just in case, do not open the bag while smoking, or near an open flame.

- Check your list on the driver's seat for anything that needs to be done before starting or driving the car.

Do these now.

- Change the engine oil again. This will assure that any internal condensation that occurred during the winter sleep is removed.

- Check all fluid levels: transmission, differential, coolant, brake fluid. Top off if needed.

- Look for any leaks that may have begun during the lay-up period.

- Check coolant hoses for condition.

- Check belts for condition and adjustment.

- Check tire pressure, and adjust to normal.

- Clean the terminal posts with a terminal tool or a medium abrasive. Clean the inside of the terminals on the cable the same way.

- Turn on the battery master switch and check the ammeter for a significant discharge that might indicate a short circuit. Check again after you turn on the ignition switch.

- Install wiper blades. If yours are easily available, replace them each year.

- Do your safety check routine.

- Start the engine. If the car has a manual transmission, engage the clutch slowly. Move the shift lever through all the gears. Move an automatic shift lever through all its positions.

- Pull the car into the driveway. Listen for unusual noises. There are bound to be some that you hadn't heard before, but most of these will go away on their own. Idle valves may stick a bit for a few minutes. Fan belts will be stiff until they've run for a while. Some noises are of more concern. Water pump noises may go away, but they may not. Make notes.

- Take the car on a short local trip. Bring along a friend to follow you, or a portable phone. Don't wander too far from home, and stay off Interstates. Apply the brakes with increasing force. When doing so, try to leave room on both sides in case the brakes pull the car to one side.

- Keep an eye on your temperature gauge, oil pressure gauge, and ammeter. Be alert for unusual smells, as well as how the car feels. If you smell something burning or see smoke, reach for the battery master switch. If you haven't installed one yet, be sure to have a wrench of the correct size on the seat next to you, so you can leap from the car and disconnect the battery terminal.

Yes, all this sounds like Caspar Milquetoast's description of how to drive a car. But if just once this routine saves you from a small or large disaster, it'll have paid you back manyfold.

CHAPTER 21
NONMETALLIC TOOLS

Some of the collector car owner's most important tools are made of paper, not steel. They include the car's original factory service manual and manual supplements published by companies like Motor and Chilton. For an older car, and especially for orphan makes, online book vendors and automotive swap meets are probably your best sources for finding such materials. Marque clubs often reprint these publications as well. Buy everything you can find that pertains to your car. You never know when you'll need the information.

Periodicals are another useful paper tool. Slick color magazines are great for seeing restored examples of collector cars. Many of these publications feature well-researched and well-illustrated historical articles. But for usable information to keep our collector cars running, I don't know of anything that compares with *Skinned Knuckles*. From the care and feeding of vacuum tank fuel systems to the latest in brake line technology, you'll find information you need in this monthly magazine. I always learn something from *SK*. You will too. *Auto Restorer* is another nonslick publication that should be in your library, and it's now printed in color. Invest in subscriptions.

The best tool of all is your car club's membership roster. Your fellow club members can be lifesavers, especially on the road. They may not be able to fix your problem, but they will know someone who can.

THE WORLD WIDE WEB

This is often referred to generically as the Internet, or online. If you are not computer savvy, the idea of getting online can be daunting. Some collector car owners still resist using a computer. Don't resist. Any computer you buy will be ready to access the Internet as soon as you take it out of its box and plug it in. All you need to do is contact your telephone company or cable TV company and they will hook you up.

Yes, there are endless possible ramifications and tweaks afterward, but the above simple process will get you

(RIGHT) *Collector car clubs offer informative and interactive websites. Get questions answered, learn history, buy, and sell parts.*

started. And there are many good books that provide novices with an easy introduction to computers and to the Internet.

The Internet is the greatest source of information that mankind has yet devised. It is also the greatest source of *mis*information that mankind has yet devised. Do not discard your common sense as you learn to "surf the Internet."

Once you're online, you might want to start with your own club's website. It may include information specific to your favorite ride. Online forums are another unique Internet feature. A forum is basically an Internet bulletin board. Users post questions, comments, and opinions on the board for other users to read. It's a great way to share or gain information about a make of car or about specific issues in which you are interested.

The Internet has changed the process of hunting for parts too. Swap meets are still fun, but they have been supplemented by eBay. This is an auction site online where you can search for specific or general items, and bid on them against unseen competitors. For a small commission, you can even sell things you don't need. While fraud is always a concern when it comes to Internet transactions, eBay's stringent rules and vigilant fraud management staff make it one of the Internet's safest locales.

In some ways, the Internet has even replaced the encyclopedia as a source of information. It certainly delivers answers faster than an encyclopedia. (For example, the Internet encyclopedia Wikipedia (http://en.wikipedia.org) contains over 2 million articles!) We all know that a fact is not necessarily correct because it's in print. This is even more true in the case of the Internet, where there are no editors or fact-checkers to protect you. On the Web, anyone can pretend they are an expert on anything. Still, there is much to be learned out there. So jump in if you haven't yet.

THE ELECTRONIC SPEEDOMETER

You may not need a GPS device to tell you how to get from place to place. Bill Hummel, a classic car driver and coincidentally the grandson of transportation entrepreneur E.L. Cord, suggests that it does have a function that you may not have considered: checking your speedometer. (If this is all you're going to use a GPS for, you'd best borrow one.)

Over time, differential gears or speedometer drive gears may have been altered on your collector car. If you change to radial tires the rolling diameter may be a bit different. In short, your speedometer reading could be way off.

An inexpensive GPS like this one can accurately check your speedometer.

Many of us have attempted to check the accuracy of our speedometers using a measured mile. That was yesterday. An excellent way to do this today is to take advantage of the 24 GPS satellites that the U.S. Department of Defense has launched into orbit at a cost of $12 billion. Your taxes paid for them, so why not use them? A GPS receiver communicates with the satellites to triangulate your position. Many GPS units can determine your location to within nine feet! This level of accuracy means you can also track the speed of your vehicle within ± 0.2 mph.

Please do not try this while driving alone. You will not get accurate results, and it is unsafe to be writing down numbers while you are driving. Here's how to use a GPS to test your speedometer:

Find a road that runs straight for a mile or so. Turn on the GPS device and be sure that it has locked onto its satellites. Navigate through the screens to the one that includes a digital speedometer. As your assistant holds the GPS near a window, get the car up to exactly 30 miles per hour on the speedometer, and hold it. Announce the speedometer speed to your assistant, and ask him or her to record the speed the GPS says you are going. Do this for 40, 50, 60 and 70 miles per hour. For a double-check, repeat the exercise. You will now know whether your speedometer is fast or slow, and by how much.

Now you can either have the speedometer recalibrated, or just do the adjustment in your head on future trips.

OIL ANALYSIS

There is an inexpensive method of keeping tabs on what's going on inside your collector car's engine without dismantling it. It involves regular analysis of your drained motor oil. Oil analysis can spot problems *before* they really hurt the engine. That's why nearly all car and truck fleet operators do regular oil analyses of their vehicles.

Blackstone Laboratories uses this plasma flame to vaporize an oil sample into wavelengths of light. Each element has its own wavelength, and the lab's computer reads these to determine the metals, additives, and other components of a sample. Blackstone Laboratories

This procedure is not just for those who drive their collector cars often. Infrequently used engines can develop corrosion problems that oil analysis can help nip in the bud.

Oil analysis involves sampling and analyzing oil for various properties and materials. The idea is to monitor wear and contamination in an engine, transmission or hydraulic system. Sampling and analyzing on a regular basis establishes a baseline of normal wear and can help indicate when abnormal wear or contamination is occurring.

One purpose of oil analysis is to provide a means of predicting possible impending failure without dismantling the equipment. Particles caused by normal wear and operation will mix with the oil. Any externally caused contamination also enters the oil. By identifying and measuring these impurities, you get an indication of the rate of wear and of any excessive contamination. You can also get an indication of impending catastrophe— bearings about to burn out, or head gaskets leaking internally. All without laying a wrench on the engine!

What follows is a list of some of the physical properties tested for and usually included in oil sample analyses. The lab's report will explain what the readings mean. The University of Nebraska-Lincoln prepared the list below:

- **Antifreeze** in the oil forms a gummy substance that may reduce oil flow. It leads to high oxidation, oil thickening, high acidity, and engine failure if not corrected.

A technician at Herguth Laboratories analyzes oil samples. Standardized American Society for Testing Materials (ASTM) standards are applied to samples received at all labs. Herguth Laboratories

BLACKSTONE LABORATORIES

OIL REPORT

LAB NUMBER:
REPORT DATE:
CODE: 20/37

UNIT ID: 1935 SSJ
CLIENT ID:
PAYMENT:

UNIT	
MAKE/MODEL: Duesenberg 8-cyl Supercharged	OIL TYPE & GRADE: Kendall 40W
FUEL TYPE: Gasoline (leaded)	OIL USE INTERVAL: 1,500
ADDITIONAL INFO:	

CLIENT

COMMENTS

Iron improved a little in this oil. We don't know if the improvement is due to a shorter oil change interval than last time, or just an improvement in the way this supercharged Duesenberg is wearing. The viscosity was fine for 40W oil, and the oil was in good shape physically, containing no contaminants that would cause a problem. Insolubles (oil oxidation due to heat, use and blow-by) were low at 0.2%, showing good oil filtration and complete combustion. Overall, we like the improvement in wear and hope to see it continue next time. Check back to monitor.

		UNIT / LOCATION AVERAGES							UNIVERSAL AVERAGES
MI/HR on Oil	1,500								
MI/HR on Unit									
Sample Date	08/10/05		9/24/2001						
Make Up Oil Added	18 qts		12 qts						
ALUMINUM	3	3	4						4
CHROMIUM	1	1	1						1
IRON	85	60	87						54
COPPER	70	63	85						67
LEAD	572	339	405						296
TIN	1	1	1						8
MOLYBDENUM	10	11	22						16
NICKEL	1	0	0						0
MANGANESE	2	1	2						1
SILVER	0	0	0						0
TITANIUM	0	0	0						0
POTASSIUM	0	0	0						0
BORON	71	60	68						45
SILICON	3	15	3						17
SODIUM	10	20	12						16
CALCIUM	74	117	166						534
MAGNESIUM	876	700	635						528
PHOSPHORUS	801	883	693						839
ZINC	855	983	735						945
BARIUM	2	2	2						1

ELEMENTS IN PARTS PER MILLION

		Values Should Be*							
SUS Viscosity @ 210°F	80.7	71-82	87.5						
cSt Viscosity @ 100°C	15.69	13.2-16.3	17.37						
Flashpoint in °F	435	>400	425						
Fuel %	<0.5	<2.0	<0.5						
Antifreeze %	0.0	0	0.0						
Water %	0.0	<0.1	0.0						
Insolubles %	0.2	<0.6	0.4						
TBN									
TAN									
ISO Code									

PROPERTIES

* THIS COLUMN APPLIES ONLY TO THE CURRENT SAMPLE

416 E. PETTIT AVE.   FORT WAYNE, IN 46806   (260) 744-2380   www.blackstone-labs.com

©COPYRIGHT BLACKSTONE LABORATORIES 2007   LIABILITY LIMITED TO COST OF ANALYSIS

NONMETALLIC TOOLS

Owners with cars as varied as Corvettes and Duesenbergs have their oil analyzed regularly. Blackstone Laboratories

- **Fuel dilution** thins oil, lowers lubricating ability, and might drop oil pressure. This usually causes higher wear.
- **Oxidation** measures gums, varnishes and oxidation products. High oxidation from oil used too hot or too long can leave sludge and varnish deposits and thicken the oil.
- **Total base number** generally indicates the acid-neutralizing capacity still in the lubricant.
- **Total solids** include ash, carbon, lead salts from gasoline engines, and oil oxidation.
- **Viscosity** is a measure of an oil's resistance to flow. Oil may thin due to shear in multiviscosity oils or by dilution with fuel. When run too long or too hot, oil may thicken from oxidation. Oil also may thicken from contamination by antifreeze and other materials.

Analyses also test for metals. Here is a list of metals and their potential sources:

- **Aluminum (Al)**: Thrust washers, bearings and pistons include this metal. High readings can be from piston skirt scuffing, excessive ring groove wear, broken thrust washers, etc.
- **Boron, Magnesium, Calcium, Barium, Phosphorous, and Zinc:** These metals are normally from the lubricating oil additive package. They involve detergents, dispersants, extreme-pressure additives, etc.
- **Chromium (CR):** Normally associated with piston rings. High levels can be caused by dirt coming through the air intake or broken rings.
- **Copper (CU), Tin (Sn):** These metals are normally from bearings or bushings and valve guides. In a new engine these results will normally be high during break-in, but will decline in a few hundred hours.
- **Iron (Fe):** This can come from many places in the engine, including camshafts, crankshaft, valve train, timing gears, etc.
- **Lead (Pb):** Also associated with bearing wear.
- **Silicon (Si):** High readings generally indicate dirt or fine sand contamination from a leaking air intake system. This would act as an abrasive, causing excessive wear.
- **Sodium (Na):** High readings of this metal are often associated with a coolant leak; an oil additive package might also be the source.

As useful as individual analysis is, its value multiplies when the lab develops a database of norms for a particular engine: a flathead Ford V-8, for example, or a Chevrolet six. This makes it possible for them to compare your engine's readings to the average reading for many engines exactly like yours, and to show this on your report.

It's important to note that the dense bypass filters discussed in Chapter 5 eventually remove nearly all the particles in the oil. They do not remove *wear metals*—the substances that oil analysis tests for. So no matter how well you filter your oil, these tests are valid.

Contact one of the labs that provides this service, and they will send you materials and instructions for collecting your oil sample. Most labs send your results back by mail. Or, if you choose, some will send it as an e-mail attachment the day the analysis is done.

Incidentally, I had a little go-round with my local post office when I shipped my most recent sample to the lab. They asked what was in it, and I told them. They told me I couldn't ship motor oil by post. I replied that I had been doing it for decades. Clerks and postmaster then diligently searched the list of prohibited substances. Motor oil is not among them. So be firm.

CHAPTER 22
AFTERWORD

Sometimes useful thoughts don't fall into the neat category of a particular chapter. I've collected them here. If nothing else, it reminds us that our collector car hobby exposes us to an amazing variety of skills and bodies of knowledge.

FASTENER LOCKING DEVICES

How can we be certain that a nut or bolt won't vibrate off? While NASA and the U.S. military are leery of the near-universal split lock washer, they do quite well for our purposes. I replace any lock washer that I remove with a new one. Cheap insurance.

There are two other fastener locking methods that work even better than a lock washer (and that are applauded by NASA and the military). The first is invisible, can supplement or replace a lock washer and can be used anywhere on your collector car. The second can replace hidden nuts.

The split lock washer has been with us for centuries. It works well enough for our purposes.

ANAEROBIC ADHESIVES

The files of the U.S. Patent Office are filled with devices intended to keep a nut from loosening on a screw. Who knew that one of the most practical answers would come in a tiny bottle? The word "anaerobic" means "without

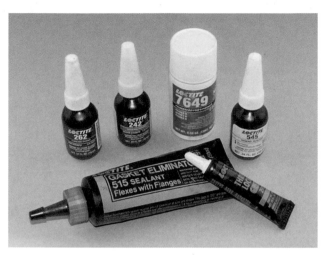

Anaerobic adhesives serve a variety of purposes. I carry these small sizes in my toolbag on trips.

air." Anaerobic adhesives refer to liquids that harden only in the absence of air. This type of threadlocker was first marketed in 1953 by a father-son team, Professor Vernon Krieble and his son Robert. Their trade name, Loctite, was contributed by the professor's wife, Nancy. Loctite has since become a huge worldwide enterprise.

A threaded part that has been properly assembled with Loctite should never loosen in use. Race car builders love it. Collector car drivers should too.

Most of Loctite's thread sealers are liquids that harden into a thermoplastic when deprived of air. They come in various strengths, usually color-coded. For most of us, the little bottle that dispenses a drop of blue liquid is the most common one. A fastener sealed with this can be removed with ordinary wrench pressure.

There is a wide range of Loctite threadlockers, adhesives and other chemicals. Their catalog describes them all. Here are a few that I use regularly:

- Threadlocker Blue. This is the popular medium-strength adhesive.
- Threadlocker Red. For use when you don't ever expect to take it off again. (Heat applied at over 300 degrees F will loosen its grip.)

- Threadlocker Green. It's very thin, and wicks its way into already assembled fasteners.

Porosity Sealer 290 is the same stuff as Threadlocker 260. It's used to seal cracks in castings and welds. Brush it on and wipe it off. I once used it to seal some hairline cracks on the outside of a rare aluminum cylinder head.

I seal pipe threads with Loctite's PST Pipe Sealant with Teflon. It's anaerobic so it seals well, but never quite hardens, which means you can move the fitting a bit to match it up to a tube. And bits of it don't get into the works the way tape can.

Anaerobic sealants are not magic. You have to properly prepare surfaces, and understand how each product is best used. So get catalogs, and read instructions. Also, Loctite is no longer the only game in town. Anaerobic technology is well understood, and no longer protected by Loctite's original patents. But Loctite and other suppliers keep improving their products. One of them may help you solve that fastener problem.

ELASTIC STOP NUTS

These devices were originally developed during World War II. Essentially, a plastic collar or pellet, usually nylon, is captured in the nut. The ID of the nylon is smaller than the internal threads of the nut, so when screwed down it deforms and seizes the threads of the bolt or machine screw. That prevents the nut from vibrating off, although it can be removed and reused using ordinary tools.

The nylon insert is usually contained in a dome-shaped protrusion on top of the nut. Thus, on our collector cars you will only want to use an elastic stop nut in a position where the nut will be entirely concealed. And since the nylon insert usually won't handle temperatures above 250 degrees F, keep it away from engines and exhaust systems.

The elastic stop nut became popular during World War II because it speeded production. Holds tight, too.

LOOKING FOR LIQUID LEAKS

There's a booming industry in pads and pans that are designed to be placed beneath your collector car when it's standing in the garage. That's because everyone knows that old cars leak.

They really don't have to. But sometimes the biggest part of the problem isn't fixing the leak; it's determining *exactly* where the motor oil, or transmission lube, or coolant is leaking from. Oil pans, transmissions and rear ends can wind up covered with escaping lubricant. Coolant sometimes drips off a frame crossmember some distance from where it's coming out of a radiator hose. Eyes alone often aren't sufficient.

There is a tested method of finding leaks. It's noninvasive and relatively modest in cost. The latest equipment can get expensive, but earlier versions often wind up at swap meets and on eBay.

The method is ultraviolet or "blacklight" leak detection. For such an effective diagnostic tool, the process is remarkably simple. To find a motor oil leak, for example, you pour about an ounce of a fluorescent tracer dye into the crankcase through the oil filler cap. Let the engine run for 15 minutes, or take the car for a drive. You want to allow sufficient time for the dye to mix thoroughly with the oil, and to start leaking out.

Stop the engine, and light up the suspect area with your ultraviolet light. (If the previously accumulated gook on your engine is really thick, you may want to wipe and scrape much of it off.) Modern 120- to 150-watt ultraviolet spotlights can be used in a lighted garage. If you're using an older 15-watt fluorescent tube, as I do, darken the garage as much as you can. The leak will leap out at you in bright color. (If you don't see it immediately, wait a while. It'll show up.)

Eyes are much more difficult to replace than any part of your car. So protect your eyes from the ultraviolet. The spotlights are pretty safe because they're easy to aim away from your eyes. I'm not so comfortable with the fluorescent tubes, which spray black light in all directions. You also get closer to them, because they're dimmer. I always wear UV-blocking safety glasses when I use my fluorescent black light. You won't find them at the discount store, but they're available online. Or, you can order a set from the maker of the test equipment.

The detection principle is the same for transmission fluid, and for coolant. Dyes are made that are compatible with fuel and automatic transmission fluid

Leaking fluids that have been treated with a fluorescent dye glow brightly in the beam of this ultraviolet lamp by Tracerline. Tracer Products

too. The colors are different for each. Happily, the dyes do no harm and may be left in until you next change the lubricant or coolant. When you wash off the outside of the dirty engine or transmission, the dye will wash off too.

HAND PROTECTION

Car maintenance involves work with many toxic substances. Few of them will kill you unless you drink them, but they're capable of making your life very unpleasant if you're careless with them. So we're usually very careful not to spray brake cleaner in our eyes, and we've learned to be more careful with asbestos and gasoline.

We sometimes don't pay enough attention to our body's largest organ—the skin. It's got immense self-protective ability; otherwise it wouldn't survive the things we do to it every day. But it still can use all the help we can give it.

I use disposable gloves whenever I work on my car. I buy them in bulk at a warehouse store. They're the same product as the exam gloves used by doctors. They fit tightly enough so I lose very little 'feel', and they're inexpensive enough to be discarded after every use.

Strong solvents soon dissolve the white latex ones. The cost of the more solvent-resistant nitrile gloves is now very close to that of latex, so I use these exclusively. Gloves come in large, medium, and small sizes. Besides

Thin Nitrile gloves can now be purchased in warehouse stores; they are white and cheap, and resist solvents well.

For heavier jobs, the familiar blue Nitrile gloves are thicker. They cost a bit more.

protecting you, you'll find that they extend your car hobby time too. With less time needed to scrub your hands and nails, you can work until closer to dinnertime.

There also are hand lotions designed to protect your skin from harsh chemicals and prevent contact dermatitis. There are numerous brands. Some claim to even protect from acids long enough to wash them off, but happily I have not had the occasion to test this.

Microfiber cloths do everything diapers used to, but better. Griot's Garage

ENGINE FLUSHING

This is a technique that's been through several incarnations over past decades, with only so-so reviews. The current offering, though, is marketed by Bilstein, a German company with a reputation for quality products. (It is best known for its shock absorbers.) The process itself is far more sophisticated than earlier attempts.

The rationale for this procedure is that even after you drain the oil from your car, about half a quart of dirty oil remains in the engine's oil galleys and in the bottom of the pan. Water, acid, wear particles and other contaminants remain behind with it. These contaminants go right back into circulation as soon as you start the engine with its crankcase full of fresh oil. Bilstein offers impressive statistics showing how their flush removes many of these contaminants.

I include this process here because collector car owners have asked me about it. Doing this very occasionally will not hurt your car—just your wallet. And it can be used only on cars that have full-flow oil filtration systems. If you change your oil regularly, I'm not convinced that this kind of service is really necessary.

THROW AWAY THE SHOP RAGS

Repair shops use fabric shop towels, or rags, because they are removed, laundered and returned to them by an outside service. Most of us do not have that luxury.

I stopped using shop rags a while ago, and switched to paper shop towels. I tried several brands, including fancy foreign ones that pull out of a vertical roll dispenser. My favorites are Scott, both their blue shop towels that fit

Disposable paper shop towels are effective and biodegradable.

in a standard holder, and their blue Rags in a Box. They are quite sturdy, and their surface is softer than kitchen paper towels.

Throw them away when you're done, and reduce the risk of getting dirty grease where it doesn't belong. The cost is competitive with washing and drying my old shop rags in a commercial coin laundry. (You didn't think I was gonna wash them in the same home washing machine that my wife washes her undies in, did you?)

INSURANCE

If your collector car is driven every day, you'll have to insure it as you would any other car. Your regular agent can handle that transaction. Be aware that you'll have difficulty getting collision, fire and theft coverage that will reimburse you for the real value in the event of total loss to a 40-year-old vehicle. There's also likely to be a deductible on these coverages.

If your collector car meets certain standards, you're eligible for one of the great bargains in auto insurance—collector car insurance. The policies of different companies vary, but generally your car must be at least 25 years old, and stored in a garage. Some companies set a limit on the number of miles you can drive. Others don't, so long as the driving is event-related. So you can drive your car across the country to a car show or take a pleasure drive on a Sunday, but you may not use it to commute to work or go shopping.

Available from several sources that specialize in this coverage, collector car insurance sets a fixed price liability, no-fault property damage, uninsured motorist coverage and medical insurance. These rates are filed by the companies for approval by each state. The minimum dollar coverage in each category is also set by each state.

For liability insurance, the ads for collector car insurance usually list rather low coverage limits by today's standards. But ask and you may find that these companies will provide higher levels of coverage. If you want even more coverage, your own insurance agent can provide an umbrella policy that sits over the regular automobile policy.

Comprehensive and collision coverages are based on an *agreed value*. You set the value on your car. If it's over $25,000, the company will usually ask for an appraisal and a photo of the car. They sometimes ask for these when you increase the coverage amount too.

If your car is totally destroyed, the company will pay the agreed amount. If there's a partial loss, the company will pay the repair costs approved by their adjuster.

Hitches only occur if the car's value appears to have been misrepresented. I have not heard of this being a serious problem.

YEAR OF MANUFACTURE PLATES

A continuing bow to America's love affair with cars, Year of Manufacture (YOM) plates are available in most states. In essence, your collector car is permitted to drive on the public way wearing a set of license plates issued in the year that the car was manufactured. Different states have different names for this arrangement. YOM plates enable the casual admirer to determine the year of your car. They add a historic touch. And, for those who drive a car of which fiberglass replicas have been made, they identify your car as the real thing.

In most states, cars more than 25 years old are eligible for YOM plates. (In one state the law has the cut-off year fixed at 1968.) Here's the typical procedure:

You need a set of license plates of the year shown on your current registration and title. If your state only required a rear plate in that year, then you only need one plate. You can get plates from vendors at most of the larger swap meets. Publications such as Hemmings Motor News also carry ads from vendors who buy and sell plates. And, of course, there are online vendors.

The plates you purchase may not be in usable condition. Or they may not be pristine enough to be worthy of installation on your beautiful car. (Some states require that the plates be in original and good condition, that is, unrestored. I've never seen this provision enforced.) License plate restoration is a minihobby in itself. For example, it's important that the colors of the

background and numbers be accurate. There are many shades of, say, orange, and no two states chose the same one. Restoration techniques vary, too. Some restorers use stencils, others use a brayer or roller method. Most will fix dents and small holes. I recommend that you ask for references before you entrust your valuable plates.

In some states the YOM procedure can be conducted by mail. In others you'll have to bring your title and registration to the local office of your state's Department of Motor Vehicles. In the latter case, be aware that the regulations regarding YOM plates are not invoked often, and you may find that the clerks you deal with are not aware of them. If your locality has more than one office, it's worth some time on the phone to identify a clerk who is familiar with the regulations before you make the trip. No matter how it's done, you can be sure that there will be a form to fill out.

Some states require that you bring the actual plates to the Motor Vehicle Department office to verify that they exist and are legible. The local office may access the state's main computer database to determine whether the number on the plates you submit are currently in use.

There are fees to be paid. (In at least one state the small fee is permanent, and you never need pay again. A car hobbyist legislator tacked this provision onto some bill many years ago, God bless him.) Some time later you'll receive your new registration. A prefix to the number indicates that these are vintage plates, for the benefit of the highway patrol officer who stops you looking for a current registration. In California, the registration is accompanied by a small metal tab that's to be mounted on the plate, to provide a place to stick the annual validation stickers. Most states also offer "historic" plates to cars more than 25 years old. These special plates often carry a lower fee than the regular registration fee. They may also have restrictions on use.

On a cross-country trip once in our 1936 Cord, we were stopped by a trooper in a Midwestern state. He said he was looking for a current license plate. As I started to explain California's laws regarding YOM plates, he smilingly waved me to silence. "I know that," he said. "I just wanted to look at the car."

APPENDIX

The listing below includes specific parts and supplies mentioned in this book. I give the website address, e-mail address and phone number, where I have them. If you must have a physical address, it's best to call or e-mail and get it from the company. They can also tell you where you can buy their product.

CHAPTER 2

Fumoto oil drain valve
Qwik Valve
www.qwikvalve.com
Info@qwikvalve.com
201-766-1557

Motor oil
Classic Car Club of America, Indiana Region
www.classiccarmotoroil.com
(317) 225-0040

American Refining Group (Brad Penn oils)
http://www.bradpennracing.com
814-368-1200

CHAPTER 3

Grease gun
Alemite LLC
www.Alemite.com
800-648-3917

Bearing packers
Lisle Corporation
www.lislecorp.com
712-542-5101

Steering gear lubricant (Penrite)
Restoration Supply Company
760-739-8843

Grease fitting caps
Niagara Caps and Plugs
www.niagaraplastics.com
info@NiagaraCapsandPlugs.com
888-227-5847

CHAPTER 5

Air filter elements
Amsoil, Inc.
www.amsoil.com
715-399-8324

K & N Engineering, Inc.
www.knfilters.com
tech@knfilters.com
800-858-3333

Remote bypass oil filters
Amsoil, Inc.
www.amsoil.com
715-399-8324

Filtakleen USA
www.filtakleen-usa.com
sales@filtakleen-usa.com
877-464-5728

We Filter It! (Frantz filter)
www.wefilterit.com
dwalkerharley@wefilterit.com
208-467-3726

Hepo Filters (Hepo/Oilguard filters)
www.hepofilters.com
tfarmer@hepofilters.com
310-260-5611

Magnetic drain plugs
C.G. Enterprises
www.cgenterprises.com
magneticdrainplugs@cgenterprises.com
800-565-9743

Lisle Corporation
www.lislecorp.com
712-542-5101

Coolant filters
Gano Automotive Coolant Filter Company
831-659-1961

MAKO Marketing (Tefba filter)
www.mako.com.au/html/tefba_filter.html

AN fittings and hoses
Earl's Performance Plumbing, Inc.
www.holley.com
800-246-5539

CHAPTER 8
Anti-corrosion additives
Applied Chemical Specialties (No-Rosion)
www.no-rosion.com
norosion@aol.com

Red Line (WaterWetter)
www.redlineoil.com
800-624-7958

Propylene glycol coolant
Evans Cooling Systems
www.evanscooling.com
610-323-3114

Thermoplastic hose clamp
Gates Corporation (PowerGrip SB clamps)
www.gates.com

Coolant test strips
Environmental Test Systems (Cooltrak)
www.cooltrak.com
574-262-2060

Fin rake
The Eastwood Company
www.eastwoodco.com
800-343-9353

CHAPTER 9
Brake tubing
Brake & Equipment Warehouse (EZ-bend brake line tubing)
www.brakeplace.com
info@brakeplace.com
800-233-4053

CHAPTER 10
Cylinder sleeving
Hagen's Hiway Auto Parts
www.hapinc.com
ecommerce@hapinc.com
253-845-7020

Brake fluid test strips
Phoenix Systems
www.brakestrip.us
866-760-5844

Brake bleeding catch bottle
Vacula Automotive Products
www.vacula.com
info.usa@vacula.com
847-263-6601

Pressure brake bleeder
KD Tools
www.kd-tools.com
kdmarketing@danahertool.com
800-688-8949

DOT 4 brake fluid
ATE-North America
www.ate-na.com
ate-customerservice@contiteves.com
502-736-0943

CHAPTER 11
Batteries
Optima
www.optimabatteries.com
questions@optimabatteries.com
888-867-8462

Antique Auto Battery Company
www.antiqueautobattery.com
info@antiqueautobattery.com
800-426-7580

CarMan's Garage
www.carmansgarage.com
800-450-5130

Custom cables (crimped)
Solar Power and Light Services
www.solarpals.com
info@acmepowercables.com
575-557-2318

The Solar Biz
www.thesolar.biz
888-826-0939

Custom cables (soldered)
The Brillman Company
www.brillman.com
brillman@shentel.net
888-274-5562

Starter rebuilding (lower voltage field coils)
The Solar Biz
www.thesolar.biz
888-826-0939

Alternators
Don's Starters & Alternators (Gener-nator)
www.gener-nator.com
gener-nator@myway.com
541-902-2255

Fifth Avenue Antique Auto Parts (alternators)
www.fifthaveinternetgarage.com
fifthave@oz-online.net
785-632-3540

Battery tools
Lisle Corporation
www.lislecorp.com
712-542-5101

Coil polarity tester
Nu-Rex (Sparklite)
www.nurex.com
330-784-5334

Master disconnect switches
Painless Performance Products
www.painlessperformance.com
tech@painlessperformance.com
817-244-6212

Hotronics
www.hotronicsproducts.com
hotronics@jps.net
714-971-8543

Uninsulated terminals
All Battery Sales and Service
Ecommerce@allbatterysalesandservice.com
www.allbatterysalesandservice.com
888-562-9501

CHAPTER 12
Reflector recoating
UVIRA
uvira@terragon.com

Halogen light bulbs
Mac's Antique Auto Parts
www.macsautoparts.com
customerservice@macsautoparts.com
800-777-0948

Bill Hirsch Auto
www.hirschauto.com
info@hirschauto.com
800-828-2061

Restoration Supply Company
760-739-8843

LED third brake light
J & L Enterprises
www.jandlenterprise.com
Jsbieback@sbcglobal.net
860-916-3582

CHAPTER 13
Rhino Ramps
www.rhinoramps.com
consumerservice@blitzusa.com
877-922-5489

Kwiklift
www.kwiklift.com
sales@kwiklift.com
800-961-5438

Jack stands and hydraulic lifts
Automotive Service Equipment
www.asedeals.com
contact@asedeals.com
800-229-6218

Easy Access stands
Backyard Buddy
www.backyardbuddy.com
800-837-9353

CHAPTER 14
Whitewall radial tires
Diamond Back Classic Radials
www.dbtires.com
wwtires@sccoast.net
888-922-1642

Coker Tire Company
www.cokertire.com
(800) 251-6336

Wheels
Stockton Wheel Service (Stockton CA)
www.stocktonwheel.com
sales1@stocktonwheel.com
800-395-9433

J.B.'s Wire Wheels (San Jose, CA)
831-465-0617

CHAPTER 15
Leaf spring paint
Superior Graphite Company
www.slipplate.com
800-366-3907

New springs
Eaton Detroit Spring, Inc.
www.eatonsprings.com
sales@eatonsprings.com
313-963-3839

Gas tank restoration
Gas Tank Renu
www.gastankrenu.com
danrenu@aol.com
800-932-2766

CHAPTER 16
Microfiber cloths, equipment, and supplies
Griot's Garage
www.griotsgarage.com
800-345-5789

Classic Motoring Accessories
www.properautocare.com
classic1@tampabay.rr.com
800-628-7596

Dry cleaning cloth
KozaK
www.kozak.com
info@kozak.com
800-237-9927

Chrome and aluminum sealant
Zoops Products, Inc. (Zoopseal)
www.zoops.com
(951) 922-2396

CHAPTER 17
Radiator cap anodes
VE-Labs (Rad Cap)
www.ve-labs.com
mike@ve-labs.com
888-483-5227

Rust controlling finishes
The Eastwood Company
www.eastwoodco.com
800-343-9353

Rust Bullet
www.rustbullet.com
info@rustbullet.com
800-245-1600

POR-15
www.por-15.com
800-726-0459

Waxoyl
Moss Motors (Starter kit)
www.mossmotors.com
800-667-7872

Robison Service (Professional application)
www.robisonservice.com
robison@robisonservice.com
413-785-1665

CHAPTER 18
Dye penetrant crack detection
Magnaflux (Spotcheck)
http://www.magnaflux.com/spotcheck.stm
847-657-5330

CHAPTER 19

Halon (recycled) fire extinguishers
H3R Clean Agents
h3rcleanagents.com
800-249-4289

Magnetic flashlight holder
Larson Electronics
www.magnalight.com
sales@magnalight.com
214-616-6180

CHAPTER 20

Car storage solutions
CarJacket
Pine Ridge Enterprise
www.carbag.com
800-522- 7224

Carcoon (the original "Carcoon" bubble)
www.carcoon.co.uk
info@carcoon.co.uk

Copperstar Products (Airchamber)
www.copperstarproducts.com
888-892-4724

Motor Inn
www.themotor inn.com
sales@themotorinn.com
203-877-4399

CHAPTER 21

Oil analysis
Blackstone Laboratories
www.blackstone-labs.com
260-744-2380

Herguth Laboratories
www.herguth.com
info@herguth.com
800-645-5227

Magazines for restorers and maintainers
Car Collector
www.custmag.com/arr
888-333-0436

Skinned Knuckles
www.skinnedknuckles.net
skpublishing@yahoo.com
714-963-1558

CHAPTER 22

Anaerobic adhesives and sealants
Henkel Loctite Corporation
www.loctite.com
248-364-4700

Ultraviolet leak detection
Tracer Products
800-641-1133

INDEX